TEXTS & DOCUMENTS
A SERIES OF THE GETTY CENTER PUBLICATION PROGRAMS

The TEXTS & DOCUMENTS series offers to the student of art, architecture, and aesthetics neglected, forgotten, or unavailable writings in English translation.

Edited according to modern standards of scholarship and framed by critical introductions and commentaries, these volumes gradually mine the past centuries for studies that retain their significance in our understanding of art and of the issues surrounding its production, reception, and interpretation.

Eminent scholars guide the Getty Center for the History of Art and the Humanities in the selection and publication of TEXTS & DOCUMENTS. Each volume acquaints readers with the broader cultural conditions at the genesis of the text and equips them with the needed apparatus for its study. Over time the series will greatly expand our horizon and deepen our understanding of critical thinking on art.

Julia Bloomfield, Kurt W. Forster, Thomas F. Reese, *Editors*
The Getty Center Publication Programs

IN WHAT
STYLE
SHOULD WE BUILD?

PUBLISHED BY THE GETTY CENTER
DISTRIBUTED BY THE UNIVERSITY OF CHICAGO PRESS

FOR THE HISTORY OF ART AND THE HUMANITIES

TEXTS & DOCUMENTS

IN WHAT
STYLE
SHOULD WE BUILD?

The German Debate on Architectural Style

Heinrich Hübsch, 1828
Rudolf Wiegmann, 1829
Carl Albert Rosenthal, 1844
Johann Heinrich Wolff, 1845
Carl Gottlieb Wilhelm Bötticher, 1846
Heinrich Hübsch, 1847

Introduction and Translation
by Wolfgang Herrmann

THE GETTY CENTER PUBLICATION PROGRAMS

Julia Bloomfield, Kurt W. Forster, Thomas F. Reese, *Editors*

TEXTS & DOCUMENTS

Architecture

Harry F. Mallgrave, Editor

In What Style Should We Build?
The German Debate on Architectural Style
David Britt, Translation and Manuscript Editor
Margarete Kühn, Editorial Consultant
Lynne Hockman, Copy Editor

Published by the Getty Center for the History of Art and the Humanities,
Santa Monica, CA 90401-1455
© 1992 by The Getty Center for the History of Art and the Humanities
All rights reserved. Published 1992
Printed in the United States of America

98 97 96 95 94 93 92   7 6 5 4 3 2 1

Publication data for the original German texts may be found in the source
notes following each translation.

Cover: Heinrich Hübsch, Polytechnische Hochschule, Karlsruhe (1833–1835).
Drawing. Karlsruhe, Generallandesarchiv Karlsruhe.

Library of Congress Cataloging-in-Publication Data is to be found on the last
printed page of this book.

TABLE OF CONTENTS

XI ACKNOWLEDGMENTS

1 WOLFGANG HERRMANN INTRODUCTION

63 HEINRICH HÜBSCH *In What Style Should We Build?*

103 RUDOLF WIEGMANN REMARKS ON THE TREATISE *In What Style Should We Build?*

113 CARL ALBERT ROSENTHAL IN WHAT STYLE SHOULD WE BUILD? A QUESTION ADDRESSED TO THE MEMBERS OF THE DEUTSCHE ARCHITEKTENVEREIN

125 JOHANN HEINRICH WOLFF REMARKS ON THE ARCHITECTURAL QUESTIONS BROACHED BY PROFESSOR STIER AT THE MEETING OF ARCHITECTS AT BAMBERG

147 CARL GOTTLIEB WILHELM BÖTTICHER THE PRINCIPLES OF THE HELLENIC AND GERMANIC WAYS OF BUILDING WITH REGARD TO THEIR APPLICATION TO OUR PRESENT WAY OF BUILDING

169 HEINRICH HÜBSCH THE DIFFERING VIEWS OF ARCHITECTURAL STYLE IN RELATION TO THE PRESENT TIME

178 BIBLIOGRAPHIES

193 BIOGRAPHIES

199 INDEX

ACKNOWLEDGMENTS

The five German texts presented here in English translation introduce the reader to a debate that preceded, and in scope surpassed, a similar English controversy. This debate was sparked off by the appearance of a book by Heinrich Hübsch entitled *In welchem Style sollen wir bauen? (In What Style Should We Build?)* in 1828. The title of Hübsch's book was also used as the title of a study by Klaus Dohmer (Munich, 1976) in which he explored the wide range of contemporary journals on architecture and art for aspects concerning controversial stylistic topics. As his subtitle indicated, Dohmer widened his search to cover the entire interval between *Klassizismus* and *Jugendstil*, whereas I confine the inquiry to a debate lasting only two decades. Dohmer's book has nevertheless been invaluable in assisting me to sift through the material relating to this short period.

I am most grateful to Harry F. Mallgrave for the fruitful discussions we had about this project and especially for the great care he took in reading the first draft of the translation and the many suggestions and corrections he made to improve it. The final text is to a considerable extent due to the skill and experience with which David Britt undertook the comprehensive task of editing. I am greatly indebted to him. I am also very grateful to Professor Margarete Kühn for her valuable advice on selecting and procuring illustrations of Karl Friedrich Schinkel's buildings. Finally, I wish to express my gratitude to Kurt W. Forster, Thomas F. Reese, and the Getty Center for the History of Art and the Humanities for entrusting me with the execution of the project and especially to Julia Bloomfield for her help, encouragement, and friendship while guiding the work through its many stages.   –W.H.

Introduction

WOLFGANG HERRMANN

HEINRICH HÜBSCH CHOSE A STRAIGHTFORWARD QUESTION AS THE TITLE FOR THE FIFTY-PAGE BOOK THAT HE PUBLISHED IN 1828. Nevertheless, a complex of problems, conflicts, and uncertainties underlay its seemingly simple wording, occupying the minds of those who, like Hübsch, were concerned about the unsatisfactory state of architecture. Over the next few decades attempts were made to answer the question or at least to consider seriously its implications. Arguments and counterarguments were advanced in quick succession; traditional values were upheld against radical proposals, and a materialistic approach was opposed by an idealistic point of view.

A lively debate, carried on in speeches and in print, arose among those whose professions and predilections inclined them toward an interest in the controversy—architects and, quite frequently, art critics and academics.

The main theme of the discussion—and the one on which this introductory essay will focus—was the question of style. Naturally, many other factors were pursued in the course of often quite elaborate argumentation, but it is those that relate most closely to the concept of style—such as construction, material, customs, or religious and aesthetic values—that are of particular interest.

Those men who were to take part in the style controversy were born around the turn of the century. During their formative years the mainly literary current of the Sturm und Drang period swelled into the full flood of Romanticism in all the arts; and in this movement they found the fulfillment of everything they longed for: escape from the confines of traditional rule and conventional order into a world that responded to their emotions. This generation chiefly owed its serious interest in medieval art and architecture to two men: Sulpiz Boisserée and Friedrich von Schlegel, the former through his collection of early German paintings, the latter through a publication describing medieval art and the deep impression that the cathedrals of Cologne and Strasbourg had made on him.[1]

The enthusiasm with which the younger generation responded to the newly revealed beauty of Gothic churches led many to choose architecture as the subject of their studies. Naturally, their teachers, who belonged to the preceding generation, firmly believed in the universal validity of the architectural canon of antiquity. Sooner or later, this was bound to lead to conflict. The way in which Heinrich Hübsch's professional life developed is a good example.

Looking back to the day when, as a twenty-year-old, he had entered Friedrich Weinbrenner's studio, Hübsch recalled how deeply impressed he had been by the "pointed-arch" style (*Spitzbogenstil*), "probably because the views of Goethe, Schlegel, and others had a strong influence on me."[2] It is therefore not surprising to hear that even after two years of studying the classical canon under Weinbrenner, he still held to his first conviction "that ancient architecture was unsuitable for our buildings, even when applied in the freest possible manner, and that it deprived them, as works of art, of the organic correlation of their parts." He admitted, however, that he was still too immature to be able to suggest something else to supersede whatever had been done hitherto.[3] He still preferred the "vivid splendor of Gothic architecture" to the "lifeless planes...of facades built in the antique style"[4] when he decided two years later, as was then quite usual, to continue his architectural education by studying the antiquities of Rome. Moreover, as the center of the Romantic German Nazarene movement, that city had an additional attraction for him.

What interested him was not so much the ancient monuments as the medieval Italian churches and the manner in which their architects had simplified the Gothic forms. He adopted these simple forms in the first year of his stay in Rome, when he worked on designing churches in the Gothic style. During his second year, he traveled to Greece. His reaction to the important event of seeing Greek architecture in its pure form, and not in the corrupted interpretation presented by succeeding generations, is most revealing. "On my return from Greece to Rome," he recounted later, "I had completely changed my views. The prolonged contemplation of Greek monuments strengthened me in my belief as to the inadequacy of Greek architecture for our extensive needs…and at the same time convinced me…that in order to establish a new style, alive to the demands made by the present, I had to proceed more radically than I had done so far."[5]

Thus, by 1819 he already had a goal that from then on would guide all his thoughts: to overcome what he called the "crisis of present-day architecture."[6] Hübsch felt that progress toward the aim he had set himself—the establishment of a new style—was impeded by the tenets of classical doctrine. One important task that he intended to undertake was to demonstrate the falsity of the notion of imitation that was so deeply ingrained in architectural thought. He developed its refutation in a book entitled *Über griechische Architectur* (*On Greek Architecture*), published in 1822. Unremittingly, he attacked the teachings of Aloys Ludwig Hirt, the leading theorist on classical antiquity. It was not the imitation of Greek art that was the object of Hübsch's critique; this ideal had lost much of the appeal that it had in Johann Winckelmann's day. The "imitation" to which he strongly objected related to the genesis of Greek architecture. According to a widely held view that had its root in Vitruvian tradition, Greek stone temples were modeled on earlier wooden buildings. Hübsch demonstrated that structural laws and the properties of the building material determined the construction as well as the form of the major parts. It was absurd, therefore, to deduce the stone structure of the Greek temple from a strange-looking, old wooden building. The idea that the trabeated system was the result of the imitation of a wooden structure ran counter to basic architectural principles.[7]

These ideas matured until in 1828, Hübsch was ready to elaborate them and to speak out against the idealistic approach to architecture. "After my final return from Italy in 1824," he wrote later, "I had a clear picture in my mind of the new style, the elements of which I then tried to develop as objectively as possible in the book…*In welchem Style sollen wir bauen?* [*In What Style Should We Build?*]."[8]

To this end he reviewed the major architectural systems. These had also been the subject of a book published a year before Hübsch's treatise by the well-known historian Christian Ludwig Stieglitz. Yet in their objectives and final conclusions the two authors differed greatly. Stieglitz gave a historical account of the manner of building as it differed among nations. Resignedly, he concluded that for the present, "all that can be done, in view of the impossibility of creating new forms, is to imitate."[9] But Hübsch, pursuing an uncharted route, undertook an analytical examination of the major styles and concluded with confidence that the new style, as outlined by him, would "freely evolve and respond to any fair demand without hesitation."[10]

Hübsch admitted four factors as the basic determinants of style: material, technical experience, climate, and present needs.[11] By limiting his analysis of ancient styles to what might be called materialistic factors, he could have found support in, and might indeed have been influenced by, a debate between Johann Karl Schorn and Carl Friedrich von Rumohr over the nature of style that had taken place in an exchange of letters published in *Kunst-Blatt* a few years earlier.[12] Rumohr (whom Hübsch knew well enough to send a drawing to from Greece)[13] countered Schorn's idealistic approach by stressing the clear distinction that had to be made between, on the one hand, the raw material to be subjected to artistic treatment and, on the other, the ideas and their artistic representation in the final work of art. Only the former, the material as treated by the artist, incorporated what Rumohr called style. While he admitted that this concept of style meant that it evolved in an inferior and merely technical sphere, he emphasized that it was just for this reason that it had a separate existence and could be perceived separately in a work of art.

Hübsch may or may not have been aware of Rumohr's theoretical arguments, but the extraordinary way in which he restricted his analysis of the major architectural systems to the technical sphere makes it evident that he too considered the concept of style to be unrelated to aesthetic qualities. Aiming at a new style, he consequently focused his attention on those four principal factors that had in the past alone determined the major styles.

Hübsch first listed the essential parts of a building: walls, ceiling, roof, supports, windows, and doors. These were the elements of style; their forms varied according to the material used.[14] The Greeks, using hard marble or ashlar as building materials, developed a system in which all parts clearly conveyed the function they were to fulfill: columns appeared only where they supported an architrave, piers only where they strengthened the wall, and the architrave only where it was needed to carry the ceiling. In this way, they developed an architecture that "excelled in simplicity of composition."[15] Next to material, it was what Hübsch called "technostatic experience" that had an important influence on the creation of style.[16] The Romans, not comprehending the logic of the structural principle on which the Greek style was based, changed it into a "mere sham and show architecture."[17] However, by using small-sized stones, they introduced the vault as a new structural element.

While architecture declined with the end of the Roman Empire, technostatic experience was never lost and even progressed.[18] Over the centuries constructions became bolder, while less material was needed to span spaces. A highly developed vaulting technique and the introduction of the pointed arch (*Spitzbogen*), created a system in which everything derived from the construction of the vault.[19] The medieval system of the vault was the opposite of the Greek post-and-lintel system. "Essentially," Hübsch concluded, "there are only two original styles: one with straight, horizontal stone architraves; the other with curved vaults and arches."[20]

The last two sections of the treatise are taken up by a comparison of two styles whose basic structural form was the arch: the rounded (i.e., the *Rundbogenstil*) and the pointed. The existence of a transitional period, in which the pointed arch was not acutely pointed and differed little from the *Rundbogen*, made it difficult for Hübsch to opt for one or the other, but in the end he decided for the latter because, he said, it conformed to the practical theory that he had developed in his book.[21] One rather suspects that it was his taste that turned the scale in favor of the *Rundbogenstil* and not the "cold logic" by which—as he said later—a new style should be judged.[22]

It is hardly surprising that Hübsch's view of the genesis of style was not accepted. Soon after his essay was published, the *Kunst-Blatt* carried a review written by Rudolf Wiegmann, who—nine years junior to Hübsch—was still on a study tour in Italy.[23] Wiegmann criticized Hübsch for attaching a meaning to the term "style" that related to material and construction. "The whole treatise," he exclaimed, "seems to be pervaded by the notion that matter dominates mind."[24]

This reproach was unjustified. It was obviously based on a misconception about the aim of Hübsch's analysis. Hübsch believed that in order to attain a style representing the present, it was necessary to probe into the factors that had determined the styles of the past, and material and construction had been the most important of these factors. He never denied that once this secure base had been established, the task of creating beauty still remained. Yet this task related to a faculty different from that of pure reflection, which was his only guide. Once, when explaining to what extent the new style would differ from the Greek style, he stopped when he realized that the reader might expect him to speak about the aesthetic aspect of the new style. He admitted that at this point it would have been fitting to discuss architectural beauty but refrained since he "would have to speak too much of feelings, and this treatise would take on too subjective...an aspect."[25] Right at the beginning of the treatise, he referred to "inessential elements" (as distinct from the basic forms): in a word, what we would call the aesthetic superstructure, where the "artist's talent and taste are mainly called upon" and where one should "let the artist's taste have free rein."[26] Shortly after, he emphasized that his investigation was concerned only with the form of the main architectural elements and that their combination was "the artist's primary task and bears witness to his talent."[27] Hübsch obviously conceived of style as a quality separate from the rest of the work and no doubt agreed with Rumohr's statement that "at times style … is the only merit of an otherwise poor work, … while a well-executed work may lack any style."[28]

Soon another critical voice joined the debate. The young Franz Kugler, editor of the newly founded journal *Museum*, wrote an article for his publication in which he regretted the lack of a characteristic contemporary architectural style while acknowledging that such a style could only arise when based on the nation's religious sensitivity.[29] He rejected the prevailing eclecticism as disgraceful and depressing and therefore welcomed recent efforts to steer clear of this confusion. He noticed two trends in particular: one represented by Leo von Klenze, the other by Hübsch.[30] He reproached Klenze for demanding the adoption of the Greek style, since this would have the same effect that adoptions of known styles had always had–the obstruction of progress and the loss of one's own creative faculty. He then turned to an examination of the other trend. Drawing on a passage of Hübsch's treatise (which he cited verbatim), he concluded that Hübsch was a representative of this trend and, in contrast to Klenze, rejected the known styles as incompatible with present needs and wanted to work out a new system based on the "technical elements of construction."[31] While Kugler did not wish to question the sincerity with which Hübsch pursued his objective and while he recognized that civil architecture would, in following these principles, be freed from unsuitable decorative overloading, he nevertheless was convinced that it was a great mistake to believe that "a work of art could ever evolve out of the material and extraneous conditions."[32]

We know of one other early reference to Hübsch's treatise. It came from a young architect, Carl Albert Rosenthal. In a book published in 1830, he noted with satisfaction that the indiscriminate enthusiasm aroused by the discovery of true Greek monuments had passed and with it the notion of a universal adoption of Greek forms. Thus, the way had been freed for an unprejudiced appraisal of medieval architecture, which had recently led to attempts at adapting it to present-day conditions, "with which Hübsch … in his treatise *In What Style Should We Build?* has made a praiseworthy, though inadequately prepared, beginning."[33] An article that Rosenthal wrote fourteen years later explains the reservations with which he acknowledged the merits of Hübsch's treatise. There, Rosenthal rejected the Romanesque style as too constrained and clumsy and called unreservedly for a reinterpretation of the Gothic or–as he named it–the Germanic style.[34]

Gradually, the quest for style gained momentum. Eduard Metzger was the first architect who, like Hübsch, tried to deduce from an analysis of past styles the effect that certain positive factors had on the genesis of style. Metzger had studied under Klenze and Friedrich von Gärtner. In 1833, shortly after his return from Greece (which he had visited together with his friend Gottfried Semper), he was appointed professor at the newly founded Polytechnikum in Munich. A few years later, he published an article "Über die Einwirkung natürlicher und struktiver Gesetze auf Formgestaltung des Bauwerkes" ("On the Influence of Natural and Structural Laws on the Configuration [*Gestaltung*] of Buildings") in which he examined in some detail the Greek and the Egyptian temple (surprisingly in this sequence) and the German cathedral.[35]

In his introduction Metzger set out the principles according to which architecture had developed throughout history. He recognized three bases from which these principles derived: national character, with worship as its focus; nature; and building material. Whereas worship and nature affected architecture in a significant, yet mainly general, way, it was specifically the way in which "the material is used and ordered, or in other words the construction," to which the architect had to pay the greatest attention. This, he reasoned, meant that a building was the result of "a rationally conceived order, based on natural and structural laws" and that its ground plan was a reflection of "all utilitarian, climatic, and structural conditions."[36] A detailed analysis of the Greek temple, which took up many pages and was supported by measured drawings, confirmed his belief that these factors were indeed "the basic means that essentially influenced the configuration of these monuments."[37]

In Metzger's opinion, natural and rational laws also explained the form and proportions of Egyptian monuments. The material, which was stone throughout, determined every essential form. "With these monuments," he declared, "Egypt paid homage to the spirit of the material and thus to the clearly manifested construction."[38]

Turning to his third paradigm, the German cathedral, Metzger found evidence of the influence of structure on form as early as the Byzantine churches of the eleventh and twelfth centuries.[39] The manner of constructing the vaults led most naturally to the pointed arch and to high buildings. The finest buildings of this style were formed according to a system of well-ordered tension, consisting of primary and secondary ribs that were closely joined to support each other, thus forming a kind of wickerwork on the surface of the vaults that needed only thin material, such as a sheathing of bricks, to cover the compartments. Function also determined the forms of the buttresses and flying buttresses, enabling the walls of the nave to withstand the pressure of the vaults and to prevent the network of ribs from fracturing;[40] had it not been for the "fairy tales" according to which these allegedly ideal forms were modeled on trees and branches, it would soon have been recognized that all these intricate forms, down to the smallest detail, followed the well thought-out structural principle of load, tension, and relief and that everything "had evolved from normal mathematical calculations."[41]

A year later, a new journal published another article by Metzger on the same subject.[42] This time he stressed—as did many others at the time—how important it was for architecture to have a scientific foundation. "Scientific knowledge alone will lead to a thorough understanding of the essence of construction," he wrote.[43] One consequence of the positive attitude toward science was this radical statement: "Once a building has been declared constructionally correct, it is essentially perfect." It was for the same reason, and contrary to Hübsch's view, that he thought the construction of the pointed arch was more perfect than that of the rounded arch.[44]

Against these statements must be set Metzger's admission that just as the framework of the human body needs to be covered by flesh and skin, so art must breathe life into the organism of the building.[45] Despite this idealistic note, Metzger's otherwise materialistic approach was still felt to be so unusual at this time that the editor thought it advisable to preface it with this caveat: "While [the author] credits technical construction with directly influencing the configuration of a building, it should not be overlooked that architecture as an art form is not just a simple reproduction of the material world but is at the same time an art subjected to the loftier influence of the freely creative genius."[46]

Within the next few years, the predominant influence of material and construction was widely accepted. The first issue of another new architectural journal included an article by its editor, Johann Andreas Romberg, who strongly believed that the promising development of a modern architecture depended on the adoption of rational principles: "Form expresses construction," he declared.[47] The study of building material and of its properties was now needed more than ever, especially in view of the great number of new industrial products; architecture, in its search for a firm base, had lately begun to turn to architectural science and pay greater attention to material and climate. With this, Romberg thought, an important step had been made to "lead architecture away from utter decline" to regeneration. The link between architecture and science ensured that "only those forms that are rooted in construction are considered to be beautiful."[48]

Anton Hallmann, an architect of great promise and author of a remarkable book, *Kunstbestrebungen der Gegenwart* (*Contemporary Artistic Trends*), was even less compromising. His book was published in 1842, a few years before his untimely death at the age of thirty-seven. "Only when the construction fits the material can we talk of style," wrote Hallmann, "and style will lack character the moment we abandon these solid supports without any reason."[49]

Many writers had by now adopted Hübsch's thesis that material determined style. Yet nobody drew the seemingly obvious conclusion. Metzger came close to it when, in reference to the mania of wanting to create something new, he wrote that it was ridiculous to talk of new architectural styles "as long as there is no new material to oust the existing style."[50] We shall return to Metzger: several years later, he was the first to realize that a new material did indeed exist.

Although some architects may have had reservations about Metzger's materialistic approach toward the problem of style, they certainly shared his opinion that it was impossible to invent a new style. All architects were concerned about the break in the sequence of styles that had become apparent at the turn of the century and were eagerly seeking ways to reform architecture; but they nevertheless knew that a quality as intangible as style could never be derived from such an extrinsic process as invention. Schlegel already warned of the consequences that would follow from attempts that aimed at "creating a new art, as it were, out of nothing."[51] Later, when the discussion about style revealed its complex nature, the idea of overcoming the difficulty by inventing a new style "at a stroke"[52] or "*par force*"[53] was thought to be "foolish"[54] and "misguided,"[55] an undertaking that far exceeded "an individual's capacity"[56] and was as unattainable as "the invention of a new language."[57] When, in 1850, by order of King Maximilian of Bavaria, the Akademie der bildenden Künste in Munich invited architects to take part in a competition "to invent a new style," the laconic reaction of the *Deutsches Kunstblatt* was: "Styles are not made; they develop."[58]

In view of these emphatic statements, it was plainly unfair of Klenze to ridicule the efforts of "some misguided German scribblers and dilettantes who believe…that they will be able to invent a new style through pamphlets, proclamations, and articles."[59] It was unfair but also a sign that he was not as much concerned about the state of architecture as were his younger contemporaries; they were painfully aware of the ill-defined and insecure part it played within the social and cultural framework of their day in comparison with the outstanding function it had fulfilled during great periods in the past. The so-called "scribblers" were motivated by the desire to reverse this decline. Whether they rejected or supported Klenze's adherence to classical ideals, they had one common aim: to work toward the establishment of an architectural style that would be a unique representation of all the material and nonmaterial factors that formed the character of their own time. Reviewing the past, they found that "every period and every nation had attained its characteristic style"[60] and that in consequence "modern art must be a clear expression of the present."[61] This, they said, was now universally demanded.[62]

To those who believed in the absolute value of Greek architecture, this was a task that while requiring a high degree of aesthetic sensitivity, could nevertheless be solved without transgressing the framework of classical doctrine. As Johann

Heinrich Wolff, the foremost representative of this faction, phrased it, all that was needed was to use the elements that ancient architecture had provided in an intelligent and reasonable way, while taking into account the admittedly changed conditions of the present.[63] Our task, he said when commenting on a lecture by Friedrich Wilhelm Ludwig Stier, can only consist of "modifying and rearranging the architectural elements that naturally evolved in antiquity."[64]

The situation was more difficult for those with opposing views, who were convinced that a break with the overpowering influence that classical doctrine had exercised over the architectural production of the past few hundred years was a precondition for a sound architectural future. This demand in no way affected their admiration for Greek architecture, which they voiced in terms that equaled those of the "classicists." Indeed, they believed, with Hübsch, that no other nation "lavished such fine qualities on its monuments" as the Greeks did during the age of Pericles[65] and, with Rosenthal, that no other nation had come "so close to the acme of perfection."[66] Wiegmann argued that even if it could be demonstrated that no future style could ever attain the supreme perfection of Greek architecture, this was no reason for holding on to the antique style.[67] Indeed, any attempts at modifying this style to meet modern conditions were bound to fail; it was just because of its perfection that the alteration of even the smallest detail would only end in disfigurement. "We must therefore accept that its time has passed."[68]

Greek architecture could therefore be of no help to architects in their search for a style characteristic of their own time. Having rejected the idea of inventing a new style or imitating a past style, they faced a frightening situation in which—as Carl Gottlieb Wilhelm Bötticher put it—"we would find ourselves alone in an immense void, having lost all the historical ground that the past has provided for us and for the future as the only basis on which further development is possible."[69] Caught in this dilemma, they reviewed the historical conditions under which postclassical styles had evolved and discovered—or persuaded themselves—that occasionally the development of a style had been interrupted for extraneous reasons. Hübsch used this argument as a justification for the application of forms in a known style. Acknowledging that the new style he had described came close to the *Rundbogenstil*, he added, "as it would have evolved, had it developed freely and spontaneously, unimpeded by all harmful reminiscences of the ancient style."[70]

Wiegmann, reviewing Hübsch's treatise shortly after its publication, was unconvinced and saw the adoption of the *Rundbogenstil* as nothing more than a change from ancient to new fetters.[71] Yet a few years later, in 1839, he recognized that many recent buildings pointed to the vitality of the *Rundbogenstil*. He still believed that it could not be directly transplanted into the present but now admitted that it had been "interrupted by outside influences" and therefore could still be adapted to meet our spiritual and material needs.[72] Semper may have had this passage in mind when he told his students in 1840 that "it was rightly said of the style that we call the Byzantine that it had not been developed to the point of perfection that it could have attained. Its development was interrupted through the influence of the pointed arch that became common toward the thirteenth century."[73]

Writing in the following year, Wiegmann was more specific about the reason why this style had never fully developed: it was, he explained, suddenly interrupted in the thirteenth century by an outbreak of eccentric rapture, an indulgence in emotion at the expense of reason, a relapse into religious mysticism. The outcome was that its promising beginnings were abandoned, although it had not come to the end of its life (*ausgelebt*); through further development it could blossom into still greater perfection.[74] It was not, he said, a natural development that had led to the Gothic style but one that occurred as the result of a powerful revolution. "If we wish to relate our art to a style of the past," he told Wolff, "then it can only be one that has been neither fully exhausted nor completely developed."[75]

It was Semper once more who took up these arguments in support of the Romanesque style that he had used in his design for the Nikolaikirche in Hamburg: "This style," he wrote in 1845, "whose truly national development was interrupted through the newly arrived element of the pointed arch, has not outlived its time as the Gothic did; it is therefore capable of being further developed."[76]

Of course, those who did look to Gothic architecture as a starting point from which to develop a style characteristic of their time had to arm themselves with similar arguments against the charge of imitating an already existing style. They declared that the "disturbance and enervation of people's lives in the thirteenth and fourteenth centuries...had interrupted the then progressive rise of German art."[77] Or, they believed that due to the domination of the priesthood, the spirit of Gothic art, as well as that of the Reformation, had remained misunderstood and unfulfilled: a conjecture that clearly marked its author as a member of Germany's Protestant church.[78] Yet there were those who, on the contrary, believed that the style of the Gothic cathedrals had run its full course and, like the Greek style, had died a natural death. "The revival of either style...is impossible."[79]

Those who upheld classical tradition and those who looked to one of the medieval styles for guidance were all sincere in their belief that they had indeed avoided the easy road of imitation. Yet the question, in what style to build, still remained unanswered; it was raised again and again and became the focus of a protracted and at times acrimonious dispute between two architects, Johann Heinrich Wolff and Rudolf Wiegmann, both academics, the first a professor at Kassel, the second at Düsseldorf.

The pages of the then-renowned journal, the *Allgemeine Bauzeitung*, primarily served as the medium for this dispute.

The controversy was triggered by a remark with which Wolff concluded a short preamble to his review of Klenze's collected architectural designs.[80] He contrasted Klenze's well-founded views, with which he wholeheartedly agreed, with the "ignorance of some architects who live under the delusion that existing architectural forms,...evolved by a nation of the highest intellectual standards, are unsuitable for our period. These architects, calling Greek and Roman architecture pagan and un-Christian, maintain that different trends should be pursued and even deem themselves destined to break new ground for our art."[81]

Wiegmann struck back at once.[82] Although Wolff had not mentioned his name, Wiegmann was convinced that the sarcastic remark about the "ignorance of some architects" who hoped to break new ground was aimed at him, because he, Wiegmann, had been the author of a treatise in which he attacked Klenze for his unswerving belief in the universal validity of ancient art.[83] In addition, he had once before clearly alluded to Klenze in his review of Hübsch's book, when, comparing the ordinary artist's work with an imitator's rehash of magnificent buildings, he concluded that the former might have broken new ground, while the latter was as unimportant as if he had never existed.[84]

He told Wolff that many shared the delusion from which he, Wiegmann, was supposed to be suffering. He could well believe that their constantly growing number could make adherents of ancient art fear that their absolute domination was endangered. However, since the views that he and Wolff held were not peculiar to them but represented those of two fairly large parties, it was sensible to hope that a discussion might lead to an understanding. To this end, he put forward a series of postulates. Those that were not challenged he would assume to be acceptable to his adversary; those that were attacked, he would try to defend. Among the many general statements (which, as Wolff in return commented, were, if not new, yet in the main correct) there was one that was clearly aimed at Wolff's position. It said: "Greek architecture...can serve us as a model, not for imitating their works without further ado, but for creating true and original works that will be as appropriate to our needs, our way of feeling and thinking, our religion and morality, and our material and climate as those created by the Hellenes were appropriate to their conditions."[85]

This declaration and the statement that from the artistic point of view a building with vaults was incompatible with the trabeated system of the Greek style and led, whenever attempted, to a "sham architecture," convinced Wolff that Wiegmann belonged to the party of those who maintained that in order to gain one's own style one must first cast off the fetters of ancient architecture and of those who not only wanted to limit what they called the "absolute domination of ancient art" but sought to persuade architects to repudiate it altogether and thus—in Wolff's view—to forgo the inheritance of the finest period of art.[86] They expected such a radical step for the simple reason that "we architects often find it necessary, in view of the wide range of present needs and different purposes, to relinquish the fine simplicity of Greek architecture…whose accomplished forms we cannot apply everywhere unless they are further developed in the spirit of the Greeks."[87] Wolff knew from earlier writings that Wiegmann took the Romanesque arch to be the embryo of a new artistic blossoming; but, as long as Wiegmann and the other members of the "opposition" could not submit some successful examples of their efforts, Wolff would still share and defend the opinion of those architects and experts who maintained that ancient architecture—both Greek and Roman—presented the elements on whose intelligent application, after proper consideration of climate and present needs, the success of modern architecture rested.[88]

Wiegmann was delighted to have scored a point: Wolff had admitted that the Greek style could not be applied unless it underwent further development.[89] But what did that mean, he asked. Did Wolff expect to bring the Greek style to a higher level of perfection? Did he really believe that the people of the nineteenth century would succeed, when the Hellenes themselves had failed to maintain the pinnacle that Greek architecture had attained under Pericles, and their work had degenerated under the Romans into mere inorganic decoration? What did "development in the Greek spirit" mean? The spirit that influenced the present was the Christian, not the Greek, spirit.[90] The ancient style had proved inadequate for the churches and great assembly halls of modern times and was even less suitable for industrial buildings, where the use of iron had begun to evoke a characteristic style that would change the physiognomy of architecture.[91]

Should his inability to name successful examples of the new trend be taken by Wolff as proof that a true work of art could not possibly arise from any other than the Greek spirit, then Wiegmann must tell him that indisputable evidence refuting this belief still existed in Speyer, Worms, and Cologne![92] If Wolff really believed that an organic integration of the vault into the trabeated system of the Greeks was possible, then he was sorry to say that Wolff had misunderstood the basic principles of classical architecture. The difference between a trabeated and an arcuated system was so great that an integration of the two was quite unthinkable. Over the course of centuries, the architrave had been totally abandoned; the vault had become the basis of a new style. In view of the construction of the majestic cathedrals between the twelfth and fifteenth centuries, there were not many architects who would deny that vaulted architecture produced original works of art. "If anyone still doubted this, the existence of universal skepticism half a century before was a sure sign that these stragglers would also soon disappear."[93] He, Wiegmann, never claimed that any of the past styles had reached the admirable perfection of Greek art and consequently was of the opinion that "even were it shown that no future style could ever reach that high degree of perfection, this would still be no reason to persuade us to hold on to antiquity and to refrain from striving after a style of our own."[94]

The second half of Wiegmann's article dealt with a recent book by August Reichensperger, the indefatigable apostle of the revival of Gothic architecture.[95] Wiegmann outlined the content of the book in great detail and then compared both calls for revival. In the end, he rejected both Reichensperger's demand for a revival of the German style of the thirteenth and fourteenth centuries and Wolff's for the adoption of the Hellenic style. In his opinion, both ignored the fact that "art as manifested at a certain time does not remain unchanged, in other words that art too has a history."[96] When Wolff called for further development of ancient architecture, he added that this should be done in the spirit of the Greeks; but, Wiegmann queried, "how could we, who are only poor bunglers compared to the Hellenes, develop architecture in their spirit? We are creatures of the nineteenth century and need great effort even to approach a scanty understanding of a different spirit, so that any attempt at production in this spirit would result in a masquerade, not a true and living art."[97]

With the rejection of both the classical and the Christian-Germanic style, which route—Wiegmann asked—should we follow? Although he was not able to give a definite answer (the need for which became more pressing every day), he could at least indicate the bounds that would have to be observed. Notwithstanding these cautionary words, he then devoted the last two pages of his paper to a description of the unique qualities of the *Rundbogenstil* and of the many advantages it offered, once its forcibly interrupted development could be resumed.[98]

Wolff, surprised that his adversary had returned to the fray after an interval of three years, decided that he ought to explain his own position yet again, in case younger colleagues might be tempted by Wiegmann's fine-sounding phrases, such as a "national" and "characteristic" style, a "new route," or the "elimination of paganism," under whose "fetters ancient architecture had languished." Apparently, no proper attention had been paid to his own frequently reiterated remarks. Why was it, Wolff asked himself, that in the aesthetic field one's views were in constant opposition to the views of one's adversaries?[99] A superficial study of architectural history had strengthened his opponents' belief that there had been many different styles over the centuries, each of which reflected the individual character of the respective nation, and that for this reason our period too must manifest its national character in new architectural forms. Wolff thought this argument misguided in principle. He believed that architecture attained full perfection only when its forms had been conditioned by the nature of the material and the construction derived from it. There were, however, only a few styles in which these factors had the all-important effect. The great variety of styles to which his opponents referred were not "true styles" but only different ways of building, aberrations and deviations from the classical products of true styles.[100] Wolff (as he made clear in the article that is translated in this volume) recognized only three periods that had created true styles—the Egyptian, the Doric, and the Ionic.[101] It was true that the other manners of building were associated with a people's distinguishing traits and had therefore gained a characteristic and, one might say, national appearance that reflected the subjective image of a nation, but this occurred only because the natural development of forms had been abandoned. Now, however, given the general acceptance of the true basis of architecture, we should, by following the correct process, arrive at forms that had previously existed, or at least come close to them.[102]

His opponents, Wolff continued, unanimously rejected the ancient style as too sensuous and pagan and therefore as inappropriate for our period; yet they disagreed over how to achieve their own aims. Some favored the revival of the Gothic style—either in its fully developed or in greatly simplified form. Others chose the Byzantine style—the one that was the crudest and least developed—as the foundation for "their new national style." Its advocates—with Wiegmann, of course, as the main target of Wolff's sarcasm—explained their eccentric choice on the basis that this style sprang from the Christian period; that small stones were used for its structures; and lastly that it had so little advanced beyond its crude beginnings that national identity, present perceptions, and modern conditions could still be implanted while it was developed in short, it was recommended because of its obvious faults. What a basis, Wolff exclaimed, on which to rest our future art![103] Although he laid no claim to the gift of prophecy, it was clear that this "aesthetic development of forms" would either lead back to Roman architecture or to the fantastic Gothic forms promoted by Reichensperger: in other words to two styles that he knew Wiegmann detested—just as he, Wolff, did not like those favored by either Wiegmann or Reichensperger.[104]

With the dispute thus ended, each contestant could claim to have successfully upheld the fundamental principle on behalf of which he had taken up the fight. This was fairly easy for Wiegmann, who simply denied the possibility that Greek architecture could in any way further the search for a new style; Wolff's position, however, was more vulnerable. He found that his call for the retention of classical ideals could only be sustained if the concept of the "Greek style" was widened. While he still subscribed in his early work to the conventional notion that Roman architecture was inferior to Greek,[105] by the time he was engaged in his dispute with Wiegmann he had accepted that ancient architecture comprised Roman as well as Greek architecture, which meant that theoretically the arch became a legitimate element of the classical system. In addition, seeing that in accordance with Hübsch's theory, material and construction played a great part in the general discussion over style, Wolff stressed the importance of both factors—but only insofar as they had been active in the genesis of the ancient styles (a fact that served as an additional justification for their adoption) and not because they determined the development of a new style, as had been central to Hübsch's perception. Lastly—near the end of the article that brought the dispute to a close—Wolff once again admitted that "due to our more complicated requirements we cannot always apply the forms created by the ancients in the same way as they did."[106]

It was strange that when Wolff challenged Wiegmann to name some notable buildings in the newly acclaimed *Rundbogenstil*, Wiegmann shifted ground and referred him to the Romanesque cathedrals of the twelfth century as evidence that the Greek spirit was not essential for the creation of true works of art. Yet for the last fifteen years prominent buildings had been erected in this style. Foremost were three buildings by Hübsch: the church of St. Cyriacus at Bulach (1834–1837), the Polytechnische Hochschule in Karlsruhe (1833–1835), and the Trinkhalle (Pump Room) in Baden-Baden (1837–1840); and three by Gärtner in Munich: the Ludwigskirche (1829–1844), the Staatsbibliothek (1831–1842), and Ludwig-Maximilians-Universität (1835–1840).

Of all those who took part in the discussion on style, Hübsch alone believed that he had devised a new one. Others were confident that the style they had chosen could be developed and would in the course of time lead to a new style, but Hübsch was sure that through his studies of Byzantine, Italian, and Gothic architecture, he had already reached that goal. In 1838, that is ten years after publication of *In welchem Style sollen wir bauen?*, he still thought that the principles he had then set out concerning the main architectural forms were irrefutable.[107]

Hübsch practiced what he preached. The composition of the extremely simple facade of the church of St. Cyriacus in Bulach expresses the structural organization of the building, mainly through pilaster strips that indicate the spatial divisions of the interior (fig. 1). In line with the first principle in art, which—Hübsch declared—was truth,[108] the walls, built from small blocks of sandstone, are not covered with plaster; and, in accordance with Gothic practice, the moderately projected cornice runs only along the inclined sides of the gable.[109] The two towers flanking the apse consist, like those in the Gothic style, of several high stories—here with round-arched windows.[110] Inside, a nave of comparatively great height is separated from the aisles by arches resting on slender polygonal pillars whose capitals and bases

1. Heinrich Hübsch, Church of St. Cyriacus, Bulach (1834–1837).
Lithograph from Heinrich Hübsch, *Bau-Werke*, 2nd ser., 1 (1852): 6.
Karlsruhe, Institut für Baugeschichte, Universität Karlsruhe.

do not project beyond the contour of the pillar (fig. 2).[111] In the same way, the transverse arches that are part of this special form of vaulting do not project beyond the capitals of the pilaster strips from which they rise. By leaving the brickwork partly uncovered, the structural parts of the vaulting and the voussoirs of the arches are strongly emphasized. The system of round-headed twin windows between the transverse arches is continued round the choir, where it produces an effect of almost Gothic lightness.

Hübsch followed the tenets of his theory with great consistency in his

2. Heinrich Hübsch, **Nave of the Church of St. Cyriacus, Bulach** (1834–1837).
Karlsruhe, Landesbildstelle Baden.

18. HERRMANN

3. Heinrich Hübsch, Polytechnische Hochschule, Karlsruhe (1833–1835). Drawing.
Karlsruhe, Generallandesarchiv Karlsruhe.

design for the Polytechnische Hochschule in Karlsruhe (fig. 3). This was a large rectangular block with a facade of "monumental repose"–to quote the architect's own
description of the building in his *Bau-Werke*.[112] He achieved monumentality by
focusing his attention upon three aspects: the texture of the walls, faced with small
blocks of red granite; the proportional rhythm of the decreasing height of the three
stories; and the emphasis given to the central block, with its vertical sequence of
arched openings: three doorways, three twin windows, and a row of eight windows on
the top floor. He refrained from applying any architectural decoration other than the

4. Heinrich Hübsch, Trinkhalle, Baden-Baden (1837–1840).
Karlsruhe, Landesbildstelle Baden.

narrow band of dentils running under the edge of the roof, two similar bands indicating the two upper stories, and rusticated lesenes at the corners of the building. Whereas at St. Cyriacus he was satisfied to present a conventional type of Christian church and therefore adopted many elements from the churches he had visited on his journeys, the Polytechnische Hochschule was a modern administrative building where he was not impeded by past traditions. The fact that he dispensed with any representational decor is remarkable, even after allowance is made for the restriction imposed by a low budget.

5. Friedrich Weinbrenner, Kurhaus, Baden-Baden (1821).
Karlsruhe, Landesbildstelle Baden.

Probably the best known of Hübsch's buildings is the Trinkhalle in Baden-Baden (fig. 4). At first glance, the overall composition seems to be less determined by Hübsch's tenets. Yet a comparison with Friedrich Weinbrenner's Kurhaus of 1821 (fig. 5), only a few hundred yards away, reveals the unconventional aspect of Hübsch's design and the great aesthetic distance between the two buildings, one Neoclassical, the other in the *Rundbogenstil*. The main feature of both is a colonnade. Yet whereas at the Kurhaus, eight tall columns form a typical portico that acts as a grand prelude to the assembly rooms inside the main building, in Hübsch's

Trinkhalle the vaulted space behind the row of sixteen columns fulfills the sole function for which it was designed, namely, to provide shelter and relaxation to those who
had filled their glasses from the source located in a small square room at the back and
center of the colonnade. The construction of Hübsch's colonnade also differs from
that of Weinbrenner's portico. "The architect," he declared in the note to the published design, "has set out to achieve something that has hitherto always been evaded,
namely to create a colonnade as light as possible by using a vaulted instead of a wooden
ceiling."[113] By using segmental instead of half-round arches to span the intervals
between the slender columns, he greatly increased the impression of airy lightness.
With its open display of the various materials used – light granite for the columns and
cornice, reddish brickwork for the vaulting, and terra-cotta tiles to face the walls –
the polychromatic Trinkhalle was Hübsch's most effective protest against the undi-
luted whiteness of the Neoclassical buildings of the recent past. The same critical
reaction had led architects interested in archaeology to discover traces of color on
Greek marble temples.

 "The Ludwigskirche and the Staatsbibliothek," wrote Kugler in 1835,
"were executed by Mr. Gärtner in the Byzantine style, which, it seems, is considered by this architect (as it is by Mr. Hübsch in Karlsruhe) to be the style that best
conforms with the requirements of our time."[114] Although the Ludwigskirche in
Munich was designed and built by royal command (fig. 6), and Hübsch's St. Cyriacus
was the parish church of a small village near Karlsruhe, the churches are in many
ways similar. These similarities are mainly due to the fact that the two architects
drew on the same source. The simplified Gothic of Italian churches had made a deep
and lasting impression on Gärtner as well as on Hübsch when they had visited Italy
early in their respective careers. Yet in addition to these recollections and adoptions of historical forms, which are especially noticeable in the interior of the Ludwigskirche, its facade presents features that are characteristic of the new style as
conceived by Hübsch. A skeleton of double lesenes clearly expresses the spatial organization of the interior building, while any ornamental decor is totally excluded.
The central part of the facade is emphasized by the simple means of a rhythmic
sequence starting from the three axes of the entrance portico, up to the five niches
with their statues and to the circular frame of the large rose window in the center of
the gabled upper wall.

 When the facade of the Ludwigskirche was completed, except for the
sculptural decor and upper story of the towers, a critic, reporting in the *Kunst-Blatt*
on recent art in Munich, thought that the church represented the beginning of a new
period "through a free adaptation of the so-called Byzantine or pre-Gothic manner,
whose essential nature was best signified by the name of Romanesque style…[and

6. Friedrich von Gärtner, Ludwigskirche, Munich (1829–1844). Lithograph.
Munich, Architekturmuseum, Technische Universität München.

7. Friedrich von Gärtner, Staatsbibliothek, Munich (1831–1842).
Oswald Hederer, *Friedrich von Gärtner 1792–1847: Leben, Werk, Schüler*
(Munich: Prestel Verlag, 1976), 122, fig. 68. Photo: Courtesy Prestel Verlag.

8. Leo von Klenze, Walhalla, near Regensburg (1830–1842).
Lithograph by Carl August Lebschée after a painting by Klenze.
Munich, Architekturmuseum, Technische Universität München.

which] as a theory had already found many adherents…until it was first put into practice in Munich."[115]

Next to the church, and built almost simultaneously, stands Gärtner's most important and best-known building, the Staatsbibliothek (fig. 7). This presented the *Rundbogenstil* in its purest form. Several circumstances came together to bring this about. In the first place, the building was to house a public library and also the official archives. Since the state had to provide the funds, it was imperative to cut the cost as far as possible. From the start, therefore, Gärtner rejected the idea that his

9. Leo von Klenze, Beifreiungshalle, near Kelheim (1836–1844).
New York, Art Resource/Bildarchiv Foto Marburg.

design for a library should resemble a "luxury" building.[116] Instead, he intended to make its exterior "very simple and serious, so that it could, as it were, be compared to a book, the cover of which should not be more sumptuous than its content."[117] In the second place, it was–surprisingly–the king who insisted that the front of the building should have "no projections, no columns, no portico–only round-arched windows."[118] Gärtner considered the royal demands unreasonable, yet may have accepted them as a challenge to show that by relying only on basic constituents, he could master the task and create a truly monumental building. In this he certainly succeeded.

PERSPECTIVE DES NEUEN MUSEUMS AM LUSTGARTEN ZU ERBAUEN·

10. Karl Friedrich Schinkel, Altes Museum, Berlin (1823–1833). Drawing.
Berlin, Staatliche Museen zu Berlin.

The most important element of the front wing, which faces onto Ludwig-
strasse, is the material. Different surface treatment emphasizes the difference between
the stories: the highly polished surface of the bare brickwork of the two upper stories
contrasts sharply with the rustication of the ground floor. By recessing the windows
and chamfering the jambs, the thickness of the walls, and thus their strength, becomes
visible. Differently profiled bands running along the window sills mark the three
horizontal blocks that make up the facade, which is crowned by a cornice resting on
a row of consoles. Not a single ornament, nor any decorative detail other than the

11. Karl Friedrich Schinkel, Nikolaikirche, Potsdam (1830–1849).
Berlin, Brandenburgisches Landesamt für Denkmalpflege.

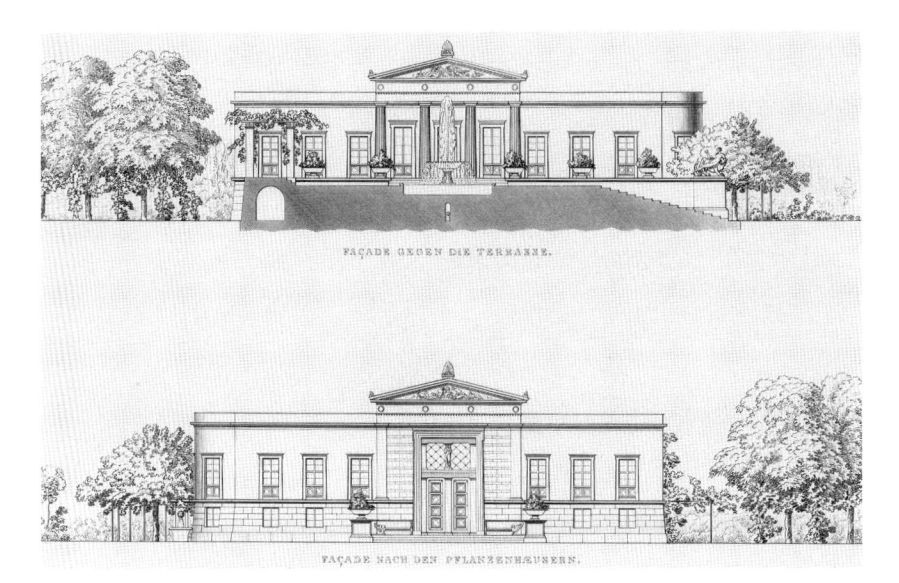

FAÇADE GEGEN DIE TERRASSE.

FAÇADE NACH DEN PFLANZENHÆUSERN.

12. Karl Friedrich Schinkel, Schloß Charlottenhof, Potsdam (1826–1835).
Engraving from Karl Friedrich Schinkel, *Sammlung architektonischer Entwürfe*
(Berlin: Ernst & Korn, 1858), 2: pl. 112. Santa Monica, The Getty Center
for the History of Art and the Humanities.

archivolts over the windows of the upper floors, distracts the eye. With great consistency, Gärtner succeeded in creating a grand public building that in its monumental stillness had no equal at the time.

These examples may suffice to draw attention to a style that represented a new trend in German architecture during the second quarter of the century.[119] It appealed to a great number of people because it seemed to take up the middle ground between those buildings that were still modeled after the Greek style during these few decades—such as Klenze's Walhalla (1830-1842) near Regensburg (fig. 8) and

13. Georg Ludwig Friedrich Laves, Royal Opera House, Hannover (1843–1852).
New York, Art Resource/Bildarchiv Foto Marburg.

30. HERRMANN

14. Karl Friedrich Schinkel, Friedrich Werdersche Kirche, Berlin (1824–1830). Drawing.
Berlin, Staatliche Museen zu Berlin.

Befreiungshalle (1836–1844) near Kelheim (fig. 9), Karl Friedrich Schinkel's Altes
Museum (1823–1833) in Berlin (fig. 10), and his Nikolaikirche (1830–1849) and Schloß
Charlottenhof (1826–1835) in Potsdam (figs. 11, 12), or Georg Ludwig Friedrich Laves's
Royal Opera House (1843–1852) in Hannover (fig. 13)–and those that represented the
neo-Gothic style, of which only a few existed at that period in Germany–Schinkel's
Friedrich Werdersche Kirche (1824–1830) in Berlin (fig. 14) and Daniel Joseph
Ohlmüller's Maria-Hilfskirche (1831–1839) in Munich (fig. 15) being the only out-
standing examples. Gärtner may have had some notion of the kind of style that was

15. Daniel Joseph Ohlmüller, Maria-Hilfskirche, Munich (1831–1839).
Engraving from *Allgemeine Bauzeitung* 7 (1842): pl. 480.
Santa Monica, The Getty Center for the History of Art and the Humanities.

needed when in a letter to his friend Martin von Wagner he expressed his belief "that something must lie between these strict Greek...rules and the purely emotive and romantic nature of the Middle Ages," something which, if it combined the two trends, would be best for the design of Christian churches.[120] This was written in January 1828, three months before Hübsch's treatise setting out the new *Rundbogenstil* was published. Thirteen years later, Wiegmann commended the Romanesque *Rundbogenstil* as deserving "the most serious consideration [since] it lies between the two extremes of the antique and the medieval trend."[121] While he believed that the task of the next era might well be the "conciliation of spirituality and sensuality,"[122] he nevertheless was convinced with regard to their architectonic realization that it was quite impossible to "fuse organically what was in fact incompatible."[123]

Three years later, the supposed incompatibility of the two architectural styles was questioned. A major theoretical work, *Die Tektonik der Hellenen* (*The Tectonics of the Hellenes*), had appeared. The author was Carl Gottlieb Wilhelm Bötticher, pupil and admirer of Schinkel and, from 1844, professor at the Bauakademie at Berlin. Taking a fresh look at the two opposite systems, he came to the conclusion that the deep gulf that seemed to divide Greek from Gothic architecture could and should be bridged. His book, the first volume of which was published in 1844, contained a comprehensive theory of the structural system of Greek architecture and the functional significance of its forms, a theory that despite Bötticher's atrocious style and contorted reasoning, remained valid for a considerable time.[124] In the opinion of its first reviewer, Ernst Curtius, "it contained the key to a new perception of ancient art."[125]

One excursus—the first of six inserted between the preface and the introduction—is of particular interest in the present context. In its twenty-six pages, Bötticher entered the discussion on styles.[126] He started from what had by then been generally recognized as the basic factor determining style—the material. The extent to which the inertia of the material had been mastered was, he declared, one criterion for judging the value of a building. In early times, only monoliths were used.[127] A steadily increased mastery over the material led step-by-step to the establishment of a fully integrated structural system, which was still based on monoliths. The covering, which seemed to be suspended, rested on beams supported by walls and on rows of freestanding columns with architraves to span the intervals between them. The structure of Greek monuments was confined to these elements. While this mastery of the material had clearly brought many advantages, the system remained restricted to the use of monoliths.

The utmost "subjugation" of the material was achieved when small blocks of stone, skillfully jointed, were used in place of monoliths.[128] This practice was based on a structural principle that was the opposite to the one that had governed Greek architecture. Its most important achievement was the introduction of a new element, the vault. Bötticher retraced the stages that marked the progress in technical skill: from the simple arch–far superior to the monolithic beam[129]–to the vaulted ceiling and the abutments that resisted the pressure and released the walls from any function other than enclosure; to the skillful handling of counterbalancing forces; and, finally, to the invention of the pointed arch, which reduced lateral pressure to a minimum and, with the help of buttresses and flying buttresses, made it possible to span spaces of great width and even greater height. This, Bötticher declared, was the highest point reached in the art of mastering the material. The structures thus created would have seemed to the Hellenes, still bound to the use of monoliths, to be supernatural phenomena.[130] After emphasizing the high cost involved and the damage inflicted to the delicate Gothic forms, and thereby somewhat qualifying his admiration for the supreme skill with which the Gothic builder had mastered the material,[131] Bötticher turned to the second criterion on which to judge the value of a style. This concerned the "art-form" (*Kunstform*), as opposed to the "core-form" (*Kernform*).[132] The criterion of "core-form" had only taken the material or mechanical side into account– the degree of efficiency with which the part fulfilled its mechanical function. What was also needed was to judge the effectiveness with which the functions were visually expressed. This was the task of the "art-form." The functions of the mechanical parts could be symbolized only by those forms that conformed to the way in which nature expresses the idea inherent in its creations; and only a style that adopted nature's analogous process could develop a universally true and eternally valid language of forms. A style that deviated from the original source would have art-forms of only temporary validity. "The art-forms of Hellenic antiquity belong to the former category; to the latter those of the architecture of the medieval pointed arch."[133] The Middle Ages never found universally valid forms. With respect to the core-form, the Greeks were artists who remained tied down to the mechanism of monolithic architecture, whereas the Germans were mechanics who mastered the material through technical contrivances. With respect to the art-form, the Germans were thoroughly energetic but uncultured mechanics who were alienated from the refining (*bildenden*) influence of nature, whereas the Hellenes were highly civilized poets, drawing inspiration from nature itself. With Bötticher thus extolling the unique qualities of the Hellenic art-forms in a poetic strain, it is obvious which side he favored.

All the more surprising and remarkable, then, are the remarks with which he concluded his excursus.[134] No longer, he declared, was it a question of whether to adopt the Hellenic monolithic system or the style of the pointed arch. Study of the monuments and a clear perception of the universally valid qualities inherent in both systems were needed in order to bring about a completely new architectural system "based on a totally different material." Although Gothic architecture formed until now the most severe contrast to the Hellenic style, this tension would not last forever. It would be resolved by present and future artistic efforts. Just as Attic art had been the synthesis of the contrasting Doric and Ionic styles, so would German art be the synthesis of ancient and medieval architecture.

The notion of resolving the contrast between Greek and Gothic styles through synthesis was first voiced by Schinkel in a memorandum published in 1811 concerning the rebuilding of the Petrikirche in Berlin, which had burnt down two years earlier.[135] Schinkel referred to the "two poles" of antique and Christian art and "their fusion...into a synthesis of art," not only at this early period in his career but again at a much later date when his advice was sought by King Maximilian of Bavaria.[136] Synthesis of the two principles of ancient and medieval art was therefore a concept with which those close to Schinkel must have been familiar. Bötticher's book, the first in which synthesis was mentioned again after the publication of Schinkel's memorandum, was an attempt to give Schinkel's vision a rational foundation from which a new architecture would eventually arise.

What Bötticher valued in Schinkel's work we learn not from the *Tektonik*, where the latter is hardly mentioned, but from Bötticher's speech in celebration of Schinkel's birthday in 1846. He admired him as the creator of "works in the severe style," works that reflected "the hieratic manner of Hellenic architecture,"[137] and as the man through whom "Hellenic tradition found a new home" in Germany.[138] He conceded that Schinkel had also built in the Gothic style but considered this a phase in his development after which he returned to "the source from which the Middle Ages too had sprung."[139] Earlier on in his speech, Bötticher had referred to an inner force through which "one aspect of architecture became prominent with the Greeks and the opposite aspect with the Middle Ages" and had proclaimed that this "process of development...must be continued by a future generation in a synthesis of both."[140] At this point Bötticher could have shown to what extent synthesis had already been achieved had he referred to one of Schinkel's latest buildings, the Bauakademie (Bauschule) in Berlin (fig. 16). His failure to do so underlines the difference between Bötticher, the theoretician, and Schinkel, the creative architect. For Schinkel the future synthesis was not, as it was for Bötticher, an interesting and fruitful concept but a task to be pursued here and now.

The Bauakademie, begun in 1831,[141] was completed within five years—a compact square block of four identical facades. It was four stories high, all of which, except the top mezzanine story, were vaulted. The structure consisted of a skeleton of strong piers whose function was to withstand the pressure of the vaults, thereby reducing the weight that the walls had to carry, which in turn made the insertion of large

16. Karl Friedrich Schinkel, Bauakademie, Berlin (1831–1836).
Berlin, Landesbildstelle Berlin.

windows possible.[142] This structural system, obviously based on Gothic principles, was clearly expressed on the exterior through the rows of lesenes that extended from their buttresslike plinth right up to the main cornice. Horizontal bands that ran underneath the windows between the lesenes created the impression of a well-balanced framework superimposed upon the flaming red brick walls of the four identical facades. The terra-cotta ornaments under and above the windows introduced a classical element. It was Schinkel's great achievement to have fused these diverse structural, as well as formal and decorative, elements into an organic whole of great character.

However, the building defied easy classification and at times caused bewilderment.

It was disliked, certainly for this reason, by Ernst Kopp, a Dresden architect. In his *Beitrag zur Darstellung eines reinen einfachen Baustyls* (*Contribution to the Representation of a Pure and Simple Style*), published in 1837 (that is, one year after the Bauakademie was completed), he declared that progress in architecture could be achieved only "by the consistent development of a basic type,...not by devising a bastard style as presented by the new Bauschule in Berlin."[143] In contrast, the judgment passed by Kugler in his Schinkel biography of 1842 was positive, although the concluding words of a detailed description betray a certain amount of uneasiness vis-à-vis this "new and surprising" building.[144] A few years later he believed it was "one of those rare creations that only a genius can achieve and that will exercise an influence for a long time."[145]

The Bauakademie became the focus of a discussion about the merits of the classical and the Gothic styles when, in the course of a parliamentary debate regarding a proposed increase of the institute's yearly subsidy, a recently elected member, August Reichensperger, seized the opportunity to vent his animosity against the classical dogma and in particular against the commanding position it held in the Prussian capital. The *Deutsches Kunstblatt* published a verbatim report of the session, followed by a detailed refutation of Reichensperger's arguments. These were mainly directed against the alleged anti-Gothic bias of the school's teaching program but also against the outward appearance of the building itself, which in Reichensperger's opinion would be more suitable on "the banks of the Ilissus than on those of the Spree." Since Reichensperger admitted that he was not acquainted with architectural problems, the editor of the journal felt free to enlighten him with the information that "the Bauschule in Berlin...is in no way an Athenian or Roman but, on the contrary, an independent and original building." As to "its construction—if one has to compare—it rather tends toward the Middle Ages, as evidenced by the vaults and the strong projection of buttresses." It surely was impossible, he thought, "to look at this building... and fail to realize that no other modern building exists that summarizes the results of all preceding architectural periods in such an admirable way."[146]

In modern times, the Bauakademie has frequently been interpreted as foreshadowing, in structure and form, principles that govern present-day buildings. In this connection, it may be interesting to compare the assessments that two writers, almost a century and a half apart, gave of the significance of Schinkel's building. One author, writing in 1842, said: "The Bauschule is one of Schinkel's most important and admirable buildings. By developing an architectural style that sprang from the natural properties of brick, he not only made great progress but took a real leap forward. It is all the more to be regretted that he had so little opportunity to pursue this path any further."[147] Another author, writing in 1981, said: "Using his conventional material, Schinkel has presented us with something that could really be produced only much later with a different material. It is not the actual technical progress that is the Bauakademie's decisive aspect, but the artistic vision of an architecture for whose realization a new technique had first to be invented."[148]

There had been two further attempts to overcome the rift that existed between those who adhered to the classical forms and those who believed that only the development of one of the medieval traditions would lead to a new style. The first of these attempts was spelled out in an article by Friedrich Wilhelm Ludwig Stier.[149] In his opinion it was vital to demonstrate the invalidity of the notion, voiced by the opponents of the antique style, that the difference between Greek and Gothic style was conditioned solely by the different building materials, monoliths as against small stones or bricks. This, he believed, even if not wholly wrong, was yet one-sided.[150] He argued that when the field of study was widened–as it should be–to include both religious and secular buildings, it would become obvious that a great variety of building materials were used in antiquity as well as in medieval times. Greek temples had wooden ceilings; Greek and Roman dwelling houses had architraves made from timber as well as columns built of brick.[151] As for vaulting, this method of covering wide spaces was already generally used in the early period of imperial Roman architecture.[152] While it was true that the church architecture of the Middle Ages was based on a structural system of vaults and arches, the secular buildings, dwellings in particular, were much freer in the choice of their structural elements. Instead of vaults, the low rooms had flat ceilings supported by beams made of timber, a material out of which whole houses were constructed. Since windows and other wall openings were bridged by lintels, horizontality prevailed, so that it would be right to say that in the Middle Ages the architrave was an element as familiar as the arch had been in Roman architecture.[153]

From these observations, Stier drew conclusions for present-day architecture. Since dwellings and, as related types, public buildings formed the preponderance of all modern architectural activity and since structural as well as aesthetic reasons led to a horizontal covering,[154] he thought it sensible and natural not to follow the principle of the arch but of the beam in the construction of our buildings: in other words to follow the principle of the Greek style.[155] However, as he stressed in the next paragraph, he was not opposed to archlike forms, whether used as vaults or in arcades: "We cannot do without either the architrave or the arch...in many buildings, both structural systems have to be used simultaneously."[156]

Stier's wide-ranging personal taste was at the root of the tolerant attitude that he adopted here and throughout the article. While he acknowledged that the form of the arch stood out as an alien element within an overall horizontality, he nevertheless agreed with the general view that too many horizontal lines tired the eye and that in the midst of all this monotony, the arch had a lively and exhilarating effect.[157]

Stier's attitude was equally ambivalent when he dealt in the second part of his article with the forms that mark the styles. As to details, Greek and Gothic architecture used the same elements, except that they differed in the way they were arranged and in the emphasis given to them in each style. Greek forms were meant to be seen at close range and were therefore appropriate for small-scale buildings; the opposite was true of the Gothic forms.[158]

The Gothic system of constructing vaults was certainly the most perfect of all, Stier wrote, and was to be recommended for monumental churches of great height. For smaller rooms, however, the simpler forms of Roman and Italian vaults were more appropriate. An unbiased study of the forms of many parts of the Greek style, such as cornice, frieze, and architrave, would confirm that these were not determined by structural, but solely by aesthetic, considerations. Since the corresponding forms that we see on Romanesque and Gothic buildings were also only loosely connected with the construction, there was no reason why we should not take the Greek forms as models. "This much is certain," he exclaimed, "whatever a nation deemed to be appropriate, when it had reached a degree of general and artistic culture as high as the Greeks had reached at the greatest period of their existence, we can imitate today without hesitation . . . even where we cannot instantly see the particular reason for it."[159]

Of course, Stier hastened to add that he did not suggest copying these forms but developing them further by skillful adaptation. That the Greek style could be developed further—despite frequently voiced opinion to the contrary—was shown by successive artistic periods and in particular by the way in which forms that derived from the trabeated Greek system had been organically joined with Roman and Italian vaults.[160]

Turning to the Gothic details and observing the various forms of pillars and columns, of bases, capitals, and friezes, and of wooden beams used on ceilings or in dwellings generally, Stier was first tempted to believe that these Gothic forms would also be suitable for present-day architecture. However, on second thought, he decided against it and instead recommended taking the ancient architectural forms as a model. He suggested this for a number of reasons, the main one being (among the "many that keep running through my head and my intuitive feeling") that an exterior with Gothic details would be out of harmony with a modern interior furnished in the English or French taste.[161]

In the last section, Stier dealt with the *Rundbogenstil*. Subjecting it to a lengthy critical analysis,[162] he showed the misjudgment of those who for the last fifteen years had preferred this style as a model to Greek, Roman, and Italian art—who, in short, had chosen to imitate "the barbaric offspring of a world," that of antiquity, whose splendid works had for centuries been hidden by dark clouds and covered by frost.[163] The ancient world had been the climax of a long historical development, the highest point that human civilization had ever reached. For that reason alone "the architecture of antiquity must remain the base for our art."[164] He justified this demand with the usual panegyric about the superior quality of Greek art and civilization.

It was typical of Stier that having made a statement in which he clearly and unambiguously indicated the stand he took in the controversy about style, he at once tried to soften the effect of his seemingly uncompromising attitude. He ended the article by saying that if one looked at the matter less seriously, took into account the monotonous appearance of our modern cities, and ignored the aim of establishing basic laws for modern architecture, then he was quite happy to allow new buildings in the Gothic and Romanesque style, since it was pleasing from time to time to encounter buildings in modern cities that recalled the style of the distant past.[165] If Stier's aim had been to bring an end to the clash between different doctrines by showing that many dogmatically upheld principles did not conform to the facts, he probably failed, since his tolerant attitude did not prevent him from repeatedly siding with the Greek ideal.

We do not know how far Stier's deductions, based on a peculiar mixture of conventional choice and personal taste, appealed to his professional colleagues. They certainly infuriated Bötticher, Stier's colleague at the Bauakademie, who wrote a long and devastating critical review.[166] His main attack was directed against Stier's failure to establish the principles at the root of the construction of both styles, one signified by the architrave and the other by the arch. To that end, it would have been necessary to examine the extent to which the properties of the particular material had been exploited, how far the material determined the forms of the structural parts, and how well these were interrelated in their function to form an integrated system. Only when this had been done was it possible to compare the two systems and come to a decision about their respective value. Stier, he found, did not deal at all with these important criteria. Instead he referred to the horizontal covering, the horizontal architrave, and the curved form of the arch and made the completely irrelevant observation that these parts were frequently made of material other than stone, particularly in secular buildings. What Bötticher, the theoretician, found most reprehensible was the fact that in a study that purported to examine architectural principles, Stier throughout allowed his personal taste to be the final arbiter. Bötticher was exasperated. "Now at last," he exclaimed, "Mr. Stier has achieved what he wanted, namely to jumble everything together, to mix the forms according to means and circumstances, fancy and inclination, and to use them as well as one was able or according to one's taste. He set out to make a contribution to the establishment of the principle that should govern present-day architecture... and in the end did not further the matter a single bit."[167] Stier, aware that he was no match for Bötticher's intellect and sarcasm, never replied.

Another attempt to ease the tension that existed among the many factions was Wolff's paper with the telling title "Ein Prinzip und keine Parteien!" ("A Principle, No Parties!"), which he read in 1846 before the Architekten Versammlung.[168] By studying the various trends, Wolff had found that although those who tried to attain a style took diverse routes, they nevertheless did share an initial approach: they all "sought to return to the original source and to follow the chief guides in our art, which are the construction and the nature of the material." In short, they wished to be truthful.[169] Therefore, any material—blocks of stone, bricks, timber, and even iron—might be used, as long as one bore in mind that the nature of the available material was the principal basis for generating form.[170] Since it could be assumed that all architects accepted that the important role assigned to the material represented one of the foremost architectural principles, it became necessary to examine the qualities and characteristic differences of the various materials in detail.[171]

Wolff presented the outlines of such an investigation in the second part of the paper. First of all there was the natural stone or ashlar. Its most important quality was heaviness, which expressed structural solidity, a quality that we at once perceive through our inborn sense of gravity and equilibrium. This, however, was not the case with structures composed of a different material, where we immediately look for the means by which the parts are bound together. When we find that mortar ensures and also makes visible the solidity of brick walls and that the components of timber and iron structures are firmly—and visibly—joined by bolts and nuts, only then does our sense for structural equilibrium feel satisfied. This need to reveal the manner of construction furnishes us at the same time with an opportunity to provide exterior forms and decorative motifs, for instance by emphasizing the joints between the bricks or by applying bands and rose-shaped patterns on timber and iron structures. Wolff grouped the qualities of the various materials under certain aspects—whether they were natural, like stone and wood, or processed like brick and iron, whether they were elastic or brittle, long lasting or easily perishable—all of which, of course, were qualities that clearly defined the forms that alone were appropriate to the particular material.[172]

While detailed research along these lines could certainly be of great value, it is difficult to see how it would lead to "a harmonious resolution of the present chaos," the stated aim of Wolff's lecture.[173] In fact, he himself ensured that his lecture would not have this effect by constantly evaluating the qualitative worth of individual materials. When he declared that "one glance is enough to know that the qualities of ashlar and the forms derived therefrom conform most easily and naturally to whatever beauty demands";[174] when, on the one hand, he recognized only in the trabeated system the full development of a harmony akin to music and, on the other hand, he invariably noted the shortcomings of all materials other than stone; and when, at the end of the article, he added a table in which stone and all its positive qualities were placed on one side and all other materials and their imperfect qualities on the other, then it is obvious that his call for a shared pursuit of truth had no bearing on the question of styles and could in no way resolve the rift between the warring factions.

In the same year Eduard Metzger wrote an article that was more likely to advance the quest for a style.[175] The article is interesting in two respects. On the one hand Metzger's belief in architectural progress considerably sharpened the contrast that existed between the viewpoints of the two sides; on the other hand, this concept of historical development led him to envisage a stage that would bring the prospect of resolving the conflict much closer. As to the first point, the consequences of the two diverging views are highlighted through a comparison of Metzger's article with a paper by Wolff, published the previous year.[176]

Both authors, Wolff as well as Metzger, review the sequence of styles throughout history. They both start with Egyptian architecture, followed by the Greek, Roman, Byzantine (Romanesque), and finally Gothic styles. Wolff recognized steady progress from Egyptian architecture to the Doric and from there to the Ionic style. At that point the rising curve of progress stopped. The Ionic style, he declared, had been the acme of perfection.[177] Everything that followed—from Roman to Gothic architecture—already contained the germ of decline. This was certainly the case with the architecture of the Romans, who abandoned the simple post-and-lintel system, replacing it by an unnatural support given by arches. This was also the case with the many subsequent styles, their structural systems derived from the vault, a vague form that produced an impression of restless immobility in sharp contrast with the classical repose of the ancient style.[178] Somewhat reluctantly, Wolff admitted that the medieval builders achieved the counterbalancing of the curved line of the arch in a manner so perfect that it had never been surpassed, but then he pointed to the boundless willfulness that ultimately led that style also into decline. As to the present, he noted with regret that the unfortunate idea of inventing a new style was still insisted upon, even though the possibility of attaining it had been precluded forever by the climax that Greek architecture had once achieved.[179]

Metzger started his review of the major styles by arranging them into three groups, allotting to each a different paradigm: the pyramid to Western Asia and Egypt, the column to Greece and Rome, and the vault to the medieval systems that extended from the fourth century to the Gothic. The vault, Metzger declared, was "the third and last art form known to the world," a statement that in its assurance equaled and almost echoed the conviction with which Wolff stated that the Ionic style was "the third and last stage in the development and progress of our art."[180] Unaffected by Wolff's pessimistic outlook for future development, Metzger's assessment of the course of history was positive: "The vault was destined…to change the physiognomy of architecture completely…the battle between the column and the vault lasted for more than a thousand years and ended only in the late Christian period with the victory of vaulted architecture."[181] This cursory review of the history of architecture confirmed Metzger's conviction that progress was a permanent process, that technical experiences always widened the field of the development of art forms, and that the fittest form of the present stage would become the form of the next stage.[182]

This evolutionary proto-Darwinism, supported by his belief that the properties of the material determined style, helped Metzger to apprehend the significance of a new material, without which—as he had declared eight years previously[183]—it would be ridiculous to talk of a new style. He now knew that the new material, from which the style of the future would develop, existed. It was iron! "I can well believe that iron construction is an abomination to the sculpturally minded architect," he exclaimed. Yet in his opinion, it would be more honorable to do battle with this new element—which was here to stay—than to resist it as long as possible and let future generations triumph.[184]

Metzger's perception of the future style was vague and did not reach far enough for him to visualize its development. Since history had taught him that a new style always arose from the last perfect style and since the monumental architecture of the fourteenth century had been the last great artistic development, the new form would derive from the pointed arch. As to structural changes resulting from the new material, he only referred in general terms to the powerful effect it would have on means of covering space, as shown by many examples in England, Belgium, and Russia of rooms spanned with iron.[185] Only once was he more specific. Refuting the idea that iron constructions would look dull, he declared that on the contrary, he imagined such buildings to present "slim and graceful contours, striving upward, strong or delicate according to circumstances, and invariably intersecting the horizontal lines": a sentence that reads like a description of the first major German iron and glass public building, completed a few years before—Gärtner's Trinkhalle (1834-1838) at Bad Kissingen (fig 17).[186] Considering the close relationship between Gärtner and Metzger,[187] it is quite possible that it was this building that made Metzger realize the important function that would devolve upon this material. However, unable to visualize the unique potentialities of the new material, all he could do was to reassure the reader (and himself) that "what he had outlined so far was sufficient to

17. Friedrich von Gärtner, Trinkhalle, Bad Kissingen (1834–1838).
Engraving by Ainmüller (1845) from Oswald Hederer, *Friedrich von Gärtner, 1792–1847: Leben, Werk, Schüler* (Munich: Prestel Verlag, 1976), 190, fig. 130.
Photo: Courtesy Prestel Verlag.

reveal the rich domain of the architecture of the future to the expert."[188]

When in the following year, 1846, Bötticher was asked to deliver a speech at the celebration of Schinkel's birthday, he chose as its theme the contrasting principles governing Greek and Gothic architecture, a subject he had dealt with a few years earlier in the first excursus of the *Tektonik*. He seized this opportunity to change his previous analysis significantly. He had since been alerted to the fact that "the totally different material," which he had formerly deduced on theoretical grounds as a precondition for a "completely new architectural system,"[189] already existed and was available for use as building material. In fact, a year earlier he had inserted in his long critical review of Stier's article a paragraph that contained a remarkable prediction of the important role that, in his opinion, iron was going to assume in the future development of architecture. He blamed Stier for not mentioning "what will gradually bring about a complete transformation of architecture, namely the use of a material... that in regard to...our architectural principle...will lift us just as far above the Greeks, Romans, Byzantines, and Germans as arch and vault lifted the Romans above the Greeks with their system of architraves made of stone. Iron is that material."[190]

In *Die Tektonik der Hellenen* Bötticher had evaluated the two styles according to two criteria, one being the thoroughness with which the material had been mastered, the other the perfection with which the art-form symbolized "the tectonic function of every part";[191] he declared Gothic superior in the first respect and Greek superior in the second. Now, in 1846, he desisted from any evaluation but classified the styles according to the "structural force that emanates from the material"; only three forces could be used architecturally—relative, reactive, and absolute strength.[192] Since the relative strength of the material was the principle of the Greek style and reactive strength that of the Gothic style, it was obvious that a new style could evolve only after the introduction of a material in which the third and so far unused force, namely absolute strength, was active. "Such a material is iron."[193]

Bötticher knew, of course, that—as always happened when dealing with a condition still in the process of developing—in this case, too, he could do no more than give some hints about the look of the future iron style. Yet it seems that he had a somewhat clearer vision of that style than Metzger. He predicted that the new material would make it possible to construct roofs of "wider spans with less weight and greater reliability" than was "possible when using stone," while a minimum of material cost would produce walls of sufficient strength to make cumbersome buttresses superfluous.[194] However, he had not changed his views with regard to art-forms. He still believed in the universal validity of the Hellenic forms and insisted that the forms appropriate to the new system would have to accord with the principles of the Hellenic style. How this could be achieved, considering the particular character of the new system, he did not say; but, like Metzger, he was quite confident that any thoughtful person would not find it too difficult to work this out.[195]

As the production of iron increased even in backward Germany, and as it became feasible to replace stone with iron as the basic element in major projects, some writers looked forward to such a radical change; others dreaded it. In 1842 Anton Hallmann, who, during a stay in England, had seen many examples of fully developed iron structures, went so far as to say that iron was the most important material of the present century and that people had begun to grow quite accustomed to it.[196] In the same year, the writer of a critical review of Klenze's newly completed Walhalla near Regensburg referred to the use of iron as a means of reducing the heavy weight of thick walls as a practice "known abroad for the last fifty years." In this connection he hailed "the new inventions and new ideas as the preliminaries to a new era," believing it to be the architect's "sacred duty to break the ground for modern art."[197]

The gulf that separated the two contesters, Wiegmann and Wolff, in their dispute about style was reflected in their attitude toward the new material. Wiegmann mentioned the evident fact that "within the last few years, through the frequent use of cast and wrought iron, the development of a particular style characteristic of those materials had begun,"[198] and he even claimed that the nineteenth century was irresistibly drawn to use metal, a material that, being subject to completely different principles, had until now hardly been taken into consideration.[199] In reply, Wolff exclaimed in exasperation: "What prospects for a new style that...arise from such a foundation!"[200] In his opinion, the use of iron next to stone violated the aesthetic sense, a sentiment that another writer, Otto Friedrich Gruppe, voiced in even stronger terms. Criticizing Hallmann's design for the Berlin cathedral, Gruppe concluded that the difference in character between an iron and a stone structure was so pronounced that an architect intent on creating a work of art would find the resulting difficulties insurmountable.[201]

It was ironic that the architect whose by now famous question had initiated the search for a contemporary style had the greatest misgivings about the state into which architecture seemed to be drifting. Almost twenty years had passed since Hübsch had published *In welchem Style sollen wir bauen?* In 1847, in his second major theoretical work, he once again reviewed the different styles of the past. When he came to deal with the future state of architecture and his hope that there would be a smooth transition to that state, he was alarmed to notice the "headlong rapidity of change" with its devastating consequences and warned that many symptoms "threaten the advent of a new and totally different period," where "instead of the monumental church, the sleek industrial hall built of cast iron will become the architectural prototype."[202]

The advent of the "iron age," confidently expected by Metzger and Bötticher and anxiously apprehended by Hübsch, did not materialize, at least not for many decades. One obvious reason for this delay was simply the lack of technical knowledge: not until the Bessemer process established modern steel production late in the century could architects make full use of iron's possibilities.

But there was another and perhaps more cogent reason why the road that promised to lead to a new era was not pursued and why history took another route. Throughout the discussion on style, there had been a very effective barrier, an inhibition by which the review of past periods was confined within well-circumscribed limits. It excluded from the order of genuine styles any artistic activities that followed on the Gothic style. All the participants in the dispute, of whatever faction, scorned the Renaissance, which, as they understood the term, comprised the architecture of the fifteenth to the eighteenth centuries.

In their historical reviews, the Renaissance was never seriously considered. Renaissance was not what Wolff called a true style.[203] Slavish imitation of the corrupt Roman architecture was the great mistake that the Renaissance had committed. The result was, according to Hübsch, that it developed into a "monstrous architecture"[204] that led to the "periwig style"; the same would happen if we were to follow the example of the Renaissance and take Roman architecture as a model.[205] Even the name "Renaissance"–rebirth of an ancient ideal–was suspect. It falsely implied a positive value and was therefore almost habitually given the prefix "so-called."[206] Johann Andreas Romberg spoke of it as the "architectural carbuncle," as the "evil that is there and cannot be argued away."[207] When Wolff tried to resolve the rift between the various factions, he declared that truth was the principle common to all styles "with the exception of Renaissance architecture, which in a way was the antithesis of all other trends, an architecture that tried to hide and, one could almost say, derided all truth."[208] It was false, because it had abandoned all the hard-won structural experience of previous centuries, and its buildings lacked structural unity.[209] Ferdinand Wilhelm Horn went so far as to call the Renaissance a "cancer" that had slowly destroyed Germanic art ("the noble German oak") from within.[210] Reichensperger condemned this "relapse into antiquity" as an insensate wish to "exchange magnificent Germanic robes for a harlequin's dress."[211]

Of course, since the two last-mentioned writers were ardent advocates of a Gothic revival and considered a movement that had succeeded the Gothic to be their natural enemy, their testimony does not carry much weight. All the more significant, then, are the remarks made by so distinguished a historian as Kugler in the introduction to the last section of his *Handbuch der Kunstgeschichte* (*Handbook of the History of Art*), where he discussed the effect of the Renaissance on the arts. It was, he said, unfortunate that in contrast to medieval times the interchange between the various branches of the arts was destroyed. From then on architecture was practiced without relating it to the other arts. What made matters worse was the fact that the study of antiquity led back to ancient architecture and ancient forms. "In this way," Kugler declared, architects "trailed the ancient forms along for many centuries, without considering that these forms…could never lead to a truly living art." This, he concluded, "is the reason why in modern times architecture plays only a minor role."[212] This may sound like an extraordinary statement to come from a writer who took a considerable interest in the architecture of his own time. However, for the purposes of his *Handbuch*, Kugler defined "modern times" as the period of the Renaissance, that is from the fifteenth to the end of the eighteenth century, and his deprecating remarks were directed only against that period and not against the present.

To learn how a critic who disliked the Renaissance style reacted to a major architectural event–the completion in 1841 of Gottfried Semper's Dresden Opera House (fig. 18), with its supreme display of Renaissance forms–we must turn to another writer, Johann Andreas Romberg, whose article "Konstruktion und Form" ("Construction and Form") has been previously mentioned. Romberg concluded his observations on this subject with a critical assessment of Semper's building as an illustration of the faults that he believed the Renaissance architects had committed. He blamed them for imitating any forms they considered beautiful without considering the reason why the great masters of the past had used them–in short, for disregarding the great principle that consisted in bringing form into harmony with construction. Instead they reversed the relationship by first choosing any form they liked and only then searching for a construction to fit the form as best it could. Above all, the architects of the sixteenth century had committed the same mistake as the Romans did when they tried to merge their own vaulted system with the Greek trabeated one–although with the difference that the "modern" architects sought to imitate a style that already consisted of a mixture of two styles.[213] Confronted now with Semper's building, Romberg was disturbed to note that the faults that he thought had been overcome with the passing of the previous century appeared yet again–empty forms that were not determined by the construction, the column treated as a decorative element, and, generally, the obvious readiness with which the corrupted Roman style had been adopted. He could not bring himself to approve the trend of which this building was an example.[214]

Romberg's criticism was motivated by his distaste for Renaissance forms, an aversion he shared with many writers. However, as the years passed, the comprehensive radicalism that "annulled four hundred years of art history" (to quote Semper)[215] was gradually lessened, and the architecture of the first century of the Renaissance was at least now thought to be worth studying. Stier recommended taking the works of Filippo Brunelleschi, Leon Battista Alberti, Donato Bramante, and Baldassare Peruzzi as models (but excluded those by Michelangelo and Andrea Palladio), because "there could be no better intermediate stage leading to antiquity than the Italian civilization of the fifteenth and sixteenth centuries."[216] Later, J. D. W. E. Engelhardt wrote an article "Über die italienische Bauart zur Zeit der Wiedergeburt der Künste (Renaissance)" ("On the Italian Way of Building at the Time of the Rebirth of the Arts [Renaissance]"), and again his appreciation stopped short of Palladio and Vincenzo Scamozzi.[217] This was also the picture Ferdinand von Quast presented in the speech he gave in 1854 at the annual Schinkel celebration. It was, he said, a period of great artistic vitality, followed by the ostentatious forms of a Michelangelo, the stiff regu-

18. Gottried Semper, Dresden Opera House (1838–1841).
Zurich, Eidgenössische Technische Hochschule.

larity of a Palladio, and utter decline in the eighteenth century.[218] These by now more frequently expressed appreciations of post-medieval architecture, notwithstanding the qualifications that accompanied them, were an indication that by the middle of the nineteenth century the barrier impeding the artistic view had been lifted. Soon all limitations disappeared, and during the second half of the century architects felt free to choose from the wide field of architectural forms whatever seemed of use to them. Total stylistic pluralism had arrived.

Of course, in the first half of the century, and especially in the three decades during which the discussion on style had taken place, all those interested in present-day architecture were aware of having a great number of styles to choose from but at the same time realized that this breadth of choice hindered architectural progress. Metzger warned that to try to grasp the essential character of all styles created great confusion and obviously harmed true art.[219] The confusion of styles was like a "second Babel"; anything that might result from this "architectural carnival" would be a badly conceived and wrongly planned building.[220] A constant complaint was that any style whatsoever was acceptable and that the arts of all nations and of all ages were adopted and used indiscriminately.[221] "Having no style of our own," argued Gruppe, "we build at one time in the Greek style, at another in the Gothic, then in the Byzantine, perhaps even in the Anglo-Saxon, Moorish, Chinese, Egyptian, and Japanese styles."[222] From these and many similar statements one would assume that the ransacking of a multitude of styles was the common practice during these decades. Yet this was not the case. The real choice lay among three styles–the classical style of Greece and Rome, the *Rundbogenstil*, and the Gothic. Phrases like "all nations and all times" turn out to be purely rhetorical. When L. Jatho, court architect at Kassel and pupil of Wolff, declared that nowadays "the results of the architectural activities of all times and all nations . . . are at the architects' disposal, who constantly make use of them," one may be inclined to think that this sentence signals eclecticism at its height. Yet further comments make it clear that by "adopting the traditional forms of preceding styles," he too meant no more than "gaining an insight into the world of forms of antiquity as well as of the Christian Middle Ages."[223]

All this changed when the range of choice in the "world of forms" steadily expanded to include the great styles of European architecture from the fifteenth to the eighteenth centuries. Before this took place, it had been commonly held that the architectural history that mattered had started two thousand years ago in Greece and had come to a definite end in the fifteenth century with the Gothic. It seemed sensible to hope that out of one of the three "legitimate" styles that made up the whole architectural past, a new style would evolve that would meet the needs and express the ideas of the present. For thirty years this had been more than a hope. Notwithstanding the many doubts that were voiced, all who maintained the discussion on style felt that one day the goal would be reached. The ground on which this confidence rested was shaken when Hübsch's "carnival" became a reality and when younger generations yielded to the temptation to exploit the rediscovered fertility of four hundred years of European architecture.[224]

The long and passionate debate on style thus ended not with the victory of the views of one or the other of the protagonists but–more unexpectedly–simply with the passing of time.

Notes

Bracketed numbers following page numbers in the bibliographic citations below refer the reader to the translation of the cited text that appears in the present volume.

1. Mathilde Boisserée, ed., *Sulpiz Boisserée*, 2 vols. (Stuttgart: Cotta, 1862); E. Firmenich-Richartz, *Die Brüder Boisserée*, vol. 1, *Sulpiz und Melchior Boisserée als Kunstsammler* (Jena: E. Diederichs, 1916). The Boisserée collection was moved in 1810 from Cologne to Heidelberg, where Goethe visited it in 1814 and 1815. Four years later, it was moved to Stuttgart to make it more accessible to the increasing numbers of people interested in medieval art. See W. D. Robson-Scott, *The Literary Background of the Gothic Revival in Germany* (Oxford: Clarendon, 1965), 161, 190, 281.

Schlegel's work was first published in *Poetisches Taschenbuch für das Jahr 1806*. Friedrich von Schlegel, "Grundzüge der gotischen Baukunst," in *Sämmtliche Werke* (Vienna, 1823), 6: 2. For a modern critical edition, see Hans Eichner, ed., *Kritische Friedrich-Schlegel-Ausgabe* (Munich, 1959), 4: 155-204.

2. Heinrich Hübsch, *Bau-Werke*, 1st ser. (Karlsruhe: Marx, 1838), 1.

3. Ibid.

4. Ibid.

5. Ibid., 2.

6. Ibid.

7. *Über griechische Architectur* (Heidelberg: J. C. B. Mohr, 1822), 17. For the dispute between Hübsch and Hirt, see Barry Bergdoll, "Archaeology vs. History: Heinrich Hübsch's Critique of Neoclassicism and the Beginnings of Historicism in German Architectural Theory," *The Oxford Art Journal* 5, no. 2 (1982): 2-12.

8. Hübsch (see note 2), 2.

9. Christian Ludwig Stieglitz, *Geschichte der Baukunst vom frühesten Alterthume bis in die neueren Zeiten* (Nuremberg: F. Campe, 1827), 467.

10. Heinrich Hübsch, *In welchem Style sollen wir bauen?* (Karlsruhe: Chr. Fr. Müller Hofbuchhandlung und Hofbuchdruckeren, 1828), 52 [99].

11. Ibid., 13 [71].

12. "Über Styl und Motive in der bildenden Kunst," *Kunst-Blatt* 6 (1825), no. 1, 1-4; no. 75, 297-300; no. 76, 301-4.

13. Carl Friedrich von Rumohr, *Italienische Forschungen* (Berlin, 1827-1831), part 3, 195: "Von Herrn Professor Hübsch zu Frankfurth erhielt ich, kurz nach Beendigung seiner fruchtbaren Reise durch Griechenland, die Seitenansicht einer Kirche in den Umgebungen von Athen...."

14. Hübsch (see note 10), 5, 7 [66, 67-68].

15. Ibid., 18 [77].

16. Ibid., 9-10 [68-69].

17. Ibid., 21 [79].

18. Ibid., 9, 31 [69, 86].

19. Ibid., 42 [93].

20. Ibid., 8 [68].

21. Ibid., 51-52 [99-100].

22. Heinrich Hübsch, *Die Architektur und ihr Verhältniß zur heutigen Malerei und Skulptur* (Stuttgart and Tübingen: J. G. Cotta, 1847), 189-90 [172-73].

23. Rudolf Wiegmann, "Bemerkungen über die Schrift: *In welchem Styl sollen wir bauen?* von H. Hübsch," *Kunst-Blatt* 10 (1829): no. 44, 173-74; no. 45, 177-79; no. 46, 181-83 [103-12].

24. Ibid., 177 [105].

25. Hübsch (see note 10), 28 [84].

26. Ibid., 3-4 [65].

27. Ibid., 6 [67].

28. *Kunst-Blatt* 6 (1825): 298.

29. Franz Kugler, "Über den Kirchenbau und seine Bedeutung für unsere Zeit," *Museum: Blätter für bildende Kunst* 2 (1834): 1-8.

30. Ibid., 3-5.

31. Ibid., 4. Kugler cites the second paragraph on page 13 of Hübsch's treatise.

32. Ibid., 5.

33. Carl Albert Rosenthal, *Über die Entstehung und Bedeutung der architektonischen Formen der Griechen* (Berlin, 1830), 1. On Rosenthal, see Eva Börsch-Supan, *Berliner Baukunst nach Schinkel: 1840-1870* (Munich: Prestel Verlag, 1977), 27, nn. 109, 110.

34. Carl Albert Rosenthal, "In welchem Style sollen wir bauen? (Eine Frage für die Mitglieder des deutschen Architektenvereins)," *Zeitschrift für praktische Baukunst* 4 (1844): 23-27 [113-23].

35. Eduard Metzger, "Über die Einwirkung natürlicher und struktiver Gesetze auf Formgestaltung des Bauwerkes," *Allgemeine Bauzeitung* 2, nos. 21-26 (1837): 169-215.

36. Ibid., 170-71.

37. Ibid., 189.

38. Ibid., 194.

39. Ibid., 195.

40. Ibid., 196.

41. Ibid., 201.

42. Eduard Metzger, "Untersuchungen im Gebiete der Architectur," *Münchner Jahrbücher für bildende Kunst* 1 (1838): 42-74; 2 (1839): 117-52.

43. Ibid., 44.

44. Ibid., 51.

45. Ibid., 53.

46. Ibid., 42.

47. Johann Andreas Romberg, "Konstruktion und Form," *Zeitschrift für praktische Baukunst* 1 (1841): 154–75.

48. Ibid., 156, 157.

49. Anton Hallmann, *Kunstbestrebungen der Gegenwart* (Berlin: Buchhandlung des Berliner Lesekabinets, 1842), 20. See Sabine Kimpel, "Der Maler-Architekt Anton Hallmann (1812–1845)" (Ph.D. diss., Ludwig-Maximilians-Universität, Munich, 1974).

50. Metzger (see note 35), 189.

51. Friedrich von Schlegel, *Deutsches Museum* (Vienna, 1812), 1: 283. See Eichner (see note 1), 1: 230.

52. Franz Kugler, *Karl Friedrich Schinkel* (Berlin: G. Gropius, 1842), republished in idem, *Kleine Schriften und Studien zur Kunstgeschichte* (Stuttgart: Ebner & Seubert, 1854), 3: 313–14.

53. L. Jatho, "Über das Streben nach einem neuen nationalen Baustyle vom Standpunkte des praktischen Architekten aus betrachtet," *Zeitschrift für praktische Baukunst* 7 (1847): 58.

54. Rudolf Wiegmann, "Polemisches," *Zeitschrift für praktische Baukunst* 2 (1842): 499.

55. Johann Heinrich Wolff, "Einige Worte über die von Herrn Professor Stier bei der Architektenversammlung zu Bamberg zur Sprache gebrachten (und im Jahrgange 1843 dieser Zeitschrift S. 301 mitgetheilten) architektonischen Fragen," *Allgemeine Bauzeitung* (*Literatur…Beilage*) 2 (1845): 269 [144].

56. Friedrich Eisenlohr, *Rede über den Baustyl der neueren Zeit* (Karlsruhe, 1833), 27.

57. J. D. W. E. Engelhardt, "Architektonische Zustände und Bestrebungen in Kurhessen," *Zeitschrift für Bauwesen* 2 (1852): 219.

58. "Ein neuer Baustyl," *Deutsches Kunstblatt* 2 (1851): 145.

59. Leo von Klenze, *Anweisung zur Architektur des christlichen Cultus* (Munich: In der liter. artist. Anstalt, 1833), 9.

60. Johann Heinrich Wolff, "Polemisches: Berichtigung," *Allgemeine Bauzeitung* 12 (1847) (*Literatur…Beilage*) 3, no. 9: 180.

61. Hübsch (see note 22), 190.

62. Ferdinand Wilhelm Horn, "Das Horn'sche System eines neugermanischen Baustyls," *Zeitschrift für praktische Baukunst* 5 (1845): 244. This is a detailed résumé of Horn's book, published in Potsdam in 1845 under the same title. See Börsch-Supan (see note 33), 192–93.

63. Johann Heinrich Wolff, "Polemisches: Entgegnung," *Allgemeine Bauzeitung* (*Literatur…Beilage*) (1843): 2.

64. Wolff (see note 55), 270 [144].

65. Hübsch (see note 10), 18 [77].

66. Rosenthal (see note 34), 24 [116].

67. Rudolf Wiegmann, "Gegensätze: Die Tendenz des Hrn. Prof. J. H. Wolff und 'Die Christlich-germanische Baukunst und ihr Verhältniß zur Gegenwart von A. Reichensperger, Trier, 1845,' nebst einer Schlussbetrachtung," *Allgemeine Bauzeitung* 11 (1846) (*Literatur... Beilage*) 3, no. 1: 4.

68. Rosenthal (see note 34), 24 [117].

69. Carl Gottlieb Wilhelm Bötticher, "Das Prinzip der hellenischen und germanischen Bauweise hinsichtlich der Übertragung in die Bauweise unserer Tage," *Allgemeine Bauzeitung* 11 (1846): 113-14 [151].

70. Hübsch (see note 10), 51 [99].

71. Wiegmann (see note 23), 173 [104].

72. Rudolf Wiegmann, *Der Ritter Leo von Klenze und unsere Kunst* (Düsseldorf: J. H. C. Schreiner, 1839), 56.

73. Semper-Archiv, Zurich, MS. 25 (1840), fol. 196.

74. Rudolf Wiegmann, "Gedanken über die Entwickelung eines zeitgemäßen nazionalen Baustyls," *Allgemeine Bauzeitung* 6 (1841): 213.

75. Wiegmann (see note 67), 18.

76. Gottfried Semper, *Über den Bau evangelischer Kirchen* (Leipzig: In Commission bei B. G. Teubner, 1845), 27.

77. "Über den Bau christlicher Kirchen," *Allgemeine Bauzeitung* 12 (1847): 283.

78. Rosenthal (see note 34), 27 [121-22]. As early as 1815 Schinkel had declared that the Gothic style had been interrupted in its prime ("nachdem die Gotik in der Blüte durch einen wunderbaren und wohltätigen Rückblick auf die Antike unterbrochen ward"; cited by G. F. Koch, "Schinkels architektonische Entwürfe im gotischen Stil 1810-1815," *Zeitschrift für Kunstgeschichte* 32 [1969]: 300). However, in contrast to the writers just quoted, Schinkel believed that the interruption was caused by the "wonderful and beneficial event of looking back to antiquity," and not by any adverse and unwelcome circumstances. See also Börsch-Supan (see note 33), 185, 201.

79. Wiegmann (see note 72), 51.

80. Johann Heinrich Wolff, *Allgemeine Bauzeitung* (*Literatur... Beilage*) (1842): 451-58. Klenze's *Sammlung architektonischer Entwürfe* was published in Munich in 1830; Wolff reviewed the first three installments.

81. Ibid., 451.

82. Wiegmann (see note 54), 498–500.

83. Wiegmann (see note 72), Preface, 9-10, 41ff., 69ff. In fact, this treatise was Wiegmann's response to the–at times–critical remarks made by Klenze in his *Aphoristische Bemerkungen* (Berlin, 1838) on Wiegmann's own study of ancient painting technique, *Die Malerei der Alten* (Hannover: Hahn, 1836).

84. Wiegmann (see note 23), 182 [110].

85. Wiegmann (see note 54), 499.

86. Wolff (see note 63), 1, 4.

87. Ibid., 1.

88. Ibid., 2.

89. Wiegmann (see note 67), 1-19.

90. Ibid., 2.

91. Ibid. (On the effect of introducing iron as a building material see pages 43-46.)

92. Ibid., 2.

93. Ibid., 3.

94. Ibid., 4.

95. August Reichensperger, *Die Christlich-germanische Baukunst und ihr Verhältniß zur Gegenwart: Nebst einem Berichte Schinkel's aus dem Jahre 1816, den Cölner Dombau betreffend* (Trier: F. Lintz, 1845).

96. Wiegmann (see note 67), 14.

97. Ibid.

98. Ibid., 18-19.

99. Wolff (see note 60), 178.

100. Ibid., 180.

101. Wolff (see note 55), 261-62 [132-34].

102. Wolff (see note 60), 180.

103. Ibid., 181.

104. Ibid., 182.

105. Wolff (see note 55), 263 [135-36].

106. Wolff (see note 60), 185.

107. Hübsch (see note 2), 2.

108. Hübsch (see note 10), 47 [96].

109. Ibid., 44 [94].

110. Ibid.

111. Ibid., 46 [96].

112. Hübsch (see note 2), vol. 2, text to design of Polytechnische Hochschule.

113. Ibid., vol. 1, text to design of Trinkhalle.

114. Franz Kugler, *Museum: Blätter für bildende Kunst* 3 (1835): 191.

115. *Kunst-Blatt* 13 (1832), 382.

116. Oswald Hederer, *Friedrich von Gärtner* (Munich: Prestel Verlag, 1976), 114.

117. Klaus Eggert, *Die Hauptwerke Friedrich v. Gärtners* (Munich: Stadtarchivs, 1963), 71.

118. The king was Ludwig I (r. 1825-1848). Hederer (see note 116), 118.

119. For studies on the *Rundbogenstil*, see Albrecht Mann, *Die Neuromanik* (Cologne: Greven, 1966); Michael Bringmann, "Studien zur neuromanischen Architektur in Deutsch-

land" (Inaugural diss., Ruprecht-Karls-Universität Heidelberg, 1968), 24ff.; and the chapter "Rundbogenstil" in the comprehensive work by Kurt Milde, *Neorenaissance in der deutsche Architektur des 19. Jahrhunderts* (Dresden: Verlag der Kunst, 1981), 116-27; also the recent article by Kathleen Curran, "The German Rundbogenstil and Reflections on the American Round-Arched Style," *Journal of the Society of Architectural Historians* 47 (1988), 341-66.

120. Eggert (see note 117), 21-22.

121. Wiegmann (see note 74), 213.

122. Ibid., 214.

123. Rudolf Wiegmann, review of Schinkel's *Werke der höheren Baukunst, Allgemeine Bauzeitung (Literatur...Beilage)*, installments 1-3 (1841): 407. Wiegmann refers here to the incompability of Schinkel's classical style and the "spirit of the Christian Era."

124. Carl Gottlieb Wilhelm Bötticher, *Die Tektonik der Hellenen* (Potsdam: Ferdinand Riegel, 1844); on this see Börsch-Supan (see note 33), 20-21, 101-2.

125. *Kunst-Blatt* 26 (1845): nos. 11-15, 46.

126. Bötticher (see note 124), 1-26.

127. Ibid., 1-8.

128. Ibid., 8-17.

129. Ibid., 11.

130. Ibid., 16.

131. Ibid., 18-21.

132. Ibid., 21-26.

133. Ibid., 23.

134. Ibid., 26.

135. On the notion of synthesis, see Norbert Knopp, "Schinkels Idee einer Stilsynthese," in *Beiträge zum Problem des Stilpluralismus*, ed. Werner Hagen and Norbert Knopp (Munich: Prestel Verlag, 1977), 245-54.

136. Ibid., 247, 252; Curran (see note 119), 361; Börsch-Supan (see note 33), n. 116 and p. 188.

137. Bötticher (see note 69), 112 [149].

138. Ibid., 121 [161].

139. Ibid., [160].

140. Ibid., 117 [156].

141. In 1831 the Bauakademie (founded in 1799) was given the name Allgemeine Bauschule, by which it was known until 1849, when its name was changed back to the original one. See Adolf Borbein, "Klassische Archäologie in Berlin vom 18. zum 20. Jahrhundert," in Deutsches Archäologisches Institut, *Berlin und die Antike: Aufsätze* (Berlin: Deutsches Archäologisches Institut, Wasmuth, 1979), 110. In 1945 the interior of Schinkel's building was destroyed by firebombs. Although the shell remained intact and work to restore it began in 1960, a subsequent decision to pull it down was carried out despite strong protests. Only the main porch,

with its decorative framework, remains; it now serves as the entrance to a restaurant.

142. Regarding its structure, see also the technical report by the supervisor Emil Flaminius, *Allgemeine Bauzeitung* 1 (1836): 1ff.

143. Ernst Kopp, *Beitrag zur Darstellung eines reinen einfachen Baustyls* (Dresden, 1837), 1: 1.

144. Kugler, 1842 (see note 52), 326-27.

145. Franz Kugler, *Kunst-Blatt* 27 (1846): 61.

146. The debate was reported and discussed in the following journals: *Deutsches Kunstblatt* 2 (1852): full report of the debate on 10, 17, and 24 April with editor's comment on 24 April (quoted passage on p. 142), on 24 May a letter by Reichensperger replying to editor's comment and a further reply by editor (quoted passage on p. 177). *Zeitschrift für Bauwesen* 2 (1852): 233-37, report of the debate and editorial critical comment. *Zeitschrift für praktische Baukunst* 12 (1852): under the heading "In welchem Style sollen wir bauen?" 192–304, prints Reichensperger's speech and the editorial comment from *Zeitschrift für Bauwesen* verbatim, together with another reply by Reichensperger published in *Organ für christliche Kunst*.

147. Otto Friedrich Gruppe, *Carl Friedrich Schinkel und der neue Berliner Dom* (Berlin, 1843), 52.

148. Erik Forssman, *Karl Friedrich Schinkel: Bauwerke und Baugedanken* (Zurich: Schnell & Steiner, 1981), 207.

149. Friedrich Wilhelm Ludwig Stier, "Beiträge zur Feststellung des Principes der Baukunst für das vaterländische Bauwesen der Gegenwart: Architrav und Bogen," *Allgemeine Bauzeitung* 8 (1843): 309-39. On Stier (1799-1856), see Thieme-Becker, *Allgemeines Künstlerlexikon* (1938), 13: 44; see also Börsch-Supan (see note 33), 19-20, 683 89.

150. Stier (see note 149), 310-11.

151. Ibid., 311-13.

152. Ibid., 317.

153. Ibid., 318.

154. Ibid., 313.

155. Ibid., 319.

156. Ibid., 319-20.

157. Ibid., 321.

158. Ibid., 325-26.

159. Ibid., 327-29.

160. Ibid., 330-31.

161. Ibid., 331-34.

162. Ibid., 334-38.

163. Ibid., 336.

164. Ibid., 338.

165. Ibid., 339.

166. Carl Gottlieb Wilhelm Bötticher, "Polemisch-Kritisches," *Allgemeine Bauzeitung* (*Literatur…Beilage*) (1845): 281-320.

167. Ibid., 297.

168. Wolff, "Ein Prinzip und keine Parteien!" *Allgemeine Bauzeitung* 11 (1846): 358-67. On this paper see Milde (see note 119), 184.

169. Wolff (see note 168), 359.

170. Ibid., 361.

171. Ibid., 362.

172. Ibid., 362-64.

173. Ibid., 361.

174. Ibid., 365-66.

175. Eduard Metzger, "Beitrag zur Zeitfrage: In welchem Stil man bauen soll?" *Allgemeine Bauzeitung* 10 (1845): 169-79.

176. Wolff (see note 55), 255-70 [125-45].

177. Ibid., 261-62 [132-34].

178. Ibid., 263-64 [134-37].

179. Ibid., 268-69 [142-44].

180. Metzger (see note 175), 172; Wolff (see note 55), 262 [134].

181. Metzger (see note 175), 172.

182. Ibid., 175.

183. Metzger (see note 35), 189.

184. Metzger (see note 175), 176.

185. Ibid., 177.

186. Hederer (see note 116), 189ff.; Metzger (see note 175), 178.

187. Hederer (see note 116), 244-45.

188. Metzger (see note 175), 177.

189. Bötticher (see note 124), 26.

190. Bötticher (see note 166), 293.

191. Bötticher (see note 124), 17-18, 23.

192. Bötticher (see note 69), 116 [154].

193. Ibid., 119 [158].

194. Ibid.

195. Ibid., 120 [159].

196. Hallmann (see note 49), 71.

197. J. Fuss, *Allgemeine Bauzeitung* 7 (1842): 531, 533.

198. Wiegmann (see note 67), 16.

199. Ibid., 2.

200. Wolff (see note 60), 187.

201. Gruppe (see note 147), 119.

202. Hübsch (see note 22), 190-91, 195 [172-73, 175].

203. See page 15 and note 101.

204. Hübsch (see note 22), 175. Hübsch used this and many other equally derogatory terms when he devoted chapter thirteen of *Die Architektur* (see note 22, 168-85) to a highly critical examination of Renaissance architecture: "sham architecture" (p. 169), "dishonest and untrue" (p. 178), "slavish imitation of Roman architecture" (p. 169), "accumulation of thick blocks of stone and heavy barrel vaultings" (p. 172).

205. Rosenthal (see note 34), 25 [118].

206. Wiegmann (see note 23), 173 [104]: "...a so-called style...arbitrarily...pieced together from the fifteenth century onward"; idem (see note 67), 18: "artistic jargon called Renaissance"; Bötticher (see note 69), 115 [153]; Wolff (see note 55), 269 [143].

207. Johann Andreas Romberg, "Fragen an die deutsche Architekten- und Ingenieur-Versammlung zu Halberstadt," *Zeitschrift für praktische Baukunst* 5 (1845): 8.

208. Wolff (see note 168), 360.

209. Hübsch (see note 22), 171, 178.

210. Horn (see note 62), 245.

211. Reichensperger (see note 95), 26 and 61, where he speaks of the Renaissance as the "pseudo-heathen growth that like ivy crept up on the mighty medieval building, entangling all forms."

212. Franz Kugler, *Handbuch der Kunstgeschichte* (Stuttgart: Ebner & Seubert, 1842), 624. The phrase about "trailing [or dragging] along the ancient forms" was taken up by Metzger in 1845 (see note 175), 176. On Kugler's treatment of Renaissance architecture see Eva Börsch-Supan, "Der Renaissancebegriff der Berliner Schule im Vergleich zu Semper," in *Gottfried Semper und die Mitte des 19. Jahrhunderts* (Basel: Birkhäuser, 1976), 162.

213. Romberg (see note 47), 159-60.

214. Ibid., 165ff.

215. Semper-Archiv, Zurich, MS. 178, fol. 61.

216. Stier (see note 149), 337-38.

217. J. D. W. E. Engelhardt, "Über die italienische Bauart zur Zeit der Wiedergeburt der Künste (Renaissance)," *Journal für die Baukunst* (1850): 209-51.

218. Cited by Börsch-Supan (see note 33), 73.

219. Metzger (see note 42), 52.

220. Wolff (see note 168), 358; Hübsch (see note 22), 186 [170].

221. Wiegmann (see note 74), 208; Wolff (see note 60), 179.

222. Gruppe (see note 147), 75.

223. Jatho (see note 53), 54-55.

224. Michael Bringmann concluded his excellent study of neo-Romanesque architecture with the observation that a clear distinction must be made between the architecture of the first and the second fifty years of the nineteenth century, because the early decades—apart from a comparatively moderate application of historical styles—had little in common with the strong impact of stylistic pluralism after the middle of the century: Bringmann (see note 119), 330–31. Börsch-Supan (see note 212), 163, also comments on the change in the art-historical conception of the Renaissance that took place around 1850.

IN WHAT
STYLE
SHOULD WE BUILD?

The German Debate on Architectural Style

Johann Anton Ramboux, *Portrait of the Architect Heinrich Hübsch*, ca. 1820.
Drawing. Darmstadt, Hessisches Landesmuseum, no. HZ 4288.

In What

Style

Should We Build?

Heinrich Hübsch

1.

Painting and sculpture have long since abandoned the life-less imitation of antiquity. Architecture alone has yet to come of age and continues to imitate the antique style. Although nearly everybody recognizes the inadequacy of that style in meeting today's needs and is dissatisfied with the buildings recently erected in it, almost all architects still adhere to it. Most of them really believe that the beauty of architectural forms is something absolute, which can remain unchanged for all times and under all circumstances, and that the antique style alone presents these forms in ideal perfection. Many architects who fully recognize the inadequacy of using the antique style nevertheless dishonestly insist on it out of vanity, since they happen to have erected several buildings in this style. Like false prophets, they claim the privilege of an inspiration—that of beauty—for which they claim to need no justification. Other architects, it is true, admit that it must first be proven that the architecture of the ancients, as universal architecture, can be as appropriate and beautiful to us as it once was to the Greeks. To this end they go to enormous and self-deceiving lengths to construct a system of specious arguments. In this way only a very limited field is allotted to sound reason and, then, only in matters of detail; as soon as reason tends to come too close to essentials, it is quickly rebutted by an authority. A few architects recognize the pointlessness of all this sophistry, but not knowing anything better to put in its place, they lose heart and despair of ever establishing firm and adequate principles of beauty. Hence, they think it impossible to create a suitable architectural style through reflection and—in sheer desperation, as it were—continue to build in the ancient style, where at least they have the sanction of an obsolete authority.

Whoever looks at architecture primarily from its decorative aspect and perhaps asks himself why he likes one form of leafwork on a capital better than another will easily despair of the possibility of establishing reliable principles. Yet whoever starts his investigation from the point of view of practical necessity will find a secure base. Now, since the size and arrangement of every building is conditioned by its purpose, which is the main reason for its existence, and since its continued existence depends on the physical properties of the material and on the resulting arrangement and formation of the individual parts, it is obvious that two criteria of functionality [*Zweckmäßigkeit*]—namely, fitness for purpose (commodity) and lasting existence (solidity)—determine the size and basic form of the essential parts of every building. These formative factors, derived from function, are surely as objective and as clear as they could possibly be. Yet they do not determine the size and basic form of the essential parts with any exactness. They present a path that is firm yet not too narrow: though clearly indicating the main direction, it still allows some latitude. For instance, if we know the number of people that a hall is to hold, this does not exactly determine the proportion of its length to its width, let alone to its height. Or, if we know the load that a pillar made of a certain material and prescribed height has to carry, this does not give us its exact diameter in inches and lines.

An open-minded person must admit, furthermore, that the factors controlling the shape of the less essential parts are by no means immutable and that they become less objective the more detailed they become. Thus, for instance, the reason why a column shaft of uniform diameter is preferred to one whose upper part is formed differently from its lower part will not be as self-evident as the principle that the shaft of a column must first of all stand vertically. Should one then ask oneself which of two shafts is more beautiful, one with twenty flutings or another with twenty-four flutings, it would be hard to give a reason for one's choice.

In this way some uncertainty and arbitrariness arises even with regard to the principal forms and appears from a narrow theoretical point of view to degrade the art. This is the reason for the frequent efforts of aestheticians to construct systems to account for the specific detail of architectural forms—efforts that must unfailingly result in empty sophisms.

If we take a more practical view, our courage revives. Though it is true that this uncertainty and arbitrariness make art into a plant that easily runs to seed, there are limits; and the danger is really not so great as may appear at first glance. The beauty of a building, like the beauty of a landscape or a symphony, is composed of many elements, all of which are not of equal importance in relation to the whole. Just as in a landscape a tree here or there might be dispensed with or replaced by another tree or in a symphony a few passages might be changed without affecting the overall impression, so two quite differently decorated capitals can be equally beautiful on the same column; and even its size, though more significant, is not as important as, say, the distance between columns, while the latter in its turn is not as important as the basic form [*Grundgestalt*] of the building as a whole. This does not mean, however, that the choice of less essential elements can be left to blind chance but rather that here the artist's talent and taste are mainly called upon.

Whoever views the monuments of different nations impartially will find that much has been formed, as it were, unconsciously, in accordance with the artist's individual taste, and that this in itself is the cause of a lively diversity that ceases when we try to place those forms for whose development no objective laws exist under the tutelage of conventional rules.

Therefore, we should not demand what has never existed and never will. We should be content that the formation of the main parts proceeds from objective principles and, for the rest, let the artist's taste have free rein.

Unbiased reflection that starts from this point of view and always verifies its own conclusions historically, by reference to the principles that truly emerge from the monuments of earlier times and nations, is bound to lead to a satisfactory conclusion. Even someone who still despairs of ever reaching such a conclusion must at least concede that a sound beginning has been deduced from obvious needs; he may then stop halfway, if he believes that the investigation is no longer sufficiently objective.

2

We shall first define the concept of style. In its familiar usage—for instance, all Greek monuments are said to be built in the Greek style, all Moorish monuments in the Moorish style—style means something general, applicable to all buildings of a nation, whether intended for divine worship, for public administration, for education, etc. The most general requirement for all kinds of buildings is the enclosure of a specific space in such a way that it is accessible and well lit; and just as its interior provides shelter, its exterior, if it is to last, must itself be protected against the weather.

Hence, we arrive at the following essential parts of a building. The enclosure requires a ceiling and its supports, which also serve either as enclosing walls or solely as supports for the ceiling. The last condition occurs when either the space that needs to be covered is too wide for a ceiling to span it unsupported from wall to wall or when simply a ceiling and no lateral enclosure—or at least not one on every side—is required (that is, an open portico). Piers or columns spanned by connecting members are then set up—in the first case between the enclosing walls and in the second case at intervals along the open sides. The spanning members stretching from pier to pier provide the ceiling with continuous support, like a wall. Their height varies according to circumstances, but their width usually corresponds to the thickness of the piers. If the ceiling is in the form of a groin vault, its ribs serve as the spanning members.

The door and window openings that are set into the walls to provide access and light are spanned in the same way as the piers; above them, the walls continue up as far as may be required. For exterior protection, the ceiling is covered by a roof (which at times is one and the same); the projection of the roof constitutes the main cornice—at least, in most cases the cornice is a continuation of the surface of the roof.

These are the essential parts of a building. They relate to the most basic task of architecture and must therefore be regarded as the elements of style. When examined historically, these architectural elements are indeed of a general character, retaining the same form in different cases. For that reason, the difference between the monuments of one nation and one period lies in the number and manifold combinations of walls, ceilings, piers or columns, doors, windows, roofs, and cornices, according to their various purposes. All vary in size and in degree of decoration: all are more or less enriched according to the importance of their purpose. Aside from these variations, however, the same type reappears again and again, even in its decorative detail. Finally, it is evident that specific needs also affect the style in that those of one nation, despite local variations, display a common character when compared to the total needs of another country.

The present investigation is, therefore, concerned only with the general form of architectural elements and their combination, not with their specific form and combination in relation to the functions of particular buildings, which is the artist's primary task and bears witness to his talent. This investigation aims at giving the artist an explanation of the essence of his subject and at providing a secure base for criticism, since in this sphere we differ so much that we do not even agree on the ABC's.

3.

Having now established what is meant by style, we must examine its manifestations in the various original forms of architecture.

The principal formative factors, as can be deduced a priori as well as confirmed historically, are climate and building material. In the first place the climate, as already mentioned, gives a uniform character to the needs of one country as compared with another. Thus, a mild southern climate makes less exacting demands than the rough climate of the north; all eastern buildings appear to be somewhat open in contrast to the anxiously closed-in buildings of the north.

Secondly, the exterior will be given greater or lesser protection, depending on the rigor or mildness of the climate; this becomes apparent in the form of the roof and of other elements. Egypt, with no rainfall at all, has buildings without any roof; the medieval buildings of the north have tall roofs, and all their projecting parts are formed in such a way that the water can easily run off.

The materials that chiefly affect the form of the architectural elements are wood and stone. Even in countries where stone is scarce, the more important buildings use stone not only for walls and piers but also for the members that connect the piers or span the openings, wherever these are exposed to weathering. Often, even large interior ceilings are made of stone so as to last.

The basic form of walls and piers is not much affected by the nature of the material, since they have to stand vertically, whether made of wood or stone, and have the same thickness from top to bottom. The material has a greater effect on the ratio of thickness to height; this is determined by the resistance of the material to compression and buckling (reactive strength). Therefore, height, load, and all other circumstances being equal, a pier of hard marble is made thinner than one made of soft tuff. The material has its greatest effect on the main form and on the proportions of spans and ceilings. Wood grows straight to a considerable length and offers strong resistance to fracture. Therefore, it is in the nature of a wooden ceiling always to be rectilinear and to have a low ratio of thickness or height to unsupported span. Stone usually breaks into cube-shaped or slablike pieces and is rarely—in many places never—found in long beamlike pieces. Stone also has little resistance to breaking (relative strength), to which must be added its considerable specific weight. It, therefore, cannot sustain its own weight over a wide horizontal span and must be thicker than a wooden beam of equal length. Yet there are great differences among the different kinds of stone. In Greek monuments, mostly built of marble (the stone with the highest elasticity and relative strength), all column lintels (architraves) and soffits consisted of stone beams and plates, so that there were continuous horizontal spans in stone like those in timber, sometimes of very light proportions. It should be noted that the architectural proportions so far dealt with should more correctly be called *technostatic* proportions, as distinct from the main proportions that derive from the purpose of the building. These latter proportions include the ratio of length to height, both in the building as a whole and in its individual rooms and sections: for instance, the relation of the width (depth) of a portico to its height.

In countries where the available varieties of stone are brittle and not found in great lengths, attempts were soon made to span the opening with more than one piece of stone. The crowning result of these attempts was the vault. With vaulting, aided by mortar, the widest openings could be spanned with pieces of almost any size, however small. The vault not only greatly influenced the form of covering, since its construction naturally followed a curve rather than the straight line of a single lintel, but also changed the form of the piers and walls on which, by resting on them, it exerted a lateral pressure. Thus almost every architectural element changed—in other words the whole style—so that it may be said that essentially there are only two original styles: one with straight, horizontal stone architraves; the other with curved vaults and arches.

4.

Building, being a skilled craft, is of course bound to improve with time. With the advance of civilization, the needs and demands for comfort expand, as do the tasks of architecture; and so people try to carry them out more efficiently and with less mechanical work. Apart from making improvements in the treatment of the material as such, they seek in the first place to obtain the necessary solidity through ingenious construction rather than through a mere accumulation of heavy masses. In the second place, even with unchanged methods of construction, they seek to reduce the mass of material, which with the growing need for comfort becomes more and more of an impediment: successive new buildings become lighter while remaining safe. In other words, lighter technostatic proportions are applied than in those older buildings that by their continued existence have proved to be of sufficient strength. This empirical progress in technostatics—or, if I may thus express it, in technostatic judgment by eye—must happen all the more regularly because a nation's previous experience is never lost but is constantly available to succeeding generations through the buildings that survive.

That this progress regularly occurs is shown by the monuments of nations known to us. It is even transmitted through a succession of nations in contact with each other. Of course the pace of progress, impeded in any case by the need for stability and by the force of custom, differs considerably among nations. It depends, in general, on how flexible and unimpeded their evolution has been and on the effect of political events. In Egypt where the priests had many workmen at their disposal, progress was very slow: all buildings were massive, and no real difference is apparent even over many centuries. The freer Greeks advanced more quickly; thus, the monuments built one to two hundred years after Pericles used considerably less material than those built before Pericles. With the Romans—who took over the architecture of the Greeks and who, having far more diverse needs, were necessarily more concerned with spaciousness and economy of material—lightness steadily increased to reach its peak in the medieval style.

Although reduction of mass and bolder construction (that is, lighter technostatic proportions) apply equally to lintels, ceilings, walls, and piers, this is less obvious in ceilings and walls, whose thickness can hardly be seen, than it is in freestanding piers with longer unsupported spans that lead to wider and bolder spacing. This is, of course, especially apparent in porticoes, where the distance between piers is least conditioned by the particular purpose of the structure.

To summarize this section: while it is true that the technostatic proportions of the architectural elements mainly derive from the material, they constantly evolve with advancing architectural experience and, in fact, are subject to permanent change. The basic forms of the architectural elements were set out in Section 3, above. In what follows we shall explain how the progress of architecture as a fine art affects the specific shape of these elements.

5

Architecture should not be called a sister of the other arts but rather their mother; this is the art that leads the way and educates the others. It begins by satisfying the most pressing needs; only later, when it produces buildings intended for a higher purpose, does it gradually rise to the level of a fine art. These buildings soon come to be planned on a grander scale with greater richness and elaboration of workmanship than is considered appropriate for utilitarian buildings. Once necessity is satisfied, there is pleasure in free creation: ornaments are added in the belief that these unnecessary adjuncts, the offspring of idleness, will in some way enhance the value of the building. A more refined treatment of architectural elements also gradually arises through the greater delicacy of form, which together with the technostatic progress already mentioned tends to do away with all mass that is unnecessary for strength and that detracts from convenience. Yet this is done as a kind of spontaneous play, so that solidity and convenience act more as indirect than as direct regulating factors.

With every human activity, the force that leads to perfection already contains the germ of decline; and so it is with architecture. On the one hand, all its parts evolve in accord with the regular progress of technostatics, of ornament, and of formal delicacy; on the other hand, it loses that truly moving simplicity and unpretentiousness of the early buildings, which never represent more than what they are. Embellishment extends beyond its true sphere, which is that of adorning (not overloading) the essential forms or elements. Yet more pernicious than this decorative overloading is the fact that the architectural elements themselves, whose origin and use are rooted solely in their true purpose, and which are meaningful only insofar as they fulfill this purpose, acquire an immediate appeal simply as skillful workmanship [*Machwerk*]. In time (as it happens so often that one forgets the goal while on the way) the architectural elements are treated more and more as embellishments or, rather, as means to make the building seem more important than its true purpose can ever make it. First, the elements are applied to places where true purpose does not call for them and where they serve a sham purpose only; then, even this fictitious purpose is dispensed with, and the architect rests content, as it were, with the sham of a sham: with completely dead forms such as blind windows, doors, etc. In order to allay misgivings, a wholly conventional aesthetic forum is postulated, which supplies the argument that this or that essential form arises, at least initially, from some real purpose. The decline of art is hastened in no small measure by the fact that quite independently, technostatic experience is constantly growing, and daring combinations of forms, driven to extremes by the craze for variation, become progressively easier to execute.

In reality, the sequence does not, of course, proceed with such regularity. Some steps are brought about very quickly by political events, while at times there is even a step backward to something better. Yet everyone who surveys the monuments of past peoples must recognize the process just described. Unfortunately, the last stage is always the most fully completed, whereas the earlier and better stage is rarely found to have developed undisturbed, since few nations have enjoyed a harmonious development from childhood to manhood without the intrusion of foreign influence. Most nations, in fact, are like cuttings transplanted in alien soil. Consequently, architectural embellishment is usually traditional and, because of its arbitrary nature, could hardly be otherwise. It is part of human nature to hold on to the familiar, not only in matters of arbitrary choice but also in necessary matters; and so, when the forms of the elements become more refined, much is accepted—or rather retained— that might, by its nature, have been given a characteristic form in line with current circumstances. Such anomalous survivals are not easily found in the Greek style, but they frequently appear in the earlier phase of the medieval style, as we shall see.

6.

Apart from the natural formative factors discussed in the preceding three sections, no others are essential. Where other, conventional factors are active, everyone will regard this activity as hostile to the consistent and harmonious development of style as soon as it goes beyond the decorative sphere. At one time, it was a common deduction in support of "xylomania" that style was indeed a result of the named fac- tors—not in the way these act at present but as they did in primeval times when the first hut was built, the event whereby original sin was fully brought into architecture.[1] Surely, all this no longer needs to be refuted. For this, I refer the reader to my book on Greek architecture.

If we wish, therefore, to attain a style that has the same qualities as the buildings of other nations that are accepted as beautiful and are much praised by us, then this cannot arise from the past but only from the present state of natural forma- tive factors—that is: first, from our usual building material; second, from the present level of technostatic experience; third, from the kind of protection that buildings need in our climate in order to last; and fourth, from the more general nature of our needs based on climate and perhaps in part on culture.

Our material—to refer for the present to Germany alone and to deal with stone buildings only—is sandstone or other types of stone, which, with regard to their relative strength, are far inferior to marble. An unsupported beam, even with nothing but its own weight to carry, can with rare exceptions span at most a distance of twelve feet, and there is always the fear that it might break at the onset of a severe frost. If a stone has to carry a load in addition to its own weight, then it must be almost as high as its unsupported length. Even ashlar blocks resting on each other in a massive wall are scarcely made longer than three times their height; if their beds are weighted more toward the edges than at the center, then the edges will chip. How different it is with marble in this respect! On Greek monuments, in order to reduce the work of dressing, only a narrow strip along the edge of each stone was finished to a close fit, while the middle part was somewhat hollowed out and left rough, so that the load rested entirely on the edges. Porticoes with ceilings constructed entirely of marble can be found to have had unsupported beams of up to twenty feet with their height barely one-seventh of their length. The unsupported beams over the portico of the Temple of Theseus in Athens, which are still in place, have a width that is only one-eleventh of their length of twelve and a half feet. We, however, must construct a relieving arch above a window lintel with only three feet of unsupported length to free it of all dead weight.

Regarding the level of our technostatic experience, we have the bold constructions of medieval buildings before us. In this respect we far surpass the Greeks. Any expert today would without hesitation (provided the circumstances are not unfavorable) set up a pier or a column with a diameter of only one-eleventh its height, whereas with even the slimmer Greek columns the diameter is rarely less than one-eighth its height. Furthermore, he would support a ceiling by constructing arcades (fig. I) with one-third fewer piers or columns than would be needed in a Greek colonnade of the same length—even one that does not have the narrowest intercolumniation (fig. II). Thus, by using vaults to support the ceiling, we require far less than half the mass of material that was used in Greek architecture without having to fear a collapse, which with our brittle stones is a constant threat in horizontal spans. Moreover, since an arch needs only small blocks of stone, whereas the stone beam of an architrave must be made from one block, and since transport and setting up is comparatively very expensive, a colonnade of normal dimensions costs about four times as much as an arcade with equally rich decoration. No expert will deny that this disparity greatly increases with larger dimensions.

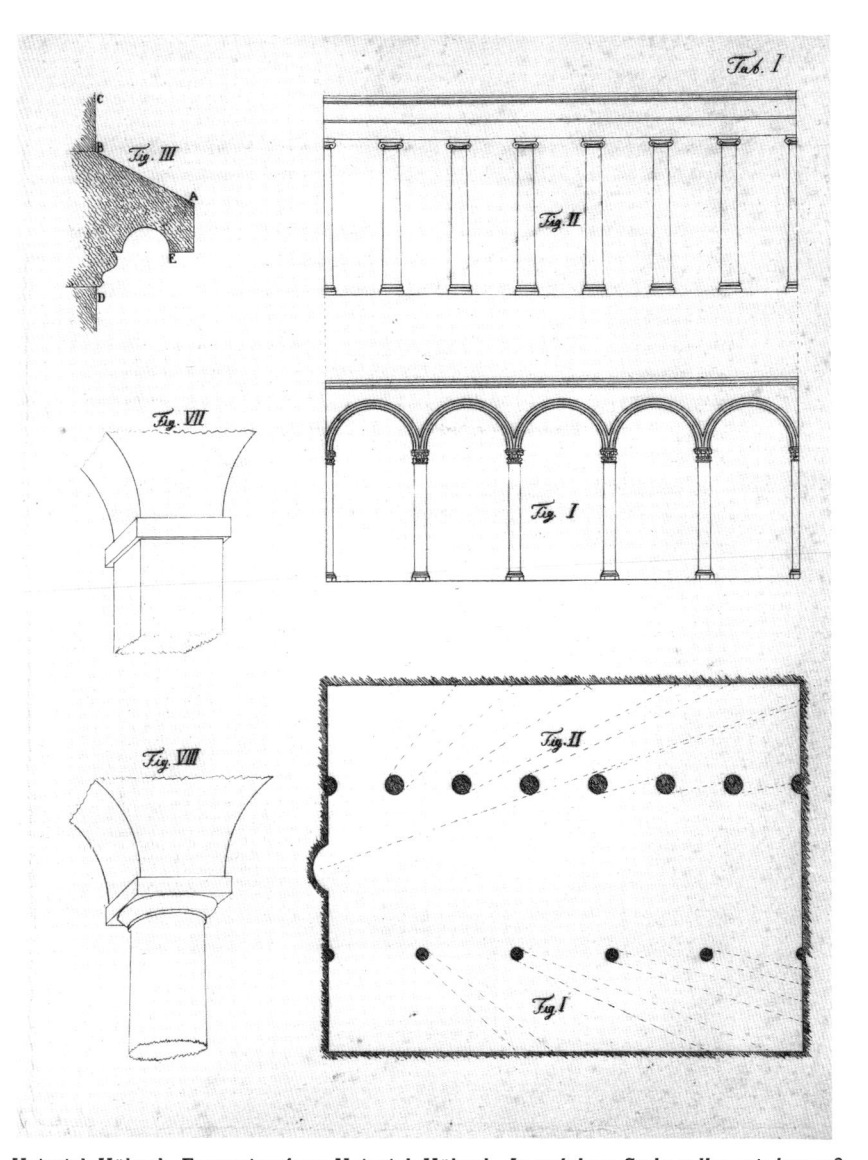

Heinrich Hübsch. Engraving from Heinrich Hübsch, *In welchem Style sollen wir bauen?*
(Karlsruhe: Chr. Fr. Müller Hofbuchhandlung und Hofbuchdruckeren, 1828),
table 1. London, Victoria and Albert Museum.

73. *IN WHAT STYLE SHOULD WE BUILD?*

Heinrich Hübsch. Engraving from Heinrich Hübsch, *In welchem Style sollen wir bauen?*
(Karlsruhe: Chr. Fr. Müller Hofbuchhandlung und Hofbuchdruckeren, 1828),
table 2. London, Victoria and Albert Museum.

74. HÜBSCH

7.

In our northern climate, more care must be taken to protect buildings against rain or snow than in the south. The pitch of the roof, normally covered with slate or perhaps even with tiles, must be steeper than on Greek monuments. Furthermore, the projecting upper surface of cornices or other similar parts must have a distinct slope for the water to run off, unless for some reason something quite different is required, as is the case with exterior flights of stairs or any projections on which something is intended to stand.

If the surface, AB (fig. III), of a projecting cornice is not sufficiently sloped, this surface itself will suffer from weathering. Decay will soon set in, mainly because rain falling on AB will splash back toward the mortar coating BC, will remain on AB after the rain has stopped, and will rise up the mortar coating BC. Furthermore, the water will run along the underside of the cornice toward the wall D and will cause damage here too, unless a groove is hollowed out on the underside of the cornice, forcing the water to drip down at E.

For today's needs we require buildings of a size that the Greeks did not remotely approach in their buildings. How small would even a fairly large Greek temple look next to the parish church of a modern town! The widest span constructed in stone was the ceiling of the Propylaea at Athens (cited by Pausanias as a rarity), and that came to twenty feet. How insignificant this is compared to our interior spaces, which, moreover, require both the slenderest pillars and the widest possible spans! If, for instance, a church were divided by two rows of columns into a nave and two aisles and the columns were arranged even according to the widest Greek intercolumniation (see fig. II), people in the aisles would be unable to see the altar or the pulpit from the third column on—even in churches where the nave is quite wide. The aisles would be of no use, unless the columns were at least as slender and as widely spaced as in fig. I.

The carriage entrances of even our ordinary houses, let alone of city gates and other public buildings, must have a width that is never found on Greek monuments with the sole exception of the central intercolumniation of the Propylaea at Athens.

A portico should provide either a dry carriageway or a shelter from the weather for pedestrians. In the first case, the piers or columns must be placed well away from the wall, so that the carriages can pass through, and the portico should not be higher than its width or depth to prevent the wind from driving the rain onto the wall. Even the widest Greek intercolumniation would not have the desired effect. In the second case, a portico can offer reasonable protection from draft only when no more than one side is open and the other three are enclosed by walls: not when three of its sides are open, as was usual with ancient porticoes. Altogether, porticoes rarely suit us, because they take away light from the interior where it is most needed. For the Greeks, on the other hand, a public building without richly decorated porticoes was scarcely thinkable, and windows were rare. Furthermore, almost all our buildings consist of several stories, whereas all Greek monuments known to us had only one story.

Therefore, the formative factors that condition today's architecture are completely different—indeed almost diametrically opposed to those that affected the Greek style. There can hardly be a greater contrast. To reiterate the main points of the preceding two sections: the Greeks had good stone of great relative strength that made a continuous horizontal span possible, whereas we have brittle stones that permit only the shortest horizontal spans, a shortcoming that is, however, amply compensated by the vault. The Greeks had few needs and made comparatively modest spatial demands, whereas we have many needs, one of which is the greatest possible spaciousness. Greek buildings had splendid colonnades and no windows and were only one story high, whereas ours rarely have porticoes, have many windows, and are several stories high.

8.

And yet we build in the Greek style, especially of late. How is this possible, if what I have said up to now is true? The riddle will be solved by inquiring into what kind of Greek style we build and how far this satisfies our needs.

The discussion of the first point will best proceed from a short review of the main qualities of the Greek style and its later development under the Romans.

Up to the time of Pericles, Greek monuments consist of the following forms. In the beginning the columns A (fig. IV) are less slender and more closely spaced than later; the tapering toward the top is more pronounced to produce greater structural stability. The capital B, especially in the Doric order, projects considerably to reduce the unsupported length of the architrave. The architrave C consists of beams that reach from the center of one column to that of the next. Above the architrave is a frieze D, of equal height, consisting of smaller pieces; its surface is decorated. Above the frieze there projects a cornice E. At about the height of the cornice is the soffit or ceiling F, of about the same thickness as the cornice. This ceiling is constructed by laying beams at regular intervals across the narrowest span to be covered. The spaces between the beams are spanned with stone plates, again across the narrowest span. All parts that belong to the covering, such as the architrave, frieze, cornice, and even ceiling, are classified under the term entablature. Since the wall is thinner than the architrave laid on top of it, it is strengthened (as at *G*) to create a pilaster (anta). This pilaster is as wide as the architrave only on those sides where the architrave rests on the wall, whereas it is very narrow on side *I*, where this width is not required.

Greek architecture excelled in simplicity of composition, in the consistently even development of all its forms, and in wise moderation in the use of decoration. The first quality arose from the simplicity of the plan. This cannot be imitated once the plan becomes more complicated. But the rest could and should be achieved under all circumstances. A sure instinct that was not tempted by the many means available to cover every empty surface with decoration or to make unlimited openings everywhere; an instinct that did not seek to impress merely by massiveness and by dimensions beyond the purpose of the building but one that rather wished to impress by a precision and neatness of execution such as we can hardly imagine today—such an instinct ought to inspire the art of all ages! Anyone who has seen the buildings of Pericles' time must acknowledge that no other people ever lavished such fine qualities on its monuments. Everything was built in a white, mirrorlike, polished marble. The blocks that made up the columns were finished so carefully that even now in many places the joints are not detectable. The walls were built of dressed stones; their various joints alternate with a delightful regularity that forms the most appropriate decoration. These monuments are like fair, ever-blossoming flowers. When Plutarch saw the Temple of Minerva [Parthenon] and the Propylaea on the Acropolis of Athens five centuries after they had been built, he said, "They seem to have a soul untouched by age." The same can be said now, two thousand years later, because any destruction these works have suffered was caused not by the might of time but by barbarian hands.

9.

This was the stage that architecture had reached at the time of Pericles. Yet those who believe that the architecture of later times remained unchanged or even place the Roman imitations in the same category as those works are lacking in discrimination. The principle of early Greek art was truth in the fullest meaning of the word. Every architectural element was formed and used in a way consistent with its true purpose: columns appeared only where they actually supported an entablature, pilasters only where the wall had to be strengthened to receive the wider architrave. The form of the pilasters was also different from that of freestanding columns, in line with their different characters. The architrave appeared where it was really needed to carry the ceiling and ended where it met a wall, because from that point on the ceiling could rest on the continuous wall. An architrave that rested in its entire length on a wall was pointless, because its height and form were governed only by the need to make it strong enough to span between columns. The cymatium M (see fig. IV) of the cornice, which projected slightly beyond the edge of the roof, bordered the inclined sides of the pediment only to prevent water from dripping down at the front; it stopped at the corner N, so that the water could drain off freely along the sides of the building.

I could cite many examples to prove that no architectural element was used superfluously. Each was formed to fit its special purpose and was never remodeled in order to be (as one says today) in better harmony with some other form or to create a kind of blind symmetry. Once the elements had been consistently arranged, the decoration was spread over them, not in order to conceal one or another of the elements but to adorn them.

The monuments of Alexander's time and those up to the conquest of Greece by the Romans make it evident that a decisive shift had taken place away from the natural instinct that I mentioned before. Unaffected simplicity, or the sight of a plain wall, was no longer to be endured. Accordingly, in places where a solid wall was required and a portico was inadmissible, we often find outlined on the wall a surrogate colonnade whose columns and architraves project by only half their thickness. These engaged columns appeared soon after Pericles. They represent the first great conventional lie in architecture, one that subsequently became the preferred practice because it allowed architects to indulge in very large dimensions, now that the architrave carried nothing and could therefore be made up of any number of small pieces. Furthermore, pilasters were no longer applied only where the architrave rested on the wall but were repeated along the entire length of the wall, each opposite a freestanding column. Above them ran an entablature in low relief, to form a kind of symmetry with the real colonnade placed before it.

However, the genius of Greek beauty was not to give way so easily. We can still enjoy the unity of even very late Greek monuments—where at least the horizontal covering was maintained—and also their tasteful, though too profuse, decoration, especially when we compare them to the distortion that Greek architecture endured at the hands of the Romans. Even before the conquest of Greece, the Romans had employed the arches that proved so advantageous to the construction of their extensive aqueducts and roads. Here the piers could be placed wider apart, and smaller stones could be used than with the horizontal covering. Although the Greeks were slavishly imitated in everything, including their architecture, the horizontal covering was bound to be unsatisfactory, especially because, for the multitude of Roman needs, the types of stone available were unsuited to this form of construction (at that time the Romans did not yet use marble for building). Vaulting was too advantageous to part with, despite all the Grecomania, and that is why the whole of Roman architecture is nothing else but a conflict between these two heterogeneous modes of construction: the arch and the Greek column.

At the beginning, when Greek models were still fresh in people's memories, the colonnade appeared on the outside of the temple still in its pure form, untouched by vaulting. The vault was allowed in the interior, where it was indispensable if a continuous stone cover was wanted. Yet soon the vault also intruded on the exterior, directly between the columns, thereby taking over their essential structural function. This caused the colonnade to degenerate into mere sham and show architecture, as for instance on the Theater of Marcellus and the Colosseum in Rome (fig. V). Here the entablature is carried only by the arches, not by the engaged columns. Those engaged columns are so shallow that they hardly differ from painted ones and cannot pass for real architectural elements. Looked upon as decoration, they in no way represent wealth but only the utmost poverty of imagination. The work of the stonemason—a pier, an architrave, etc.—when used simply as decoration is the most wretched thing of all and is inferior to the most monotonous leafwork, not to mention the higher forms of painting and sculpture. Is not the plain lateral wall K of a Greek temple (see fig. IV) with its frieze of figures in bas-relief a more precious work than a wall on which the money needed for a bas-relief has been squandered on a row of pilasters? Figures IV and VI show clearly that the Greek colonnade and the arcade serve the same purpose and that the use of both in the same place (as in fig. V) must therefore be considered the most unfortunate pleonasm possible.

10.

From the descriptions given in the two preceding sections, it is easy to see how we must build today if we intend to imitate the Greek style. Will our architecture then have an advantage over Roman architecture? On the contrary, it must be inferior, because the Romans at least had the same climate, had similar though more extensive needs, and in later years mostly built in marble. Since the Greek monuments have become better known, people nowadays assume that we are far superior to the Romans. However, our recent architectural improvements, which are thought to be so important, concern only matters of detail. What does it matter if we exchange the shallow profiles of the Roman cornice for the stronger Greek profiles, or choose a Greek Corinthian capital instead of a Roman Corinthian capital, or generally copy individual parts of the colonnade not from Roman but from Greek monuments? This is to catch the small fry and let the big fish swim away. Could we, like the logical Greeks, manage with the horizontal covering and dispense with vaulting? Architects try hard and do not shrink from roundabout ways of constructing the outside of the building, at least, without vaults—lest the crass inconsistency become too obvious. At the sight of an arcade together with a colonnade, the latter less than half as spacious but requiring two or three times the quantity of material, any child would ask, "Why not use an arcade here too, instead of a colonnade, since after all we do know how to build vaults?" But even if we manage to build a facade without vaulting, the contradiction is not disposed of but only deferred. For how amazed will the spectator be when, having squeezed through the narrow colonnades outside, he is confronted inside with spacious vaults!

Also, is a single story sufficient for our buildings as it was for the Greeks? What a Scylla and Charybdis we encounter with a building of several stories! If we simply place several rows of columns one above the other, we do not achieve a whole but a pile of as many buildings as there are stories, because the main cornice that unites everything below into a whole is lacking. The cornice of the uppermost row of columns cannot be taken for a main cornice, since in depth and projection it is no different from those of the lower rows of columns. The alternative approach, whereby a building of several stories is given only one row of columns extending up to the roof, is equally wrong. It gives the impression that the columns originally existed on their own and that little stories were later built between them. In Italy ancient monuments have actually been used in this way.

Everything must yield to the column. Of all parts the column alone is thought to embody beauty, and it is used in such profusion that the grand impression of free space is completely lost. Besides, architects try to make the columns as big as possible in the belief that this will enhance the impression, whereas it usually has the opposite effect. True colonnades can rarely be used on the exterior of our buildings, since there is hardly ever a reason for open porticoes. That is why architects usually resort to an architecture of bas-relief, that is, to engaged columns and pilasters.

11

If an unbiased person is amazed at how such a makeshift and mendacious style can possibly be called Greek and thought to be beautiful, then his amazement will reach its highest pitch when he realizes to what extent convenience, solidity, and economy have been sacrificed for the sake of all this patched and borrowed finery.

Whereas the architect, in periods when a natural style prevailed, was well acquainted with the needs of his time, which he regarded as the prime mover of his creations, today he considers our many needs as so many enemies and as an impediment to his designs. A perfectly ordinary carriage entrance, as required in any sizable dwelling, embarrasses him when designing one for a grand palace. For how can he combine such spaciousness with his Greek portico? Although one entrance is in fact already too much for him, either he talks himself into believing that two are needed, which he shifts to the wings (provided these can be spared from having porticoes), or he places a single entrance on the lateral facade. This then has the result that the important facade is there for the minor people arriving on foot, while important people arriving by carriage must make do with a minor facade. If the building can be placed on a high podium, then some place for the gateway may be found at the foot of the colonnade.[2] Yet should a portico be demanded in which carriages can turn, then the architect must simply despair of solving the problem with stone architraves.

In a church built in the antique style, even with slender and widely spaced columns, people in the aisles from the third column back cannot see the altar or pulpit, as already mentioned. Furthermore, does a Greek portico provide the slightest protection in our climate? Since a portico based on Greek proportions is not very deep in relation to its height, the slightest wind will drive the rain and snow between the columns to the back wall.

How can it be said that architecture has enjoyed a great resurgence in the last decades? The revived imitation of ancient architecture in Italy in the fifteenth century was confined in the beginning only to minor details. When whole rows of columns and pilasters were eventually imitated, the purpose of the building primarily determined its principal forms, to which fragments of ancient architecture were superficially attached. That is why church interiors by Brunelleschi[3] and most of those built in the following century are just as satisfactory in use as the older churches built in the medieval style, because they still consist of a vaulted nave and side aisles supported by very slender and widely spaced columns. Their only defect is that the principal forms are not configured and decorated to go with the interior but that an architecture derived from an alien way of construction has been tacked onto them as best it can be. Brunelleschi and the architects who followed him could never have passed all at once from almost unlimited medieval spaciousness to the constraint that went with ancient colonnades—much though they extolled the beauty of ancient architecture. After all, the unprejudiced majority is mainly concerned with the practicality of the building. When it becomes obvious that what passes for architecture, far from being the creator and friend of function (as it ought to be and as all architects proclaim), actually regards function as its worst enemy, then such an architecture must seem to ordinary people as something they can do without.

The arbitrary application of antique architecture simply as decoration soon caused facades to become nonsensical, especially when the abstract line of beauty became the dominant principle. The models had hitherto been Roman monuments, which themselves frequently display similar absurdities. Eventually, the discovery of the best Greek monuments opened people's eyes to the abominations that had been committed. Architects recognized the senselessness of applying isolated fragments and tried to imitate the integrated whole; but then, as has previously been explained, they forgot the present in their concern for the past. Is the new point of view preferable to the earlier one? A building with a sham facade but with an interior that conforms exactly to its use may sooner find admirers than a building with a so-called pure facade for the sake of which the whole interior is either too high or too low and whose function is everywhere impaired by Greek proportions.

12.

As to the expense entailed by building in the ancient style, it quite often happens that the main building costs less than the porticoes. It has already been said, in Section 6, that a portico in the Greek style, completely useless to us, costs at least four times as much as a useful and just as richly decorated hall formed with arches. This stands in strong contradiction to our architects' usual complaints today over the financial restrictions they experience when executing their designs. Architects have never had unlimited resources at their disposal. Yet when huge sums are spent on cumbersome columns and heavy cornices running around the entire building (because the architect has the vague feeling that this would look well), then of course nothing is left over to construct vaults in buildings that ought to be fireproof or to use ashlar quoins to protect the corners from damage.

The outlook for durability is not much better. Unsupported stone beams easily fracture during our cold winter months. They will wear badly, since age makes the stone crumble. Buildings in the antique style are so badly protected from the weather that it would be a good thing to cover such offspring of a southern clime with a special structure during the rough season, in the same way that one preserves exotic plants. Without sinning too much against the antique form of moldings, one cannot give the projecting cornices either a slope above or a drip molding beneath to shed the water from the wall (as was shown to be necessary in Section 7). Consequently, the rendering above and below the cornice will soon perish, and water will easily penetrate into the joints and drive the stones apart.

The very gentle slope of ancient gables is not possible for our slated or even tile-hung roofs. For that reason, architects are often forced to resort to a metal roofing that easily costs ten to twenty times as much. Otherwise, the considerable depth and comparatively modest height of our buildings (that is, if they are built in the ancient style) make the roofs too conspicuous, which of course is incompatible with the essence of this style. Therefore, architects often have recourse to flat roofs, which, even when covered with copper plates, are in constant need of repair. Otherwise, the timber construction underneath is quickly ruined.

Many similar shortcomings could be cited. Yet our best witnesses are the recent buildings themselves, which without exception and in just a few decades have reached such a state that they will hardly survive the beginning of their second century.

13.

Having explained in detail that present needs and the northern climate make it impossible for architects to fulfill their task in the Greek style and that so far all attempts to imitate this style correctly or to fulfill these needs satisfactorily have failed, we now return with all the more confidence to the conclusions that according to Section 6 follow from the present state of the formative factors. According to these conclusions, the main quality by which the new style differs from the Greek style is this: instead of the horizontal stone lintel, we have a vault; or rather, instead of a colonnade with a horizontal entablature we have an arcade. The second definition better illustrates what is meant by the statement without detracting from its general validity, because the several forms of the support and its covering are visually the most conspicuous and constructively the most important ones that lend every style its distinctive character. Consequently, as soon as arches are used, the horizontal stone covering plays only a subordinate part. It is used only to bridge a short opening of no more than three or four feet; or, if wider, it is relieved of its great load by an arch placed above it.

Some people who no longer doubt the fitness for purpose of such a style may yet demand to be convinced, at their leisure, that it will also be beautiful. It is true that this would be the right place to explain what does and does not constitute architectural beauty. However, in that case I would have to speak too much of feelings, and this treatise would take on too subjective, and thus too vulnerable, an aspect. The field of artistic feeling is a chaotic domain ruled by a great deal of outworn and feebleminded stubbornness and little sincerity, since it is one in which one can never be caught in a lie. Besides, there is no end to the human capacity for self-deception in matters of feeling. Although time can easily change cool reflection into warm emotion, this cannot be forced to happen all at once. Thus the wisest course for the time being will be to avoid a direct discussion of where to find beauty, a subject on which opinions are much divided, and to present the argument indirectly, as follows.

Although not everything that is fit for its purpose [*zweckmäßig*] is beautiful, anything that is unfit cannot possibly be considered beautiful, unless one wants to turn architecture into a kind of crocodile paradox in which the impossibility of a satisfactory solution is inherent in the premise.[4] Therefore, those who cannot contradict the conclusions reached so far must decide to bid farewell to the antique style and accept at least the basis of the new style, unless they can show that the line of the arch is absolutely ugly or less beautiful than the straight horizontal line. This cannot possibly be proven, even by those who adhere fanatically to the theory of the abstract line of beauty; for, as is well known, according to this theory the serpentine or wavelike line is the most beautiful, and this line is certainly closer to the line of the arch than to the straight line.[5]

Once the basis of the new style has been accepted, the rest may be reconciled with the most diverse views on beauty. Anyone who seeks beauty only in decoration and regards it as a process of formal creation quite independent of function (with the main forms or architectural elements only providing a kind of framework) will be able to overornament an arcade as readily as a colonnade. True, he will have to choose objects that really are decorative and not be obsessed with pilasters and entablatures in relief, which even in his own view cannot be beautiful. For if the main forms (which certainly include elements such as entablatures and piers) cannot be beautiful, then fictive versions of those same forms cannot be beautiful either, unless beauty were to be defined as the very opposite of function.

Those who seek beauty mainly in symmetry, rhythm, and proportion can find these qualities in an arcade just as well as in a colonnade.

Those who see architectural beauty more in function—that is, in the characteristic manifestation and generous fulfillment of purpose, rather than in individual forms—will of course get along best.

For an authoritative justification of the new style, we refer to the fact that within the last few decades medieval art has generally become much appreciated, and hardly anyone still dares to revile it. Now, a form of architecture that already shares a basis—namely, the dominant method of construction, which is vaulting—with the medieval style will therefore never turn out to be very different; nor will it readily be considered ugly.

Finally, it may be an eye-opener for some to learn how inconsistent they are in their feelings about beauty. Even the most single-minded adherents of the antique in architecture can be heard to speak highly of the characteristic forms of rural buildings that have developed quite naturally from their actual purpose and traditional construction. Yet when it is a question of urban buildings, the same people will hear nothing of a natural influence of the present but seek to achieve beauty through a slavish imitation of a completely alien past!

14.

Having established the basis of the new style in every respect, it remains to define more precisely the form of the architectural elements. For this we turn once again to history in order to observe the gradually changing forms of vaulting and how they influenced every element. We shall trace this development up to the time when all reminiscences of ancient architecture disappeared and the form of each element was derived in an organic way from the vault, a stage finally reached in medieval architecture.

We left Roman architecture in Section 9 as a sort of hybrid in which two mutually exclusive methods of construction—the Greek colonnade and the arcade—appear at one and the same place (see fig. V). Later on, as the rules deduced from earlier monuments became more and more obsolete and the influence of the present became more dominant, the entablature was reduced to such a degree that only a short piece of it, a sample as it were, projected from the wall above each column, with the vault resting directly on it, as in the Baths of Diocletian and the so-called Temple of Peace.[6] In the end this piece also disappeared, and the arch rested directly on the capital of the column. As far as I know, this construction first appeared on the Palace of Diocletian at Spalato but was soon applied in all the earliest Christian churches in Italy, especially in Rome.

In keeping with the new form of worship, these churches had to accommodate the whole community, and they were therefore extraordinarily large by comparison with the *cellae* of the pagan temples. They were usually oblong in form with a ceiling supported by two or four rows of piers, thus creating two or four side aisles. At the front were one or more entrances and frequently a spacious vestibule. At the opposite end, the nave terminated in a great semicircular recess that formed the choir, in front of which stood the altar and the presbytery with pulpits. The nave was wider and higher than the aisles. The difference in height made it possible to have windows in the walls above the arcades. The first churches were based on the Roman lawcourts, which had a similar form and were known as basilicas; this name was transferred to the newly built Christian churches.

At the time when these were built, the aesthetic rules that governed antique architecture had become extinct along with the political reign of paganism, so that architects, quite unbiased, resolved the main function of the building in the most direct way, using the technology of the time. Notwithstanding the decline of antique architecture, technostatic experience had not been lost: architects dared to build high and heavy walls on a row of slim supports. Nevertheless, this style incorporated many heterogeneous details reused from antique monuments. In particular, there was a plentiful supply of columns made of excellent stone, and these were used as supports. For the sake of space, these columns were placed as far apart as was considered safe and were joined by arches made from brick, then the commonly used building material. Rarely, such architraves as came to hand were used instead of arches. This row of slender arches carried the wall on which the ceiling of the nave rested. The wall contained arched window openings that were usually filled in, not with glass but with thin marble plates pierced with small holes, probably covered with a transparent material. The naves of some basilicas had a double row of columns one above the other, with the upper row forming a gallery. The ceiling was a very simple timber construction; it was identical with the roof (which even today in Italy is very carefully preserved within a double layer of tiles), so that the whole timber framework of the roof was visible.

Among the churches known to me that were built in the basilican style, the church of Santa Balbina on the Aventine in Rome is the only one where no antique fragments were used and where the vaulting style appears in its purest and simplest form.[7] This moderately sized church originally had a nave and two side aisles. The piers as well as the arches and walls are built of brick. They are square and rather thick and are set wider apart than are the ancient columns in the other churches. The walls that rise above the piers, wherever an intermediate tie or principal rafter rests on them, are strengthened by piers or pilasters projecting from the outside face of the wall. The windows are almost as wide as the span of the arches. The cornice of the nave is embellished by a course of small corbels; that of the choir is formed, as is usual in this style, with several courses of brick laid in different directions.

The type of Christian church that evolved in the eastern Roman Empire was different from the one just described. There, better political conditions made a greater expenditure possible. Not content with a wooden ceiling, the whole interior was vaulted. The cupola was chosen because it had the advantage of needing neither the use of centering during construction nor sustaining walls as thick as those necessary for barrel vaults of the same span. The central part of the church was then laid out on a circular plan with four short wings, so that the whole did not form a rectangle like the basilicas but a Greek cross, yet with arcades in the four arms like those in the basilicas. The first and at the same time the largest of these buildings in the early Byzantine style was Hagia Sophia in Constantinople. It served as a model for many other churches and was even imitated by the Muslims, for whom the dome still ranks as a main feature of their architecture.

For all the rightness of the arrangement and design of the early Byzantine style, the initial use of many ancient fragments and, later, the mechanical copying of their forms led the style into a great muddle. This had less effect on the plainer basilican style of the western empire with its great simplicity and economy of ornament. The wealth of the eastern empire was childishly misused by pasting embellishments over the main forms like a pattern card. For the same reason, ancient monuments were robbed of columns made of precious material, of which there were many. These could not be used as supports for the large domes and vaults in the same way as for the light wooden ceilings of the basilicas. Instead, they were often used to form completely superfluous arches placed between the heavy piers and vaults. If the shafts of the columns were not tall enough, then several columns were set on top of each other (which incidentally might have been the reason for the later ringlike ornament); or a piece of cntablature was added to increase the height; or the brick arch was stilted to stretch it as high as possible. Often two to four columns were coupled, or four smaller ones were placed on top of a larger one, as in the church of San Marco in Venice. In order to overcome the plainness of the large wall surfaces, which had only small windows, the facades of many churches were crammed with colonnettes joined by arches to form small galleries. In most cases, however, these were so narrow that a person could barely squeeze into them, and there was in any case frequently no access. There exist buildings, the facades of which are composed of such galleries one above the other. These small columns are quite different in their proportions from those of normal size. In particular, the capital and base are very large in relation to the shaft; otherwise the decorative details would have become indistinct. Also, the capitals project rather far to receive the comparatively heavy impost of the arch. The fact that column shafts originally consisted of very strong material may be the reason for this particular proportion.

However, there are also very simple buildings in Greece and Italy whose architectural elements were little affected by the disturbing influence of ancient architecture. For instance, there is a cistern in Constantinople, probably built in a later century and called by the Turks the Cistern of the Thousand Columns, that has slender columns with hardly any taper and with the cushion capitals that later become common in the West. The cushion form, like the Greek Doric capital, is a transition from the round to the square capital.

15.

Although buildings in the Byzantine style differ from those in the basilican style in overall plan and form, the elements of both styles are practically the same. Just as no rigid division can be observed between countries during the early period, so we find a mixture of both kinds of planning in the Western churches that from the tenth century on were built in the style known as neo-Greek, pre-Gothic, or rounded-arch style (*Rundbogenstil*). They have domes, but instead of a Greek cross, with four equally long arms, they form a Latin cross, with one arm considerably extended, creating a long building like a basilica. Two rows of piers divide it into a nave and two side aisles. In the beginning it often has a timber ceiling and later a groin vault. In the former case the piers stand closer together than they do in the basilicas; they support the walls of the nave, which is always higher than the aisles, and are either square or circular, like columns.

In the second case, the piers stand farther apart but are much thicker because they have to withstand the full lateral pressure of the groin vault. The core of the pier is usually square and as wide as the wall of the main nave. On the back of the pier, a half-column projects, on which the ribs of the groin vault of the aisles meet, as they do on a console at the opposite side of the aisle. The moldings of the base plate of the capital and often all the decorative parts of the capital continue around all four sides of the pier. The groin vaults of the nave are generally twice as wide as those of the aisles, so that the ribs meet only on every second pier; here another half-column projects, and this continues past the capital or impost, up the wall of the nave, to the point where the ribs of the main vault meet. These projecting half-columns, which support the ribs of the groin vaults, must under no circumstances be placed in the same category as the engaged columns or pilasters of ancient architecture, which did not carry anything.

At those points in the interior where the ribs of the groin vaults abut and where all lateral pressure is concentrated, there are buttresses on the outside, which extend in uniform width and depth up to the main cornice. In the intervals between the buttresses this cornice rests on a row of small arches, which form a straight line under the edge of the roof and have the same projection from the face of the wall as the buttresses. Originally, these arches arose out of the construction, as we can see on old castles, where they acted as supports for the battlements and were built of small blocks, mainly of brick. This had the advantage that only a few large blocks of stone were needed for the whole length: these formed the corbels on which the arches rested. Later, these arches were retained even where they were smaller and everything was built in ashlar.

There are also other forms that are highly decorated in parts. Under the main cornice of the nave, apse, dome, and towers, there is often an arcade or gallery supported by small columns, for which there are abundant examples among the buildings in the early Byzantine style. This gallery is, of course, always interrupted by the buttresses extending up to the main cornice and fills the empty space between the vertical outer wall and the vaulted ceiling inside.

The windows are generally arched and in most cases are very high in relation to their width, although round windows, or roses, and even half-roses are not at all unusual. To admit the greatest possible amount of light, the jambs of the windows are splayed on both sides of the pane and are either left quite plain or, if decorated, do not project beyond the face of the wall. The jambs of those window openings that are not glazed are less necessary for lighting the interior and are therefore not splayed. In most cases two window openings are coupled, so that their arches rest on a common pier or, more frequently, on a column (if the wall is thick enough, on two columns, one behind the other). Up to three window openings may be grouped in this way, with a larger arch constructed above them to relieve the small columns of the weight of the wall.

The richly decorated jambs of the entrances, in particular those of the main doorway, are very wide and, starting from the deeply recessed door, are chamfered at a greater angle than the window jambs, as if to invite people to enter. The outermost jambs often project beyond the face of the wall; they then receive a small canopy. Because it is easier to construct a square wooden door that can easily swing back against the jambs, the part with the shortest distance between the jambs (in other words the actual door frame) is spanned with a straight piece. In order to divert the load from this piece, an arch is built above, the line of which is followed by each concentric member of the frame within. The empty semicircular area above the door either serves as a window or is closed by a stone plate carrying some sculptural decoration.

The towers that were built after bells came into use are generally not very high in relation to the nave and dome, though they are very numerous. They have small paired window openings of the type just described, consist of many short stories (reckoned by the number of window rows and stringcourses), are round or square, and generally have a pointed but not very high stone roof. The roof of the nave and the transepts is usually sloped at an angle of forty-five degrees.

The secular buildings erected in this style also often have open galleries with colonnettes and vaults throughout and mostly very small windows.

16.

All monuments of the *Rundbogenstil* in Western Europe share the qualities enumerated here but differ greatly in the particular formation of their architectural elements. As a rule, we find these elements progressively closer in form to the accompanying technique of vault construction; the transference of details from the Byzantine or, rather, the ancient style became increasingly rare. The construction became bolder and the vaults wider, employing less material and supported by slimmer piers or columns. Yet older monuments are often superior in this respect to later ones, which were the work of derivative architects who went on unthinkingly regurgitating—and misapplying—the principles of their teachers.

With regard to the more objective aspect of architecture—namely, the design and development of its elements—monuments vary widely in artistic value, depending on whether they are the work of good or bad architects (of whom the latter have at all times been in the majority); and this is even more the case with regard to the overall plan and the arrangement of particular parts and decorative forms. Many buildings display a truly mindless randomness: windows, galleries, and cornices are thrown together unrelated to each other, so that one would think it the work of several architects, each working in ignorance of the others. On the other hand, there are many buildings so simply arranged that they are among the most successful works of art and can rival the monuments of the Greeks.

Altogether, the *Rundbogenstil* was in many respects governed by the same spirit that gave life to the Greek style: both have many plain walls, which, notwithstanding the ample scope that they offer, are not overloaded with superfluous little cornices, stringcourses, and the like; rather, they impress us by the beauty and precision of their ashlar construction. The decoration in most cases still adorns and does not mask the essential parts. The decorative elements are very small compared to the parts they adorn and thus create the character of delicate yet sober grandeur.

Toward the end of the twelfth century, the church of the Benedictine abbey of Maria Laach near Koblenz was built in the fully developed *Rundbogenstil*.[8] Here the piers of the naves and aisles are as slim and widely spaced as in the later churches of the *Spitzbogenstil*. This very large church, with five towers, a dome, and a forecourt, looks as if it had been built at one stroke in a most careful ashlar construction according to a single plan. The decorations, which in monuments of this style are often incredibly clumsy and rather disfigure than embellish the fabric, are conceived and executed here in excellent taste. I must declare this church to be the most beautiful I have ever seen. Although not everyone may agree with this assertion, they will admit, at least, that this church is the crowning achievement of the *Rundbogenstil*, as the monuments of the Periclean age were of the Greek style. The church is unfortunately in a very poor state at present; and it will collapse within a few years unless the roof is repaired and iron ties are added, which could be done at very little cost. I shall count myself fortunate if these lines were to induce His Majesty the King of Prussia, who has done so much for the preservation of medieval works of art, to save this church too from impending ruin.[9]

17.

In the thirteenth century appeared the so-called Gothic or Old-German style, in which the arches and vaults no longer formed a semicircle or *Rundbogen* but two segments of a circle, the so-called pointed arch or *Spitzbogen* (hence the most fitting name, *Spitzbogenstil*), and in which all parts give an impression of lightness and extend to a remarkable height. These two qualities (the origin of which we can leave undecided) clearly set the new style apart from the old, as did the characteristic nature of its decoration, which consisted mainly of lacy fretwork and sharp points. Yet the difference was not as fundamental as may appear at first glance, since in the construction and composition of the elements, the same principle was maintained. Furthermore, in the transitional period when both styles were often merged and used together on the same building, the pointed arch was not so pointed and differed little from the *Rundbogen*; nor were the lightness, the delicate tracery, and the upward impulse of the *Spitzbogenstil* as dominant at the beginning as they became in the later stages.

With few exceptions, all Gothic churches have groin vaults to ensure that the lateral pressure is concentrated at a few points. The sharply projecting ribs of the vault, springing from the piers or columns like branches from a stem, are found here in greater number than in the *Rundbogenstil*. These ribs intersect one another in various ways, dividing the surface of the vault into small cells, each with its own shallowly curved and extremely thin vault held up by the ribs. The basic form of the pier varies: sometimes it is a square, sometimes an octagon or polygon, sometimes a circle. The piers of larger churches are square, though placed diagonally; their four sides are surrounded by as many columns as there are ribs that spring from the top of the columns toward the vault. They thus resemble a bundle of extremely slender columns that are not really freestanding but are connected at the back to the shaft of the pier. When the aisles are lower than the nave, as is usually the case, the majority of these columns stop at the point where they support the ribs of the aisle vaults as well as the imposts of the arches on which the walls of the nave rest. Here these columns have capitals, whereas those that support the ribs of the higher nave vault continue up the walls to the point where these ribs begin.

Because the walls are very thin, the supporting buttresses project from the face of the wall more than they do in the *Rundbogenstil*. They terminate in various ways: either they are joined to the main cornice, as in the *Rundbogenstil* (a feature chiefly seen on Italian churches); or they stop below the main cornice and have a cap of their own; or they extend beyond the parapet of the roof and end in decorative pinnacles. From the buttresses of the walls of the aisles, arches usually spring toward the higher walls of the nave, which are supported by the interior piers of the church; thereby, the lateral pressure of the nave vault is concentrated on the buttresses. The main cornice, basically a large concave molding and frequently ornamented with leaves, runs round each buttress. The roof is slightly set back, thus producing a narrow passage between the roof and the parapet of the cornice. The water streaming down from the roof runs along this passage in hewn channels and is thrown off at various points by gargoyles.

The very tall towers are generally square at the bottom and change into octagons at the top; their roofs form sharply pointed octagonal pyramids, which on more important churches are built of stone. All other roofs and gables are also high and steep.

The windows of many churches are so wide that they take up all the space between the buttresses. Notwithstanding the great number of large window openings, the stained glass and the intersecting and variously arranged tracery of the windows admit only a very subdued light to the interior of these churches. The heads of these long windows extend to great heights and are all pointed, although there are also circular windows, or roses, and some with heads formed by segmental arches. The narrower windows of domestic buildings usually have straight lintels and are often combined in groups of two or three. The jambs are splayed like those of the

Rundbogenstil and are often decorated with many ornaments that do not project from the face of the wall. The main entrances have the same form as those of the *Rundbogenstil*, except that the heads are not round but pointed. Smaller doors often have straight lintels with no arch above, but in most cases the length of the free span is reduced by two corbels projecting into the width of the opening, directly below the lintel.

Admittedly, a great number of buildings with small cornices and other randomly attached forms are the work of mere artisan builders and consequently even more deficient in order than the most confused buildings of the *Rundbogenstil*. Yet everyone must rank the better buildings, and above all the Cologne cathedral, among the most beautiful works of art, comparable to a finely constructed poem in which not a single syllable strikes a discordant note.[10] Nevertheless, the unbiased observer will confess that there is usually much overloading, produced by an endless array of decorative shapes that hide the essential forms of the building. The tracery has been greatly overdone; even the roofs of towers are perforated, so that proper roofs have had to be constructed beneath them. Some forms have been used purely conventionally, such as sham gargoyles and gables and blind windows. The *Rundbogenstil* relates to these buildings as a pre-Raphael painting relates to a post-Raphael one. In the former, the incorrect way of drawing is disturbing; but in the latter, where nothing is left wanting in this respect, we nevertheless look in vain for the moving simplicity of the former.

However, let us learn from the one undisputed merit of the *Spitzbogenstil*: the way in which its forms, down to the smallest detail, derive in a consistent and organic manner from the construction of the vault, completely eliminating those reminiscences of the antique that here and there still disturb us in the *Rundbogenstil*.

First the tapering of the shaft of the column disappeared, as had already often happened in the *Rundbogenstil*. The conical form of the shaft, although it adds strength, belongs to an earlier stage of technostatic experience, which the bold vaulting style had left far behind. This form was unsuited to the spaciousness now required; for, if one takes the greater diameter at the bottom of the shaft as the necessary dimension, the diminution at the top pointlessly increases the distance that the vault has to span. Yet in most cases there was no need to worry about adequate resistance to the comparatively strong lateral pressure of the vault, in the way the Greek architect had to pay attention to the resistance of the column to earthquakes or other possible lateral pressures. Now that several arches, in different directions, rested on the shaft, their lateral pressures canceled each other out, and the column needed only to have reactive strength, for which a wider diameter below is the last thing needed.

Furthermore, the arches were profiled in such a way that at the point where they rested on the pier, they nowhere projected over its basic form to any significant extent. Because a spontaneous tendency toward lightness, independent of tradition, causes the corners of a square pier (fig. VII) to be chamfered and thus changed into an octagonal or round one, the same chamfer, or at least a similar contour, must continue along the arch that rests on that pier (see fig. VI). This ensures that the impost of the arch does not project too far beyond the pier when seen from an angle, as shown in fig. VIII. Otherwise, the heavy load may indeed cause a fracture. Apart from a few exceptions, the *Rundbogenstil* did not observe this practice. Here, the manner of the early Byzantine or basilican style was retained, where plain angular arches built of brick were supported by ancient round columns. People had become used to this combination of forms and did not feel the lack of harmony.

Thereafter, the base plates of the capitals, as well as the bases of the piers, were made polygonal instead of square, since square corners, projecting too far over the round form, obstructed the free space. Because the capital no longer served a structural purpose, as it had done in ancient architecture, and in fact did not support anything, its projection was reduced. It was really nothing more than a decoration, and therefore the capital or impost block was often omitted.

In ancient architecture the gable or pediment was bounded by the main cornice, not only along the inclined sides but also along its horizontal base (see *E* on fig. IV). The reason for the latter arrangement was that on Greek monuments the figures in the tympanum rested on this base. Yet the moment it ceased to have this purpose, as was usually the case in Roman architecture, the placing of two projecting main cornices so close together became a reprehensible pleonasm. Although in the Byzantine, Basilican, and *Rundbogen* styles the projection of the cornices is less pronounced and the fault therefore less obvious, it is met there quite frequently; but it is consistently avoided in the *Spitzbogenstil*. Here the cornice runs along the inclined sides of the gable but not at the bottom; or if it does, then the inclined sides are treated in a different way. Besides, as already mentioned, the cornices project to a much lesser extent than in the Greek style, where the strong projection is probably a reminiscence of the timber construction. In the *Rundbogenstil* the moldings of the cornices still resemble those of the flat Roman cornices; on the monuments of the northern *Spitzbogenstil*, greater attention is paid to throwing off the water; and this, by hollowing out the moldings more deeply, also improves the visual effect.

Finally, one more improvement should be mentioned here. The *Spitzbogenstil* had a better understanding of the essential character of church towers, and these were built not by piling up many low stories but by forming a framework of a few, though much higher, stories and windows.

18

The description of the successive vaulting styles contained in the four preceding sections has traced so distinctly the principles according to which the architectural elements of the new style must be formed that we cannot easily go astray.

Nowadays, as mentioned in Section 6, there can be no question of spanning the distance between pillars with a single stone, like an antique entablature. The span must always be vaulted and follow the line of an arch, because the piers or columns employed as supports for the ceiling, both inside and outside at the open side of a portico, are naturally spaced as far apart as possible, that is, more than six feet even in the most confined space. Should one choose a pointed arch instead of a semicircular arch, this would produce an organic style equally well; yet, practice would soon convince everybody that the exceedingly steep proportions of the *Spitzbogenstil* are incompatible with our needs, which normally point to the opposite, the use of the segmental or semicircular arch. In some cases, however, the *Spitzbogen* may be preferable. The catenary curve has an advantage only when applied to ceilings, and specifically to those that are of the same thickness throughout and receive no extra support at the points where the circular arch would be its weakest and would tend to collapse outward. In the case of a wooden ceiling, one pier need carry only two arches (see fig. I), whose intrados must be profiled in accordance with the basic form of the pier or column, as explained in the previous section. With single-story buildings, the spandrels between one arch and the next need to be bricked in only up to a height that allows the ceiling and exterior cornice to find horizontal support. With multi-story buildings, one should either place a second row of arches atop the lower one (with the ceiling of the first serving as the floor of the second) or build a wall above the row of arches. This wall, like one resting on the ground, must of course be of a thickness commensurate with its height and unsupported span, and the arcade must be of the same thickness. The wider the span of the arch, the flatter its curve, and the heavier its load, the greater must be its thickness (which should not be confused with the depth or intrados, determined by the thickness of the wall); and, as a result, the greater will be the lateral pressure that it exerts on the abutments.

A wooden ceiling, because of the nature of its material, must have a straight and not a curved surface. How absurd it is to waste effort and material on forming wooden ceilings into arches, while seeking to avoid the arch in stone construction by using straight architraves! Those whose taste is uncorrupted will not be disturbed by the contrast between a flat ceiling constructed in timber and stone arches spanning the piers. They will prefer the vaulted ceiling not because its form resembles the arches but because of its greater solidity and lavish appearance. With a stone ceiling, one can use any kind of vaulting, with or without ribs or bands (a description of which would be too elaborate), depending on which type is considered the most appropriate for a particular room or is preferred for other reasons.

The basic form of the pier that supports either the arches under wooden ceilings, or the ribs of vaulted ceilings, or the groins of plain vaults is governed by the contour that is outlined by these parts on the pier. As explained in the preceding section, the basic form of these parts must not project beyond the pier. It follows that the piers can have very different forms: they can be round, square, octagonal, and even polygonal, or a combination of all these shapes, with concave as well as convex corners. However, this should not be carried to extremes, as is done in the *Spitzbogenstil* where the outline of the pier is hollowed out to such an extent that it resembles a bundle of stalklike columns barely attached to the core, so that they seem to be freestanding. It is true, however, that in the Gothic style this type of pier is in full harmony with other parts whose lightness and openness verge on the miraculous. That the shaft of the pier or column must have no swelling at all was shown in the preceding section. The foot or base of the pier must not obstruct the space and must therefore not have corners that project too far, unless required by special circumstances. On the other hand, there is no need to make the base meticulously follow the concave corners of the pier: it should rather simplify the complicated basic form, as was done so well in the Gothic style. As explained in the preceding section, the capital or impost block must not project as much as ancient capitals and can perhaps be omitted altogether. The abacus of the capital should also not protrude too far and thereby conceal the place where the arches or ribs rest on the capital.

The proportion of the thickness of the pier to its height is not as restricted as it was on Greek monuments, which only had one story, and where the columns had to carry a comparatively balanced load. Piers that have to withstand lateral pressure must be proportionally thicker in relation to the increase in pressure, although, of course, less so as the specific weight of the material increases and the pier is constructed with fewer pieces. With the lateral pressure of the arches and ribs coming from opposite directions and thus being canceled out (as is usually the case), the thickness of the pier (with length unchanged) does not increase in proportion to its load and to the distance between the piers. This is because only reactive strength is involved here, which, however, varies greatly with different types of stone.

Because the first principle in art must be truth, we must not overlay bare yet functional walls with feigned constructions. We must adopt the point of view of those who in both the ancient Greek style and the *Rundbogenstil* aimed for beauty and opulence in walls not through frequent projections but through long-lasting and careful construction, fine surface treatment, and (especially in Italy) interior mural paintings. If a wall has not been strengthened for some other reason (as may often be the case) to withstand the lateral pressure of the vaults (with the ribs resting on imposts as shown on A, see fig. VI), then walls with vaults that direct their pressure toward certain points must naturally be strengthened at these points by abutments. These form projections on either the inner or the outer face of the walls or on both at the same time. Inside, they are placed opposite the freestanding piers as wall piers; they carry about half the number of ribs of those that rest on the freestanding piers and, accordingly, are shaped like a halved freestanding pier. These wall piers, which have a real load to carry, must not be confused with the engaged columns and pilasters of ancient architecture, which carried nothing at all. On the outside the reinforcement projecting from the face of the wall consists of buttresses that either extend up and join with the main cornice (a simple form that is generally found in the *Rundbogenstil* and frequently also in the *Spitzbogenstil*) or stop below the main cornice and must then be given their own termination. Buttresses extending above the main cornice and terminating in a decorated pinnacle, a type seen on larger churches in the Gothic style, will be in harmony with the whole only if all other parts take on spiked and pointed forms. To allay the fears of those who foresee the new style as consisting of exceedingly long plain walls, it should be said that even if the ceiling is not vaulted and therefore no lateral pressure bears on particular points of the wall, it nevertheless would definitely be better in most cases to place pilasters here and there at the corners and along the walls, because the walls could then be made much thinner. The main socle of the building, whose considerable height enhances the appearance of the whole, can, like the base of a pier, simplify the outline by omitting the returns created by minor projections of the wall.

The slope of the roof depends on the material used. If covered with tiles, it cannot be inclined much less than forty-five degrees; if with slate, it can be less than thirty degrees; if with metal, it can be very flat. The extremely steep gables and roofs of the *Spitzbogenstil*, though often covered with metal, were more a consequence of the upward striving that affected every part and certainly did not come about because of the northern climate, as is proved by the less-steep roofs of the *Rundbogenstil*, which are well preserved despite their great age.

If the cornice is made of stone, it cannot project as if made of wood. It has to be hollowed out in such a way that the water is forced to run off the outer edge of its contour, which, as the main profile, can be enriched by adding various minor moldings (see fig. III). The projecting supports between the buttresses form part of the cornice. In the medieval style these usually consisted of a row of small arches, as previously described, though other richly decorated forms have also been used and new ones could easily be devised. Even the plain corbels seen on old churches are appropriate. A wooden cornice, formed by the projecting heads of the rafters and beams, has (apart from the greater overhang) a different look, mainly because of the variously carved heads of the rafters and beams. As explained in the preceding section, the same main cornice must not run along both the inclined sides of the gable and horizontally under the gable.

The openings for doors, above which the wall continues, must be vaulted like the spans between the piers, with the possible exception of smaller openings. Since, however, it is easier to construct and to open a square door, it is generally better, especially at the main entrance, to separate the space circumscribed by the arch from the actual door opening. This space will then either be made into a window or be completely closed to provide a suitable place for inscriptions, architectural decorations, and (provided the actual door is sufficiently recessed from the face of the wall) the display of sculptures or paintings that no one entering can overlook. The jamb of the door must be chamfered to allow people coming from the side to enter comfortably, and this chamfer can be plain or stepped.

Larger window openings must also be vaulted. Straight lintels might be used for smaller openings up to a width of four feet, if they have wooden frames and are made to be opened. This was the usual form for dwelling houses in the Gothic style, and this subordinate use of the horizontal stone covering was not regarded as a disturbing inconsistency. The jambs of the windows must be splayed both inside and outside to admit more light. They are very suitable places for ornamental decor, although its use in dwelling houses should be carefully considered, since the jambs on the outside will be covered by the shutters when open. Unless objects are to be placed on the outer window sills, these must be shaped (like all projecting parts, such as cornices, bands, socles, etc.) in such a way that the water can run off, and they must be given a drip molding that will prevent the rainwater from running down the face of the wall and soiling it with the dust from the frames and sills that the rain carries with it.

It takes little effort to achieve a great effect with deeply cut and finely curved moldings, as we can learn from the Greek and Gothic styles, which are in amazing agreement on this point. Sculptural decoration, when not excessive, is almost exclusively an adornment of the essential parts and in every style is chiefly applied to those parts that are particularly conspicuous. Thus, in the Greek style, the door frames behind the columns had very simple decorations; whereas the portal in the medieval style, unless hidden by a porch, was the most elaborately decorated part of the building—and this is also the case with present-day buildings.

*   *   *

We have now reached the goal that we tried to attain and have established a strictly objective skeleton for the new style, sufficiently articulated, I believe, for the artist to enliven with his own individuality.

Everyone will realize at once that the new style must come closest to the *Rundbogenstil*—that it is, in fact, essentially the *Rundbogenstil* as it would have evolved had it developed freely and spontaneously, unimpeded by all harmful reminiscences of the ancient style. This resemblance arises from the nature of things and was not brought about by authoritarian influence or individual preference. All the qualities of the new style described in this last section have either been substantiated by what has been said in the earlier sections or are based on structural laws that for the sake of brevity have been assumed to be known. Where the same task allowed several solutions, all have been accepted. The influence of reality in all its complexity has consistently been upheld. No rule that had proved correct in only a few cases or that in itself could not possibly be generally valid has been heedlessly proclaimed as a far-reaching principle applicable to all cases. The theory of art developed here is not, therefore, like those scholarly theories that relate to reality in only a few issues and in which rules abstracted from such theories are unhesitatingly made into general laws. This theory is thoroughly practical.

The new style will thus afford the most direct solution for the most diverse problems. Probably the least likely of all the faults for which the new style may be blamed by its opponents is that of being a motley assortment of forms. The style will freely evolve and respond to any fair demand without hesitation. The architect will not feel as helpless with this style as with the limited means of Greek architecture; he will not feel like a painter who has to depict the wide-ranging subjects of Christian art with a restricted number of ancient physiognomies. The buildings of the new style will no longer have a historical and conventional character, so that emotional response is impossible without prior instruction in archaeology: they will have a truly natural character, and the layman will feel what the educated artist feels.

The decoration of buildings will depend on the imagination of the individual artists and will therefore be manifold. However, this will not endanger the new style, as was pointed out in the first section. Even in countries where a uniform and consistent taste has prevailed, there is a great variety in decoration. This will be even more so with us, who know all things past and present and are so fond of novelty and diversity. The crowd of imitators will anyhow soon lend authority to these products of a happy imagination. In every case buildings logically designed in their basic elements will rank much higher as works of art, even with the most infelicitous decorations, than the most exact imitations of ancient architecture.

Source Note: Heinrich Hübsch, *In welchem Style sollen wir bauen?* (Karlsruhe: Chr. Fr. Müller Hofbuchhandlung und Hofbuchdruckeren, 1828).

Translator's Notes

1. Xylomania: from Greek ξύλον = timber. This term refers to the obsession, once common among archaeologists, with tracing all the elements of the Greek stone temple to an imaginary primordial wooden hut: an idea first propounded by Vitruvius and reiterated in modern times, especially in the mid-eighteenth century by Marc-Antoine Laugier. Since this theory presupposed a translation from a structural system derived from one kind of material to another system based on a different material—in other words, a process of imitation—it was strongly opposed by Hübsch, who developed his arguments in a book entitled *Über griechische Architectur* (Heidelberg: J. C. B. Mohr, 1822). His critique was mainly directed against the teachings of Aloys Ludwig Hirt. The result was an angry dispute between Hirt (*Verteidigung der griechischen Architektur gegen H. Hübsch*) and Hübsch (*Verteidigung der griechischen Architektur gegen A. Hirt*), published as an appendix to the second edition of *Über griechische Architectur* in 1824.

2. This might refer to Karl Friedrich Schinkel's Schauspielhaus (1818–1821) in Berlin, a particular feature of which was the covered carriage passage under the flight of outdoor steps. In 1821 Schinkel published the building in his *Sammlung architektonischer Entwürfe*, vol. 2, which was then reviewed by Johann Heinrich Wolff in *Göttingische gelehrte Anzeigen* 1 (1827): 441–62. Wolff praised the practical advantage that this arrangement had insofar as persons using the side entrances were not inconvenienced by the carriages setting down others at the main carriage entrance but criticized it for the bad effect it had on certain exterior aspects (the exceedingly steep rise of the flight of outdoor steps and the unusually large distance between the columns and the main wall of the building).

3. Filippo Brunelleschi (1377–1446), Florentine architect and engineer.

4. The "crocodile paradox" is the name given to a sophism devised by ancient logicians: A crocodile has seized a child; it will hand it back provided the mother guesses correctly whether the crocodile does or does not intend to return the child. This creates a dilemma for the mother: her two possible guesses are contradictory yet they may lead to the same conclusion.

5. The theory to which Hübsch referred—in this place and also a few pages earlier—was William Hogarth's *Analysis of Beauty* (London, 1753). Of all the various straight and curved lines, there is, according to Hogarth, only one, the waving line, that is the line of beauty, and only one, the serpentine line, that is the line of grace (pp. 28, X). During the eighteenth century this theory became, in

Hübsch's opinion, "the dominant principle."

6. The Temple of Peace near the Arch of Titus is described by Antoine Desgodets, *Les édifices antiques de Rome* (Paris: C.-A. Jombert, 1779), 45.

7. Santa Balbina, situated near the Baths of Caracalla, is a simple early Christian hall church of the fifth century.

8. The Benedictine abbey of Maria Laach near Koblenz was built from 1093 to 1230. It is the most perfect example of Romanesque architecture in Germany. The church was pillaged in 1802, and by 1815 the first steps were taken to restore it.

9. King Friedrich Wilhelm III (r. 1797–1840).

10. When Hübsch wrote these lines, the Cologne cathedral consisted of a choir (begun in 1248 and completed in 1322) and part of one tower, still in the unfinished state in which it had been in 1560 when work on it had been abandoned. Hübsch could also have had a vivid picture of the cathedral as it would be when completed, from the original designs as reproduced in the superb illustrations of Sulpiz Boisserée's great work *Ansichten: Risse und einzelne Theile des Doms von Köln*, which was published in Stuttgart in 1823. It was due to Boisserée and these illustrations that the decision was made to proceed with the completion of the cathedral. For the next twenty years, however, work was confined to the repair of the existing building. The actual completion took forty years—from 1841 to 1880. See: Arnold Wolff, "Die Baugeschichte des Kölner Domes im 19. Jahrhundert," in *Der Kölner Dom im Jahrhundert seiner Vollendung*, ed. Hugo Berger (Cologne: Historische Museen der Stadt, 1980), 2: 24–34; and W. D. Robson-Scott, *The Literary Background of the Gothic Revival in Germany* (Oxford: Clarendon, 1965), 287–301.

REMARKS ON THE TREATISE

IN WHAT STYLE

SHOULD WE BUILD?

RUDOLF WIEGMANN

IF AN UNBIASED PERSON CASTS A GLANCE AT THE ARCHITECTURE OF THE PRESENT TIME, HE IS BOUND TO SAY THAT IT IS IN A WORSE STATE THAN ANY OF THE OTHER ARTS. In its degeneration—on crutches and in the rags of every nation and period—it makes itself conspicuous in a manner at times ridiculous, at other times obnoxious. Architecture claims a right to an enhanced position, the more so since the other arts—which, unlike architecture, do not even affect our material needs—are daily attracting an increasingly enthusiastic public. Therefore, to say a few words about a treatise that aims to heal those shortcomings needs no justification.

Closer acquaintance with Greek masterpieces has clearly brought to architecture a confusion that nobody could have foreseen. Far from opening the artists' eyes to their slavish imitation of a so-called style that had arbitrarily been pieced together from the fifteenth century onward, far from inducing them to follow a rational principle commensurate with the means available and with their own age (as the Greeks had done in theirs), the spirited, autonomous, and consistent art of Greece has been degraded to the status of a dead model for desultory imitation by unimaginative architects. But the contradiction between this imitation and the needs of our time is too glaring not to have aroused general doubts as to the suitability of ancient art for our time and for our needs. The consequence of this was a tendency to vacillate and to snatch at the possessions of almost every nation and period. This heterogeneous assortment was then thoroughly jumbled to ensure that it was called an original creation. Greek, Roman, Byzantine, Old-German, and Egyptian styles were used not only side by side but even within the same building; and then it came as a surprise that the work was not regarded as that of a genius! Art became a senseless rehash of historical fragments, nothing but efforts without principle or aim. Nobody could deny that these anachronistic products were monsters—ridiculous parodies and caricatures that aroused only disgust when compared with the ancient originals, their noble and beautiful language, and the general tenor of their time. Even something that is beautiful in itself can make a ridiculous and foolish impression simply because it is anachronistic and manifestly contradictory, just as a great tragic line would certainly evoke laughter in a comedy.

Since painting and sculpture, the sisters of architecture, have long since put their vagaries behind them and are presently treated in a way commensurate with their character, it is certainly time to free architecture from constraint but also from arbitrariness. An art of our time and for our people will then arise from true principles: a spirited and independent art that does not steal from history for history's sake.

Greek art, sculpture as well as architecture, is for us the most perfect model. Yet it is not a model for blind imitation but for the consistent development of an art that should be as characteristic of our time, our climate, our material, and our needs as the Greek works were of their own period. Whoever maintains that the Greek style is the right one for us is saying that it was not the right style for its time.

This leads to a reproach to which the author [Heinrich Hübsch] leaves himself open. He wants to banish the Greek style and instead recommends the Byzantine arch style—although only as it would have been if its development had been carried through. Yet would our present art gain anything by exchanging one set of fetters for another? Is it possible to imagine any art that is valid for all times? Beauty is beyond time and place—unlike art, which is a human endeavor. Art is like a living book in which nations faithfully record—as they must—their lives, their feelings, and the trends of the time. I am sure that art has an organic life, as has mankind itself, that it has stages and periods that are closely and inseparably bound to those of mankind, and that it cannot possibly be severed from these without the most disastrous conflict between art and truth. To prescribe what kind of art a period should have is therefore no different from prescribing to a child what life it should lead; every movement has an undisputed right to its own life and art.

It would not have been a departure from the aim that the author sets himself, if he had spoken of, or even touched upon, the essential quality that makes an architect and perhaps art in general—what it sets out to do and what it can do. He would then have assumed a better vantage point from which to recognize the new danger that threatens his eager and laudable endeavor to free architecture of its degrading fetters. Many things that now seem to belong to the material aspect of architecture would thus have acquired a higher and more spiritual significance. Many of his statements would have been qualified and would not have been uttered so categorically. The whole treatise seems to be pervaded by the notion that matter dominates mind, whereas almost the reverse is true. As soon as mind relinquishes its control over matter, it also loses control over form and collapses into itself. It is true that matter, in the fine arts, sets up insuperable limitations that affect the creation of form. Yet these are so remote and so contingent that they cannot possibly be reduced to a few unalterable proportions.

Before entering into details, we wish to make a few remarks about the term "style," which are absolutely necessary in order to arrive at an understanding with H. H. Throughout, he attaches to the term "style" a meaning that relates to material and construction, whereas in everyday language it is used in a spiritual sense only. Style is not a definite and unalterable system of construction and decoration; even less does it exclusively signify two different approaches to spanning—the arch and the straight architrave. In aesthetics, style has only two possible meanings: first, the signal character of a nation and an epoch, which is always reflected in any work of art (one speaks, for instance, of the Greek style, the Old-German style, or the Raphaelite style); second, a distinctive mode of expression or specific quality (in this sense, one speaks of a light, a sublime, or a grave style). In the latter meaning, it has nothing at all to do with construction, since the light, the sublime, and the grave style can appear in an arch just as well as in a straight architrave.

Consequently, a period cannot strive for a single style. In the first sense of the word, each period will automatically have a style of its own; in the second sense, it will include them all. The art of the Middle Ages, of the age of Pericles, and even that of the periwig age left an unmistakable impression of the time and its point of view—that is, of what we call style—although at those periods no conscious effort was made to strive for a particular style. Instead, style crystallized organically out of the time and the circumstances. Yet in every style in the first sense, there are various specific qualities that signify style in the second sense.

This being granted, the author cannot have meant anything by the new style that he wishes to establish but a matter of material and construction. Precepts of this kind nip artistic creation in the bud, clip the wings of genius, and lead it down a false and narrow path when, left to itself, it would create works that would be admired. Only what is already known can be prescribed; an original work is born unassisted. If the works of the most inspired masters of any art had been obliged to follow a pattern devised by others, what would they then have been like? The artist must create as a free man; he must obey only the spirit of his time and be the master of his material. He should master it but not tyrannize it. He should be obedient to the spirit of the time; but this spirit also lives in him. These are the conditions that will always bring forth true works of art. If the construction, which is a rational matter, is prescribed, the resulting works will of course be rational. But will that make them beautiful? With beautiful works, on the other hand, rationality may be taken for granted. The history of art shows that construction is not the cause but the result of the formal idea. If the ancient Greeks had wanted to create a building according to the idea of a medieval cathedral, they would have been just as unable to manage it with their system of construction as the Old-German masters would have been if they had planned a work according to the idea of the Parthenon. In both periods the construction was attuned to the total character of the architecture; and although both manners of construction were rational, they were poles apart. If a system of construction were to be laid down dogmatically, this would act as a barrier against ideas and ideals. Therefore, construction follows the idea. This is a universally valid law. If a person believes that one particular system of construction is adequate for the present time, this is only his personal belief, and he should therefore allow others the same right that he has arrogated to himself. There may be only one path to an ideal, but who wants to subscribe to one particular ideal and not acknowledge another equally sublime?

However, with the buildings we require and the materials we have, arched construction will in most cases conform best with the idea and execution, and for this H. H. advances many arguments. Yet because such a construction will be the best in many cases, should that lead us to insist on it in every case?

I maintain that it is impossible to express a light and spontaneous grace with arched construction. The reason may be the following: in arched construction, solidity and structural equilibrium arise from the balance of different forces acting in different directions and canceling each other out. The slightest cause that upsets this balance—for instance, a buttress or a voussoir giving way—releases forces with the power to destroy the whole. Balance is maintained as long as the constantly active forces destroy only each other, but it is just this conflict of forces that the onlooker senses. It may be that this will finally bring about solidity but never a light, virginal naïveté. Instinctively and unconsciously, we calculate the thrust and counterthrust: in short, we engage as it were in a dialogue with the material. When we find in many Greek works those charming qualities that arched construction lacks, then it is obvious that the horizontal covering, which ensures solidity through the structural repose of all parts, must be more appropriate. In Greek works, the idea appears free of all material; in the *Rundbogenstil*, the material is clearly dominant. Furthermore, since the buttresses, indispensable in arched construction, are not hidden, they easily impart to the whole a feeling of heaviness that hardly accords with the lightness intended elsewhere. The Greek architect had nothing to hide. Where there is something to hide, something is wrong. No doubt, there will always be architectural tasks of this kind, and—one may ask—should one then reject a type of construction that has once already been proved right for the task?

For a character of imposing grandeur, such as a church should convey, there is nothing better than arched construction, because here the masses must never be so delicate as not to withstand the thrust of the vaults or not to give complete assurance of structural balance at first glance. In many other cases, this type of construction offers practical advantages that justify its application, even where the straight covering would be equally beautiful. However, one can think of many cases where practicality and function (not to mention the aesthetic aspect previously mentioned) in themselves provide a reason to reject arched construction and prefer the straight covering. That we need porticoes, for instance, on many buildings, more than the Greeks and Romans did, is due to our climate. Obviously, the delicate character of such porticoes is not achieved with the heavy piers that would be necessary to withstand the pressure of a vault. What then should we do in such a case? The columns would have to be tied together and fixed to the wall with iron rods to prevent them being overturned by the vaults. Those who advocate this method can take it a long way and end by suspending a house in midair. H. H. rejects porticoes with a straight entablature because they cannot be deep enough. But, in the kind of weather against which these do not give enough protection, porticoes are surely little frequented. Besides, deep porticoes deprive windows of light and impart a dark and oppressive character to the whole building.

Both methods of construction can certainly be combined, and if this seems to be impossible, it is not because of the nature of things but because of a too narrowly conceived idea of harmony. Why blindly follow a rule—however apparently sacrosanct—which lays down that if one opening is arched, all must be so, even if expediency, construction, and beauty of expression cry out against it? When the arch is warranted by nothing but an arbitrary conception of consistency and harmony, in the face of contradictions and absurdities affecting construction and function, then that same feeling for consistency and harmony would—close to semicircular arches[1]—also demand entablatures and other lines that could hardly be more objectionable than the use of monolithic stone arches to span small openings. Why should someone who has jumped over a wide ditch take the same running jump when he encounters a wagon rut? Harmony, however, is an earthwork erected to protect prejudices and fixed ideas of beauty from any attack.

Thus, where the purpose of the building imperatively demands it, an arch is unquestionably to be used; but why do so always, when one need not and—as with the portico mentioned above—cannot do so?

We are convinced that both methods of spanning an opening are justified in their respective places and permit a perfect harmony that is not exclusively dependent on construction and the material nature of art. Of course, an arbitrary combination of heterogeneous forms is just as indicative of a lack of feeling for harmony and beauty.

The author is partly of the same opinion when he proposes a straight lintel for the heads of ordinary windows. If such a lintel can carry a thick wall, even more can an architrave carry the entablature. If the straight termination is inharmonious in the latter case, then it is no less so in the former.

When H. H. says that the new style will be the Byzantine arch style, he is certainly right in adding: as it would have been had it fully evolved. Because in the form that it finally achieved, it retained too much that could only have arisen in that childish period (for us merely of historical interest) for us to adopt it unconditionally in its present form. When we look at its masses and proportions, we find too little harmony; when we compare one form with another, we find a harmony that is too narrowly circumscribed. Everyone will admit that the subordinate forms and their details are rarely in harmony with the main masses and are often even fussy and in bad taste. If the great architect of the Speyer cathedral—that first and most admirable masterwork of Byzantine art—had endowed the exterior with the same simple grandeur that impresses us in the interior, then we would have been totally relieved of the sight of these old inherited defects, and that period would have bequeathed to us a monument that would match in every respect the greatest works of any nation—whereas we can now make this claim only for the interior.[2]

Those who seek to revive the Byzantine style on the grounds that it was a native style should bear in mind that it originated in foreign lands and flourished there as much as it did with us. But above all, they ought to consider whether this style is congenial to our own time. If it was beautiful and characteristic for its time, how could it possibly be so now, in an age that has little or nothing in common with that time? Our art must represent our time, just as past art represented its time. Has this not been so in the art of every period and nation, without conscious effort? The seventeenth and eighteenth centuries are characterized by periwigs, and it is therefore not by chance that the arts reflect the very same spirit, because a period impresses its mark on every sphere of activity without distinction. From costume to poetry, we find great uniformity. This inevitable concurrence of all that is contemporaneous is perhaps the reason why our own time, the age of the cravat, has produced nothing of architectural importance by comparison with other periods. Everything that an age brings forth belongs to it; but, of course, the child resembles the mother. History demonstrates that great epochs were followed by periods of relaxation and repose: times in which to recuperate and digest, as it were. Hence also the mindless imitation of the great masters: the masters sought an ideal after their own heart, but their followers looked up to them as lawgivers and did nothing but imitate them. Presently, our age seems to live by the enjoyment and elaboration of the past, yet it ought never to lose sight of the great objective that once was paramount—namely, to make one's own time into a great one.

This forbids a helpless clinging to the past. Just as we cannot make time stand still, so we cannot detain its spirit, which is inseparable from it. Both are gone forever, because in the worlds of nature and the spirit, where all is in eternal flux, there is no lasting rest. To demand the resurrection of the Byzantine or any art of the past is to seek to disrupt by force the organic process of evolution. We must create something new that fits our time, just as in the preceding centuries something new was created that fitted their time. If the Germans of the twelfth century had thought as people generally think today, they would have retained the arched style that had been introduced by their eastern empress and would never have developed the wonderful German style.[3] The paintings of Cimabue and of Fiesole[4] are admirable and beautiful for their time, but the Italians of the sixteenth century wanted their age to be portrayed for posterity by a Raphael and a Michelangelo. Struggle as we may with the Raphaels of the thirteenth century, they will never be right for the sixteenth century; and they will be equally wrong for the twentieth.

The main reason why the Byzantine style has found so many adherents in recent times is that its buildings are highly picturesque. Whether the picturesque is a necessary requirement in architecture is not difficult to decide. Were this quality a sole condition of value, then the generally esteemed Florentine palaces would have very little value and the works of the Greeks none at all. By contrast, the Byzantine style holds first place in this respect, even surpassing the Old-German style, because it presents a greater mass to light and shadow without disrupting both with too many details. Yet, using this as a criterion, we would also have to assign architectural value to a miserable cottage, such as we see every day, and deny it to a Parthenon. Architecture is an autonomous art that presents beauty in its own way and therefore has no need to consult another, and totally different, art. If a sculptor were to make his works picturesque, he would sin against the essential principle of his art, and he would have every right to demand sculptural paintings from a painter. It is true that picturesque beauty can exist alongside architectural beauty, but it is not a constituent element of the latter.

The picturesque aspect of the Byzantine style should not, therefore, induce us to take it up again. Nor can its purely architectonic aspect do so, as we have explained already. These considerations apart, would it not be a very poor art that was not permitted to go beyond a few forms and types of construction? The only field left to the artist in which to show his originality would be a little arrangement and decoration—something very subordinate to the true idea of art. If, however, art means the creation of works whose beauty (in close relation to their purpose) appeals to the emotions and conveys to the onlooker the artist's idea (to which the works owe their existence), then it must create from a base dependent only on the time, the means, and the artist's individuality. It is for the artist to reconcile need and necessity with his ideal. Even if by thus relying on his own resources he creates something that is not perfect, more is gained by this work than by an imitator's rehash of magnificent works that do not arise from his mind or from his time. The former artist, with his imperfect work, may have broken the ground from which great things will arise, whereas the latter might as well not have existed; he has, as it were, lived outside time.

It would be foolish to insist that an original work must not at all resemble an already existing one. Many buildings, because they serve the same or similar purposes (as do churches), have so much in common that they can differ only in proportions, subordinate forms, and decorations. Walls, piers, or columns—three age-old means—serve as supports. To cover the building, there is the roof, which is thousands of years old and so conditioned by its purpose that its form is also given. Windows are needed to light the rooms. To comply with physical laws, the main lines of the building must be either horizontal or vertical. Not much of this can be changed, because it is all a matter of necessity. Even the forms of specific parts are determined by some cause—as, for instance, the gable is the simplest way to construct the roof. A portico is often indispensable in front of entrances, etc. It must have a gable, so that the water does not run down in front of the entrance. Those who build in this way do not imitate the Greeks, since they only submit to circumstances and needs. Even if no one in antiquity had built in this way, some clever man would have thought of it when confronted with such a task. An art that is as rationally developed as Greek art and that contains nothing arbitrary, accidental, or conventional, is bound to be later touched upon, simply because it is a rational art. The demand to avoid the rational, solely because the Greeks or other nations have previously adopted it, is nonsense.

Although many of the points raised here are not contested by H. H. in his essay, and although he no doubt largely shares our point of view, nevertheless this seems to be the right place to make some suggestions that might serve to prevent the revival of past artistic systems (which is spreading more and more) and clear the way for true art. All systems are based on the records and facts of past ages. For that reason, a living art has no system as such. We should thus strive to attain a living art that faithfully reflects and is nourished by the character of our own time. Admittedly, architecture is also better fitted than any other art to express the character of the present time, which might be described as lacking in independence. To attain this independence and to transform and shape the age is now the supreme duty of an artist, nay of a man. Success depends on circumstances, and it would be futile to imagine that a few individuals could bring about a salutary reform. Not until the artist encounters true artistic sense, pure taste among the people, and a warm and encouraging response to what he has to offer can a single person—however right and however sincere he might be—achieve anything of importance. Nevertheless, while the time of fulfillment has not arrived, he ought to give his loyal support to preparatory work. He must, however, look upon history as history and not as a source for precepts! The idea thus embodied may find some fortuitous historical counterpart; but it still belongs to its own time, whose freeborn child it is. It makes no difference whether columns, arches, or architraves carry the load. Every means of spanning space can, in its proper place, be the best and the most beautiful. When art is no longer directed solely by arbitrary human laws, when its principles and its essence are in harmony with the artist's spirit and with that of his age, then art will have found not only a solid basis but also a freedom that ensures its fullest blossoming.

Source Note: Rudolf Wiegmann, "Bemerkungen über die Schrift: *In welchem Styl sollen wir bauen?* von H. Hübsch," *Kunst-Blatt* 10 (1829): no. 44, 173–74; no. 45, 177–79; no. 46, 181–83.

Translator's Notes

1. The words *"nach Kreisbögen"* make no sense. After vain attempts to arrive at a sensible translation by applying one of the many meanings that *nach* has in German (directional, temporal, consequential, etc.), I came to the conclusion that "nach" is a misprint for "nah" or "nahe" (next to, near to, close by), a reading that makes Wiegmann's argumentation meaningful.

2. The Speyer cathedral was built between 1030 and 1100. In 1689 it was severely damaged during the War of Succession; the central section of the nave was completely destroyed. From 1772 to 1775 the building was restored according to plans submitted by Franz Ignaz Michael Neumann (son of Balthasar Neumann, the great architect of the German Baroque). He rebuilt the interior of the nave by closely following the forms of the undamaged section but gave the western front a new facade, which, in the words of the authors of the monograph on the Speyer cathedral, was like an effective and "imaginative theater decoration." This was the state of the cathedral at the time when Wiegmann praised the interior as a genuine Romanesque work, while his criticism of the exterior suggests that he was not aware of the damage it had suffered through war and Baroque additions. In 1854 Hübsch was charged with the restoration of the western facade. He destroyed Neumann's work and replaced it with a front that accorded well with his ideas of the *Rundbogenstil* (see H. E. Kubach and W. Haas, *Der Dom zu Speyer* [Berlin, 1972], 827–28). Wiegmann reviewed Hübsch's facade in *Deutsches Kunstblatt* (1855): 324ff.; he praised it as a "perfect organism" but had reservations about the use of differently colored stones.

3. Berta von Sulzbach, sister-in-law of the German Emperor Konrad III, became Empress Irene through her marriage to the Byzantine Emperor Manuel I.

4. Fra Angelico da Fiesole (1387–1455), Florentine painter.

In What

STYLE

Should We Build?[*]

A Question Addressed to the Members of the Deutsche Architektenverein

Carl Albert Rosenthal

The question that I herewith submit for serious consideration to all architects, and especially to German architects, is in no way
a new one. It is nevertheless a question that is vital to our art and important enough
to be raised time and time again. For many architects, of course, it has become superfluous. But so long as we do not all strive together toward the same goal—so long as

[*] *We understand by style neither the artist's manner nor the character of the building with regard to its purpose
but the aspect common to all buildings of the same nation, the same country, and the same period.—C.A.R.*

one architect applies one style, a second another, a third different styles simulta-neously, and a fourth builds without any style or even submits several designs for the same building in different styles—so long as this is so, it is the architect's urgent duty to address this question with ever more serious application and not to desist until it has been settled. It is perhaps most necessary, and also most rewarding, to raise the question just now, when architecture has made such encouraging strides, while diverging—in spite of isolated efforts to the contrary—in all directions. I am certain that there has never been a more competent judge to decide the question than the Deutsche Architektenverein [Association of German Architects], for whose members this article is intended.

Strange, is it not? If someone, on being asked this question, were simply to reply, "In every style or in none," architects would declare such an answer to be a joke or even utter nonsense; and yet, we calmly sit back and watch how architecture itself every day gives that very answer by what is actually built. It is therefore neces-sary to ask first another seemingly superfluous question, namely, "Is it really necessary or desirable to limit ourselves to one style, in the sense suggested above?"

It could perhaps be argued that just as we have not hesitated to use the scientific inventions of the nations that have preceded us, we are also entitled to appro-priate their artistic creations. But have we adopted and accepted as true everything that the ancients thought to be true, or rather only what is still true? We may adopt from earlier art only the beauty that is still beautiful for us. But here art differs from science, and architecture from the other arts. In science there are some truths that are absolute—they are valid for all times and all nations; in the other arts, too, indi-vidual details can under certain conditions be as beautiful now as they were in high antiquity. Not so with architecture. We learn from history that the only nations that have achieved something truly excellent have been those that, apart from fulfilling the general laws of beauty, have infused their creations with their own spirit. This neces-sarily follows from the very nature of architecture. Its tasks derive directly from the manners and customs, from the life and inner essence, of the nation; and climate and the material available must also be considered. Architectural works will therefore express the character of the nation, of the period, and of the country more clearly than do the works of other arts, which often depict subjects foreign to that character. It is true that every artist is affected by the national spirit; his works, apart from the char-acter demanded by the subject, also unconsciously express the same spirit. This must be particularly so in architecture where all subjects are national, and character is only a subcategory of style. Without a well-defined national style, the architect can nei-ther accurately capture the character of his building nor clearly convey its purpose, and it therefore lacks an essential element of beauty: appropriate expression, or Truth.

114. ROSENTHAL

Matters have changed greatly. Ancient peoples were left more to themselves and only gradually outgrew their childhood. Their religion in particular, the main support of art, arose from and developed with the national character. Christianity with its elevated viewpoint was not so much influenced by national character as influential upon national character, which it often greatly changed. A gradual intellectual development emanating from a natural balance of emotional forces, one that automatically ensures the homogeneous progress of intellectual activities and cultural changes, is no longer possible. Communication between nations has increasingly blurred national differences. It follows, on the one hand, that it will become more difficult than previously to find the right style and, on the other hand, that the styles of the modern Christian nations will be closely related—or rather that as in the Middle Ages, there might be only one style for the whole of Christendom, one with slight regional and national variations but with more marked distinctions between religious and secular buildings. What does not follow is that any style, no matter what, would be right for us or that we could use different styles at the same time. On the contrary, an even stricter distinction between the Christian style and the style of non-Christian nations, those of antiquity in particular, is bound to impose itself. Certainly, only one style can be appropriate for us. In fact, seen from a more elevated viewpoint, there can be only one style that leads directly to architectural beauty, just as there can be only one kind of culture that leads unerringly to infinite perfection.

Would it not be preferable, however, for architecture itself to find the right style through practice? This would certainly be the best way, if it were possible to forget past styles and begin anew and if modern nations were not so lacking in that youthful freshness of feeling without which there can be no favorable outcome. The further elaboration of the style itself, which is the most essential task, must of course take place in the realm of practice; but it would be useful first to engage in some research in order to find the right path.

Whether it will become necessary to invent a completely new style or whether one of the past styles—with whatever modifications—might be used, is a question that need not concern us here. As things are at present, we must first consider the second alternative. Since a revival of the styles of the earliest peoples is out of the question, we shall confine ourselves to a short survey of the Greek, Roman, Romanesque, Arabic, and Germanic styles. It is obvious that modern styles cannot be considered, because we have declared them to be styleless or debased versions of the styles just mentioned. The only significant one would be the Renaissance style, which may be discussed together with the Roman style.

1. The Greek Style

This is the style that outshines all others in its inner perfection. Why, therefore, look any further? How can we do better than imitate the Greeks, who by general agreement achieved more in art than any other nation and who came so close to the acme of perfection? Very well—but what is meant by "imitate the Greeks"? Does it mean that their style is to be introduced without more ado, or does it not in fact mean to build with the same fitness for purpose and the same beauty in relation to our own conditions as the Greeks did in relation to their conditions? Does it not mean to develop in this way a characteristic style, as they did, and adhere to it as they did? Or do we really have the same needs and climate, do we lead the same life, and above all, do we have the same religion as the Greeks? Finally, did Greek art really fall so short of perfection that we could make the essential changes that are evidently necessary without causing its total ruin? As to the last question, present buildings supply ample proof that to alter even the smallest detail is to distort the masterworks of the Periclean age; and as to the first question, its assumptions are so much contradicted by the facts that in order to use the Greek style, we would literally have to tear it apart.

No, no! We cannot possibly build in a Greek style but only in a modern style with Greek details, and even these would lose their original significance in our hands. But perhaps we could go back to the elements of the Greek style and from them develop a style appropriate for us—a style such as the Greeks might have developed under present-day circumstances? Disregarding for the moment the obvious contradiction that the Greeks in our circumstances would no longer be Greeks, let us look for the basic principle of the Greek style. The Greeks, as has been said many times before, were happy and cheerful children of nature; joy was in their lifeblood, beauty was their dominant, if not their only, aim, and for this reason their beauty was purely sensuous. Higher spiritual beauty was foreign to them, and they could have no notion of infinite truth and infinite goodness. In apprehending beauty, they loved fulfillment not excitement. From thence evolved "serenity" as the basic trait of their character and "perfect equilibrium" as the basic principle of their building style.[1] This principle is most simply and tangibly expressed in the way a horizontal load is held up by vertical supports (entablature and column) with no hint of upward striving. Could the sensuous beauty of the Greeks ever satisfy the Christian—his vision raised toward the infinite? Could the equilibrium and the resulting simplicity, even uniformity, of the Greek style ever satisfy the aspiring modern spirit? No, no! Not even the basic principle of the Greek style is right for us! What is more, sensuous beauty, like all things sensuous, is attainable; and the Greeks attained it. Any further step must necessarily lead to decline; and since this decline is intrinsic to the basic principle from the beginning, we need hardly regret in the present situation that Greek art has passed away.

For all that, the Greek style has one quality that, superficially taken, seems to ensure its adaptability forever. This is the subtle yet precise expression of the structural significance of forms—in other words, its strict architectonic character. The form as a whole, as well as the smallest detail, conveys the purpose of the construction at once, more distinctly and clearly than any rational analysis of the construction itself could do. Yet it is the business of all architecture to express its construction, and this must be done in every style. If this is especially the case in the Greek style, the reason lies in the great simplicity of Greek constructions, dictated by the basic principle, and is also due to the fact that the higher spiritual beauty expressed in upward striving forms is lacking. In short, the Greek style is perfect as far as it goes, that is, within its sensuous limitation. This limitation makes it totally incapable of becoming the artistic aim of Christian nations. All elements of beauty are embodied to perfection in Greek art, except one—infinity. We must therefore accept that its time has passed and that its revival will benefit neither us nor Greek art.

2. THE ROMAN STYLE

The Roman style corresponds to our needs far more closely than the Greek style but mainly because it lacks inner consistency and a characteristic development. In the beginning the Romans adopted the very ancient Etruscan manner of building and might well have developed it into a style with broad, angular masses, daring spans of arches and domes, and lively grouping of the parts, which would have expressed their warlike spirit perfectly. Although the Romans were a skillful and industrious people, who greatly advanced the science of building and later erected splendid and exceedingly magnificent buildings, they lacked a true feeling for art. Having later adopted the Greek columnar style, they did not hesitate to combine it with elements of their own arcuated style and thus provoked a battle between the two styles that ended with the decline of the Greek columnar style, of which almost nothing remained except the column as an inappropriate support for the arch. This spontaneous onslaught on Greek art and culture seems to have constituted the historical mission of the Romans, in preparation for the advent of Christian culture. The *Rundbogenstil* with clearly indicated imposts is, of all arch forms, the one that best conveys the character of repose and also one whereby the harmful consequences of its introduction into the columnar style could escape notice, especially with a people so artistically insensitive as the Romans. However, in contrast to the columnar style, the *Rundbogenstil* displays a decidedly upward-aspiring tendency, so that the two styles are virtually incompatible and demand a very different development.

If, notwithstanding its imperfection, we wished to adopt the Roman style, we would have to decide from the start which of its two inherent trends to adopt for the further development that undoubtedly would become necessary. One trend points to the Greek style, to which we must not return; the development of the arcuated style would lead us forward to the Romanesque, and then it would be easier to start with this style right away. If we want to see what becomes of the Roman style under the influence of Christian ideas, while avoiding the Romanesque style, we have only to look at the Renaissance. It led to the periwig style and would do so again. The two conflicting tendencies, arch and column—and even more the conflict between the spirit of antiquity and that of Christianity—cannot possibly be combined without producing utter nonsense. This is all that need be said about the Renaissance, which in any case was only possible so long as purely Greek models were unknown.

3. THE ROMANESQUE STYLE

The Romanesque style, or rather the different Romanesque styles (including the Byzantine), tried in varying degrees to give architectural expression to the new spirit aroused by Christianity. Yet these attempts failed because it long remained necessary to make do with the miserable remnants of the last period of the Roman manner of building. Several centuries had to pass before a lifeless art recovered, and many more before it assumed a character of its own. True, antique forms were increasingly suppressed: cornices became less dominant and were profiled differently; the characteristic frieze of delicate arches made its appearance; pilasters became lesenes; sharp edges were rounded off; columns were first given cushion capitals and later became compound piers; round arches began to change into pointed arches; and a lively sculptural and ornamental decoration appeared.

Through all of this, however, the new forms retained unmistakable signs of their antique origins; it is clear that these were not free developments but only modifications. Although in the end the whole had taken on a more varied and lively aspect and was different in character, it lacked consistent development and—as usual in such cases—also lacked a strict architectonic character. Masses already tended to strive upward, but forms still looked heavy. Details were either clumsy or too delicate, decorations were arbitrary, and forms were without any structural significance. Furthermore, there was constant vacillation; progress slowed down at times, speeded up at other times. There was some Arabic influence and finally a marked rapprochement with antiquity. While it is true that the early medieval response to Christianity was warm and sincere, it was yet too somber, one-sided, and uninspired. Christianity was too priest-ridden to be able to express itself freely in artistic matters. Late Romanesque buildings give the impression that a new, and perhaps Christian, spirit was now prevalent; but it was not yet a free spirit, and architecture, emerging from the remnants of antiquity, was even less able to express itself freely. It becomes apparent that the task was not accomplished and could not be accomplished without a total change of form. Once again, we are shown the way forward toward the Germanic style. If the Romanesque style was too severe and somber for the thirteenth century, too constrained and clumsy, too arbitrary, and architectonically lacking in meaning, it must be even more so for our time.

4. THE ARABIC STYLE

The Arabic style is more appropriate for us than one would imagine: perhaps more than any other style, at least insofar as the lively, varied, and ceaselessly striving spirit of our time finds its analogous expression in the fanciful formations of the Arabs. Yet apart from its lack of the Christian element, the style has one fault that prevents it from being recommended for general approval: an almost total disregard for the symbolic expression of structural forces; that is, the lack of architectonic character. When the free sons of the desert, aroused to fanatical zeal by Mohammed, surged forward to conquer and convert the world, they had no architectural style of their own. From the scientific point of view, they had to turn to the existing manner of building. It was different with the art to which they were attracted by the innate poetry of their character. They covered the simple Byzantine buildings, which were the first they happened to come across, with such an abundance of new and ingenious (even if arbitrary) decoration that it seems that the wonders of their own fairy tales have come alive. Yet no systematic development of a specific style could be expected in this way. The Arabian style is confined to pure decoration, which looks all the more strange as their religion prohibits figurative work. The style is charming, although never more than a lively play of fancy. When the Crusades brought the Eastern and Western, Christian and Moslem civilizations closer together, the historical mission of Arabic architecture and culture consisted in stimulating the slower and more serious Christian culture and art to rise to a higher spiritual level.

5. The Germanic Style

In contrast to the heavy, unwieldy masses of the ancient Egyptian and the equilibrium of the Greek style, the basic principle of the Germanic style is the upward striving and the dominance of form over mass, which symbolizes the dominance of spirit over matter and of spirituality over sensuousness. Once again we stop and ask, "Why look any further?" Can we do better than adopt a style whose basic principle fits us so well? No one who has ever been lost in devotion in the lofty and somber spaces of a simple medieval cathedral, filled with humility and joyful hope, can deny that these spaces are pervaded with the spirit of pure Christianity. No one who has admired the rich formations, the curiously entwined rosettes and tracery, the rising piers and turrets, can behold it all without being spiritually inspired; all these forms are truly architectural with no imitation of Nature and yet create so wonderful an organic whole that the stone seems to have turned into a plant. No one who contemplates the vigorous striving of arches and vaults, of buttresses and flying buttresses, governed by equilibrium and resolving themselves into a harmonious, mighty upsurge of masses and forms, can fail to realize not only that here the powerfully striving spirit of our time is clearly revealed but also that here he can learn for himself how to pursue the highest and most exalted goal.

We have seen that the intervening styles (wherever we may choose to begin) lead us back either to the Greek style or forward to the Germanic; and we must therefore choose one or the other. The Greek style has been shown to be unsuitable, but the contrary is true with the Germanic style in every respect. This style is closer to us in time, national character, and religion. Our needs, if not the same, are very similar; we create buildings for the same climate and use the same materials. We need not fear breaking up a style that is complete in itself, because the Germanic style was not systematically developed during the Middle Ages but interrupted midway. Therefore, it will be quite safe for us to make the few changes that will be necessary without impairing its unique character or beauty. Also, the forms of the Germanic style do not lack structural significance, although the dominant spiritual qualities of the style make it less noticeable than in the Greek. Structural equilibrium, as an expression of spiritual equilibrium, was achieved here also, although not in the very simple way dictated by the Greek style. Most important of all: here we are not constantly confronted—as we are by the Greek style—with the prospect of future decline. The spiritual beauty that is the aim of the Germanic style is unattainable; an infinite striving for perfection is thus possible, and there is no inherent cause of decline.

It is true that the Germanic style too was abandoned and forgotten, but only through external circumstances. Perhaps its temporary suppression was necessary to allow it to escape the incipient process of degeneration, so that under more favorable circumstances it could flourish again with greater beauty and purity. If this can be proven, any doubts about the expediency of its revival will disappear. It may even be that this style was almost invented for us and for those who follow us. This would also explain why medieval buildings are still so much alive and why many things in medieval architecture strike a familiar chord with us.

We have seen that throughout the entire period of Romanesque architecture the dominant aim had been to express the idea of Christianity, especially in churches, and that this aim could not be achieved with Roman forms or their derivations or under the oppressive influence of the hierarchy. After spiritual progress had long prepared the ground, a new spirit awakened with the Crusades and their aftermath, particularly in the encounter with the more advanced, flourishing Arab culture. This new spirit stirred the whole of Europe to intense spiritual activity, to a struggle against hierarchical fetters that started hesitantly but, gaining force, led to ultimate victory and the birth of a pure and spiritual conception of the teachings of Jesus.

The same spirit undoubtedly gave birth to the Germanic style. It appeared completely formed for the first time in Germany (although a few forms appeared at an earlier date in France, following that country's early participation in the Crusades).[2] From the beginning, Christianity had taken deepest and strongest root in Germany; here, too, the long conflicts between emperor and pope had prepared the ground; and here, ultimately, the Reformation was born. That the effect of the new ideas was felt in art earlier than in life is not surprising; emotional reactions are quick and spontaneous, and there they did not cause any conflict or encounter any resistance. On the contrary, the clergy was eager to heighten the splendor of the outer form of divine worship with the help of the elaborate new style, disregarding completely the many obvious hints of the stonemasons' figures mocking them. This failure of understanding, coupled with excessive enrichment, endangered the Germanic style at the outset. Without sufficient time for the steady and consistent development, which would have allowed the Germanic style to free itself of all reminiscences of the older Romanesque style, its essential character became obscured, so that only its spiritual integrity saved it from total collapse. This spirit shines forth victoriously in all the jumbled forms of later buildings and puts us at our ease with a sense of familiarity.

Such an understanding was not to be expected in the first excitement of the battle between the fiercely contending parties, and it was quite natural that when after many unsuccessful attempts, the Reformation arrived four hundred years later, the Germanic style, forced off its right track and almost corrupted by opulence, received no recognition—despite its close relationship to the Reformation. It was soon condemned and abandoned as a product of Catholicism; especially as the Reformation came under the sway of a cold rationalism with unfortunate results for all true art and for imaginative Germanic art in particular. The Reformation, whose final aim cannot possibly be to split the Church, is still not completed; neither is the Germanic style. Both have still to be reinterpreted and carried onward to fruition; and this is the task of the present and the immediate future. May art, reconciling and mediating as always, be successful in finding and showing the right way!

Therefore, we will make the Germanic style our own, not as it developed historically but as it would have developed and would still be developing under more favorable circumstances, that is, without the distorting influence of the former harsh Catholicism and hand in hand with the Reformation—if only this too had not gone over to a false extreme.

We need not look far to find the starting point or the direction that we must take. This knowledge has been bequeathed to us by our ancestors, especially where church building is concerned. From this starting point and with the basic principles always in view, spurred on by the feeling that we walk on native soil, touched by the holy breath of ancient times but also fully aware of the new, eagerly striving order of the world and its nations, we shall advance step-by-step toward the infinitely distant but also infinitely sublime goal!

Source Note: Carl Albert Rosenthal, "In welchem Style sollen wir bauen? (Eine Frage für die Mitglieder des deutschen Architektenvereins)," *Zeitschrift für praktische Baukunst* 4 (1844): 23–27.

Translator's Notes

1. Although the German words "*heitre Ruhe*" and "*vollkommenes Gleichgewicht*" sound as if they were quotations from Winckelmann, this does not seem to be the case. Nor do they occur in *Gedanken über die Schönheit* (Zurich: Orell, Geßner, Füßlin, 1774) by Raphael Mengs, whom Rosenthal quoted on another occasion.

2. The admission that a few Gothic forms appeared in France at a date prior to the creation of this style in Germany reflects the reluctance with which the work of Franz Mertens on the French origin of the Gothic style was accepted and the commonly held belief in the German origin abandoned. Wiegmann strongly rejected the notion of an early French influence in his book *Über den Ursprung des Spitzbogenstils* (Düsseldorf: J. Buddeus, 1842), 45–57. Merten's first reports were pub-

lished in the *Allgemeine Bauzeitung* in 1843. See Eva Börsch-Supan, *Berliner Baukunst nach Schinkel: 1840–1870* (Munich: Prestel Verlag, 1977), 168–72; and Georg Germann, *Gothic Revival* (London: Lund Humphries with The Architectural Association, 1972), 151–52.

Remarks on the

Architectural Questions

Broached by Professor Stier

at the

Meeting of Architects at Bamberg [1]

Johann Heinrich Wolff

Fully convinced that it is of great importance to bring unity to the efforts that are being made concerning the art and the science of architecture, I have tried through many years of literary work to contribute to the verification and establishment of objective rules that the art of architecture should observe. For this reason I was delighted to hear of the annual meetings of German architects. This, I hope, will mean that a great step has been taken to direct the scattered activities that prevail in no other branch of human knowledge and skill so much as, unfortunately, they do in architecture.

I sincerely hope that these gatherings will be fruitful.

The greatest benefit that meetings of this kind could render, in my opinion, would be to lead to the formation of a German school of art and to a theoretical consensus on certain basic truths and a practical consensus on certain basic rules for the practice of art. Founded on the unalterable laws of optics and on the invariable demands of the normal aesthetic sense, these basic truths and rules would not restrict artistic freedom but would set a limit to arbitrariness; and they ought to become the criteria by which to distinguish between creations that are thoroughly sound and the productions of mere caprice.

These preliminary remarks have been prompted by the questions submitted by Professor Stier of Berlin to the meeting of architects at Bamberg, because they signal the beginning of the kind of discussion I desire. My only regret is that those present did not at once set about answering them. It would have been a good occasion for the association to show that its competence extended to artistic matters, and it would have been of interest to hear the exchange of differing views among professional colleagues and the principles that would have emerged from it. These questions are now, for the majority of our rising young architects, likely to remain a puzzle for at least a year or longer. This was surely not what Professor Stier intended in giving his lecture, since I am sure he feels as strongly as I do that there is already too much that puzzles most architects. For my part, I particularly regret that this appeal for public debate was not taken up, because the lecturer was not given the opportunity to present his own views on the subject—views that, I am convinced, were the fruit of mature reflection, since all that he does deserves credit for a laudable effort to achieve thoroughness.

In order to show my own readiness to involve myself whenever there is a prospect of a real and well-directed advance in our art, I have chosen the platform of this periodical to initiate a debate that I expect will bear fruit in many ways. I propose to take up the three questions raised by Professor Stier and hope for some response to my examination of these questions at one of the future meetings or on some other occasion.

Let us take the first of the three points put forward by Professor Stier. It concerns "the basic principle, the idea of architecture in general."

Our old textbooks tell us that the basic principle of architecture is to create long-lasting, comfortable, and inexpensive dwellings; beauty is mentioned only in passing. This is an interpretation that cannot be pursued here; our concern is with the "artistic nature" of architecture. The textbooks deal only with the artisanal aspect, not primarily with art and not at all with the idea of architecture. Therefore, the question is this: What is its aesthetic purpose? What is its function in developing and perfecting the human race, and what importance, in this respect, has its future evolution for us?

To apprehend the spirit inherent in nature, in other words to apprehend perfection, is one of the duties imposed on man. By obeying it, man shows himself worthy of his unique privilege as the only creature endowed with a Godlike spirit. The more deeply we reflect and explore, the more clearly we recognize the inner spiritual coherence of all things. To represent and convey this coherence is the sacred impulse of the nobler and more gifted members of the human race, not only for their own satisfaction but in the hope that their enthusiasm will bring others closer to an understanding of eternal truths.

A large share in these efforts has fallen to the talented artist. He must grasp and give artistic form to the infinite harmony and meaning inherent in the visible, physical forms of nature. The artist's supreme task is therefore to probe into the profoundest inner truths, the eternal laws of form, that nature has always followed and still follows. These laws and truths (closely joined to the supreme spiritual expression that must be immanent in the concept of the work) must be made convincingly visible and intelligible. Among the fine arts, it is architecture that, by virtue of its particular quality (in relating material directly to form, as we shall see later), displays in the simplest and clearest manner the fundamental rules to which all arts must have recourse. It forms the basic harmony, as it were, the thoroughbass of all the fine arts, and it acts as their choragus. The ancients have named it the principal art, the αρχιτεκτονική τέχνη. No independent work of fine art—indeed, no work of art—can do without the architectonic in its higher sense. This has been recognized not only by the great painters and sculptors but also by musicians and poets in relation to their creations in word or sound. When a work of art lacks the architectonic quality, it collapses or is nothing but a fragment. It will never form an organic whole; whatever other merits it may have, it will arouse only a passing pleasure and then only in the masses and in those who are biased. It will never stand up before the judgment of professional criticism.

This, then, is the high standing of architecture: it should not only serve the material needs of life but also uplift the spirit, arouse and strengthen the sense for measure and law in general, and thus form the foundation for everything that art produces. In order that present-day architecture may fulfill this aim in a better way than hitherto and in this respect, as in others, once more approach ancient art, we must above all cease to let caprice have the upper hand. For how is architecture to prescribe laws to the other arts, if it is lawless itself? To search for and establish such objective rules (which at the beginning of this article I declared to be a principal purpose of professional meetings) was already my intention in 1831 in a brochure entitled *Beiträge zur Aesthetik der Baukunst* [*Contributions to the Aesthetics of Architecture*], published in 1834. Later, in a series of reviews, I took the opportunity of applying the rules that I had proposed with the appropriate modifications and explanations. In this way they were once more confirmed, since their effect was exemplified by buildings that were generally approved. I hope that the zeal with which I pursued this preliminary work will not prove to have been wasted when the time comes to deliberate on the establishment and general acceptance of a basic architectural theory. I like to believe that one or the other of the principles elaborated therein may form the basis on which, after a general discussion and with modifications, a magnificent monument to concord will be erected that will transcend all the conflicting opinions and vacillations that abound within our profession. Should our art attain this goal, then it may be hoped that this will mark the dawn of a new age when architecture will powerfully influence the activities of the sister arts and will once more worthily fulfill its supreme task—the ennoblement of the human spirit through the medium of the senses.

The first question was general in nature; the second question that was submitted for discussion referred to certain basic architectural principles on which those present were asked to express their opinion: namely, as Professor Stier phrased it, "on the usual definition and application of symmetry and on the traditional definition of the beauty of proportions."

To take the former aspect first, that of the correctness of the usual definition and application of symmetry (whereby, it seems, only bilateral symmetry is meant): it may seem strange to find that these rules, which derive from the most basic architectural concepts, are now called into question, so that in a sense one must go back to first principles; but it must be admitted that the question is an entirely apposite one in view of the practice of some young architects, who indeed hold some very confused ideas on this matter. Those who consider symmetry to be irrelevant and even harmful would not be inconsistent if they blamed the Creator for not making the human figure, as well as those of all the more highly evolved creatures, asymmetrical, so as to conform to the interior of the body (where, as is known, the parts do not exactly correspond on both sides). With regard to architecture, they even argue in the following way: since a ruin, for instance, can have great picturesque beauty, an unequal composition of dissimilar major parts and details in a building might also be equally satisfying. In fact, they say, we are tired of so much symmetry and should try to produce new forms that offer more variety, etc. The grotesque buildings near Braunschweig by Ottmer and others are due to this crazy notion.[2] With unseemly frivolity, they have taken the multiple and confused overall compositions that are occasionally to be seen in medieval castles built on high rocks (where the inequalities in the parts of the building stem from the uneven terrain and often also from piecemeal construction) and have repeated them on flat land, so that they cannot even be called picturesque but defy all reason and sense.

Buildings of this type demean themselves in serving as mere accessories to the landscape, whereas on the contrary the landscape should only be an accompaniment to the work of art. Such buildings deny the sense of order in man, who strives to make his work into a serious, dignified, well-considered whole that echoes the harmonic order and the symmetrical arrangement of his models, the organic creations of a higher order. These disparate parts seem to have been thrown together by chance. They continue the comparatively weak impression made by the landscape, instead of contrasting the landscape with a more highly organized work so that the one will heighten the attraction of the other.

How far bilateral symmetry is basically architectonic, because it particularly satisfies our innate sense of equilibrium, I have explained at great length in *Beiträge zur Aesthetik der Baukunst*, where I presented it as one of the principal laws governing the creation of beautiful works of architecture. In the same work—to pass to the second part of the question cited previously—I also discussed a number of laws that determine those proportions that are considered to be pleasing or beautiful and dealt with their application to architecture. That brochure also contains some results of my research on the subject touched upon in question two; I shall return to this later, but first I will examine how the question is to be understood and how it can be defined.

When Professor Stier talks about the traditional concept of the beauty of proportions, this can only refer to the rules that one finds in the old architectural textbooks. In my young days, these were presented to us as the key to the secret of beauty in architecture. In the belief that beauty could be captured through complicated ratios, writers had either abstracted these rules from a comparative examination of the Roman monuments or had adopted the laws of music, which had been reduced to a theory of seven basic ratios, in the correct assumption that conformity existed between the two noble senses, that of the eye and of the ear.* Yet in both arts no one really knew what to do with these presumed ratios, which were supposed to be valuable but which proved unproductive. They could not be used, as had been hoped, as guides to structures of sound and form without coming into conflict with man's inborn sense of rightness: so that, instead of clarifying matters, they obscured them. In theory, these ratios long continued to prevail in both arts, because no one

---

*Quite recently, Wolfram stated this in his treatise on architecture, published in 1838. [*Ludwig Friedrich Wolfram*, Vollständiges Lehrbuch der gesammten Baukunst *(Stuttgart, 1833–1845).*]

knew what to put in their place. In practice, however, artists were always compelled to deviate and to be guided by their own senses. This was less disadvantageous in music than in our art, because the ear is more sensitive than the eye, which is blunted by constantly looking at imperfect objects. For this reason, good care was taken not to hurt the ear by exposing it to jarring sounds as frequently as the eye is presented with architectural and structural deformities.

If—as I must assume—Professor Stier intended in posing his question to find whether these traditional concepts of the beauty of proportions are "indeed correct," then I am grateful to him for provoking the formulation and publication of a better system, which had been my wish for a long time. I was keenly aware of the inadequacy of the information given in the old textbooks on this subject. This moved me to examine the true capacity of the eye and ascertain which proportions it easily discerns and therefore recognizes as the basic proportions and which for this reason are the only ones that will give complete satisfaction. Examining the work done in this field, I soon found out to my surprise that in the attempt to establish general rules, authors had made the mistake of overlooking what was simple and obvious. They began by looking at the specific detail that pleases the eye while disregarding the context in which it appears (and which alone causes the pleasant impression), instead of examining the true reasons for this pleasure and the true capabilities of the eye. The result was that they became involved in thousands upon thousands of contradictions. I myself took an interest in this subject as far back as the 1820s. My own studies convinced me that we can perceive only that height equals width—or, at most, and under certain conditions, that one dimension is twice the other. Therefore all statements made with regard to more complicated ratios, such as 2:3, 3:5, etc.—and probably also 1:6 and 1:8, which are supposed to give particular pleasure—are completely invalid and derive, as mentioned before, from a merely deductive process.*

In which way these ratios, which I assume to be basic harmonies, can be

* When in 1832 I mentioned to my learned friend Moriz Hauptmann that according to my studies about proportions, complicated ratios are inadmissible, it turned out that Hauptmann, who at present is principal of the famous Schule St. Thomas at Leipzig and a worthy successor to Sebastian Bach, discovered at about the same time that for basic musical proportions, on which the whole tone structure rests, the only right and applicable ratios—in music too—are those that are reduced to 1:1 and 1:2. It emerged that the triad can only be analyzed into these ratios, so that, remarkably, the concordance of the basic rules of both arts, always assumed though only dimly felt, was confirmed for both of us. [Wolff continues the footnote with a reproduction of a long letter by Hauptmann in which he exposes the fallacy of an arithmetical determination of concordant sounds. On Hauptmann (1792–1868), see The New Grove Dictionary of Music and Musicians (London: Macmillan Press Ltd.; Washington, D.C.: Grove's Dictionaries of Music, Inc., 1980), 8: 307.]

applied to architecture; how everything else depends on these; and how diversity has been introduced into this unity, all this I have, as I said, discussed in greater detail in 1834, in my *Beiträge zur Aesthetik der Baukunst* and later in articles published in this journal. May the suggestions put forward by Professor Stier prompt a few of my fellow artists to examine what I wrote and either to accept or to refute it, to correct or to complete it! Whether one or the other, this would be a sign of progress.

The third question, set out here in three parts, will certainly be well received and carefully considered today, especially by architects, because it relates to a subject that architects constantly have in mind, like a haunting tune that one hums and hums again—the question of originality! I have to admit that I am glad to have the opportunity to set out my own views once more in a more connected way, because it is only by a thorough discussion of these issues that the efforts that architects nowadays make to be original at any price can be shown in the right light—efforts that have brought so much confusion into architecture.

The parts of the question as phrased by Professor Stier are:

a. "What are the preconditions for an original style?"

b. "How far, during the great artistic periods, was originality considered to be a progressive quality, and how did it manifest itself?"

c. "How is this element (originality) manifested in present-day architecture, and what is the proper manner in which it can be so manifested?"

For a better understanding of these somewhat succinct formulations, I have tried to elaborate them as follows:

a. What set of conditions, what combination of circumstances—material, artistic, or spiritual—is needed to produce an original style? (Professor Stier's words might also mean: "What are the features that define an original style?" But I believe that by rephrasing it I have kept closer to the sense of the whole.)

b. To what extent, in the great architectural epochs (the only ones that concern us here) was it thought to be essential and even necessary to be original, that is, to deviate from all preceding styles (even from those whose excellence was acknowledged) and to invent a new style, characteristic for the period; and how far and with what effect was this achieved in the various periods?

c. To what extent has originality been sought and achieved

in our times? To what style are we drawn by virtue of character, historical circumstances, vocation, and today's technical resources? What kind of originality can we expect to find in present-day architecture?

It is evident that we now enter the wide field of architectural history; only history can provide the answers to these questions. All that I can do, therefore, is to single out the factors that are most relevant, though I regret being somewhat hampered in this work by the restricted space that I can expect this journal, considering its main tendency, to allow for such an investigation.

Let us first turn to Egypt, the cradle of our art. I shall completely disregard the learned controversy between those scholars who claim priority for the buildings of India and those who (undoubtedly with better reason) favor the monuments of Egypt. I pass this over, because I am not concerned with archaeological research but with the first development of architecture; and this begins only where, for the first time, separate elements are assembled into a building. The Indian practice was to hollow buildings out of rocks, a practice that belongs to sculpture and can therefore be of no use to us.

This may also explain why, in suggestions I made earlier (in my brochure, *Über Plan und Methode bei dem Studium der Architektur* [*On Planning and Method in the Study of Architecture*] [Darmstadt: Leske, 1831]), I began with a review of the Egyptian style in the belief that I could ignore the buildings of the other nations of antiquity, not only those of the Indians, but also of the Babylonians, Phoenicians, Persians, Jews, etc. It is true that in Babylon as well as in Egypt there are indications of an early development of architecture (whereas, for the buildings of the other people named, it must be assumed from the buildings still standing or recorded by history that they adopted the forms of an already existing style). Yet the Babylonians depended on an inferior material (bricks) that did not encourage the invention of artistic motifs to be applied to the main forms (see our review of brick buildings by Schinkel, *Literatur… Beilage* of the *Allgemeine Bauzeitung*, 1843). For this reason I refrain from reviewing their monuments, which are known to us in any case only through records and a few remnants—at least until such time as new excavations furnish firm indications of their characteristic features and historical context.

The dawn of architecture therefore starts more than three thousand years ago in Egypt. Here, man first learned to handle the material on which all nations at all times have depended to satisfy their innate urge to erect (for religious or political purposes, in particular) buildings that will last as long as possible: a material whose nature and composition constitute the only correct basis for an art that in the selection of its forms must not fall victim to arbitrariness but be guided by natural analogies.

In Egypt where, as mentioned, we find the beginnings of the joining of single blocks of stone, we can observe how, step-by-step, the material itself taught man the form. The specific weight of the material resulted in the perpendicularity of the piers and of the space-enclosing walls—to which, however, as contributing factors, must be added human instinct and the human form. Other qualities, such as its brittleness, led, where large rooms had to be covered, to the use of freestanding piers as supports for horizontal architraves made of stone. The chamfering of the piers was partly the result of expediency and partly again the result of the brittleness of the material. Here was the first approach toward organic form—round, upright, and tapering—as observed in the vegetable realm, a form that in its development became more refined without, however, encroaching upon the true nature of the material.

I hope that these few suggestions (set out at greater length in the above-mentioned article on brick buildings) may suffice to show that allowance has to be made for the great influence that the material exerts on the creation of form. Of course, it goes without saying that I do not deny in any way the great influence of the specific conditions of a country, nation, and religion as the source of many symbolic forms. I feel, however, that there is no need for me to list them, because this is done—more or less satisfactorily—in every history of art.*

Accepting the rise of architecture in Egypt as the first period of our art, we must turn to Greece to look for an advance on these beginnings. There is, however, no need to assume that the Greeks were familiar with Egyptian architecture and that they only modified and adjusted it to their needs. This may have been so; but it is equally possible that Greek forms developed quite independently out of the material—which was the same in both countries—and other relevant conditions. In either case, we cannot deny that in Greece the Egyptian beginnings underwent a basic modification as a result of the climate, which demanded a sloping roof. This brought about a more complicated system (the entablature consisting of three parts), which—unimpeded by the symbolic influences that prevailed in Egypt—evolved to a high degree of perfection in the early Doric style.† This was therefore the first advance, the first expansion and development of the original forms, that arose in a natural way. With it there began a new chapter—if you will, the second period of the development of architecture.

It reached its climax with the Ionians, whose exquisite artistic sense had

---

*An essential fault in recent books on art history seems to me that their authors—who, it is true, are rarely architects—wish to explain the various styles by reflecting on philosophical notions and subtle psychological observations, while often overlooking the most obvious material reasons that led to the creation of form.
†See Beiträge zur Aesthetik der Baukunst, 55ff.

been formed through a concurrence of most fortunate circumstances and conditions.* It was here that the proportion of the height to the width of the column—until then considered as no more than a structural support, the main form of which approaches a plantlike character—was all at once doubled (from about four-and-a-half to nine diameters). This proportion was thought to recall that of the human figure, which is the only individual form the proportions of which, the same all over the world, are stereotypically, as it were, fixed within us. The type of the column was thereby established forever; in turn, it brought to perfection the Doric shaft, the height of which was increased to about six diameters in order to conform to male strength and force, just as female grace and charm, together with a resistant strength, were expressed in the Ionic order.† Thus the column, which had hitherto figured within the formal system only as a vertical line, acquired an analogical relationship that lent it a new importance within the main proportions. A more complete harmony was found for the colonnade (greater variety within unity) through the division of the square into three intervals.[3] Again I can only refer to the detailed explanation in my brochure *Beiträge zur Aesthetik der Baukunst*. There I also dealt extensively with the artistic development of the Greek style in all its details, both in the later Doric and the Ionic order, a development that had some bearing on the changed shape of the column (and finally I also discussed the invention of the Corinthian order as an enhancement and further refinement of the Ionic style). All I wish to say of this golden age of Greek art is this: the Greeks of this period with their pure sense of form made full use of the obvious formal resources offered by the nature of the material and all the other unchanging conditions; they clearly and fully recognized the creative properties of the material, which the Egyptians had already dimly sensed; and they allowed us, as it were, to look into the workshop of the spirit, whence all forms emerge as they are and no other way. This period represents the third and *last* stage in the development and progress of our art.‡

The series of those magnificent artistic inventions that made a true contribution to the aesthetic part of architecture and its truly original principle had thus come to an end. What followed brought some amplification, it is true; but in its remoteness from simple and obvious themes it already contained the germ of decline. Various attempts to develop the new additions and blend them with the integral sys-

*Karl Ottfried Müller in his Handbuch der Archäologie der Kunst, 2nd ed., 17, gives a very good description of the character of a nation that would greatly favor artistic development.

†The so-called Tuscan and Roman Ionic orders used later by the Romans were adapted both in proportion and in detail from the Doric and Ionic orders respectively and represented, in fact, a mixture of both. The columns are really hybrids that represent neither male strength nor female grace; they are evidence only of a coarse taste.

tem of the Greek world of forms soon led to the dissolution of the spiritual harmony that pervaded it.

To justify this assertion, let us now look briefly at the history of Roman architecture.

The Romans acquired their knowledge of the arch through a fortunate chain of circumstances, either by inventing it themselves or, as many believe, by adopting it from the Etruscans or from another, even older, nation. Whether the discovery came to them by chance or by their own calculation (to which the practice of using small blocks of building material may also have led), it was admirably suited to their purposes. At the beginning, this invention was primarily used to satisfy material needs in the construction of sewers and other underground works; but it soon entered the aesthetic field and was used to span wide spaces, not only to widen the passages through which the crowd reached the great public events that frequently took place in Rome—the focus of Roman grandeur and power—but also for the construction of the wide halls needed for the same purpose. The interiors of these were free of the columns and pillars required by the trabeated system, and their coverings were as durable as any that the Greeks and Egyptians could contrive by using stone beams. But the Romans used the vault to satisfy not only their real needs but also their inclination toward colossal dimensions and everything that appealed to a vulgar taste. This explains why they made their temples larger without having any need for it. Another reason why they wished to introduce this characteristic element into their style may have been, as I once expressed it, that they saw in the all-embracing roundness of the arch an image of their own grandeur and status in the world.

Yet the introduction of this spheric covering—the construction of which was possible only through complicated calculations that remained hidden—shifted

‡*I find strong support for this view in Bötticher's recently published, masterly book on Greek architecture, in which, after an appreciation of its great achievements, he writes:* "The poet and the artist, the thoughtful and the imaginative man love the Hellenes so much for their orderly spirit of invention, because it made them sense the miracle of nature's creations and listen to the law governing their existence with which they so infused their own works that a new and spiritually more enlightened generation could only arise out of their world, and even out of its ruins—a world to which every future generation must turn again to learn sophrosyne, the idea and form, the order and measure for poetry and art." *[Die Tektonik der Hellenen* (Potsdam: Ferdinand Riegel, 1844), 1st excursus, p. 25.] Professor Stier also—in an article published in this journal in 1843—repeatedly emphasizes the necessity of a return to ancient architecture. I am glad to find that other writers are also coming to recognize and appreciate the spirit and the merits of ancient architecture, on which I have long sought to shed light. It is to be hoped that these views, on which the salvation of present-day architecture depends, will in time find general acceptance.*

the form away from the realm of calm and orderly contemplation that was the basic character of classical art into the realm of Romanticism. Restrictions were indeed lifted, and limits expanded; but, with these salutary barriers, art disappeared too. When the earlier practice with its clear expression of the simple nature of the material was abandoned, and the simple method of joining stones vertically or in horizontal layers to support the horizontal parts was replaced by an unnatural support through arches and purely mental calculations, then man's intuitive sense, on which all artistic impressions depend, could no longer follow.

The Greek and Roman styles thus differ greatly in their basic ideas, and the difference in form is just as noticeable. With the Greeks, the architectural skeleton, if we may use the expression, is strictly stereometric, mineral, and inorganic in its main lineaments; it consists of squares formed by horizontal and vertical lines. With the Romans, it is shifted toward the organic aspect, or rather, the lower (vegetable) forms of organic life pervade the whole, although mainly through the linear contours.

The first consequence of the adoption of the rounded arch was that the piers or supports, one of the most essential parts of Greek architecture, came to be subordinated to the covering. So far they had been freely developed and had, through analogies and in an appropriate and sensible manner, been given a beautiful shape, manifesting the supreme artistic spirit of the Greeks. Now, they were thrust from the stage of evolution at which they had gained, as it were, the status of a higher organism back to an inorganic and crystalline state, at least with regard to their mass. For the arch does not only require a vertical support for structural reasons, its formal outline must also be in direct connection with a vertical line: structurally, because it exerts pressure; formally, because half a circle is an incomplete form, which, whenever it cannot be completed by adding the other half (as had been done in the case of the Byzantine rose windows), must be directly joined with a line from which it seems to evolve in a plantlike manner. The self-contained form of the column could not meet this demand; a perpendicular axis runs through the center of its mass but does not appear as a line—as it would have to do in order to merge with the contour of the arch. In the arcuated style, the support or pier reverted to an inorganic shape and was really nothing but a piece of wall; but its profiles assumed, one might say, a plantlike character through being merged with the organic profile of the arch (a character clearly expressed later in the Germanic style). As previously mentioned, this has the result that the semiorganic character communicated itself to the whole arch form, even though the most flexible part—the freestanding support—was, at least conceptually, changed back into a dead and rigid mass.

Yet, even with the contour of the arch continued by a perpendicular line, the arcaded form still gives the displeasing impression of something that is incomplete: an impression that is dispelled only after the semicircle has been framed by complementary forms. The Romans felt this, and this (along with the wish to make their buildings look opulent) led them to frame their openings with horizontal and vertical lines, which, being tangential to the contour of the arch, reconciled the semicircle with the main directions [horizontal and vertical] and thus resolved dissonance and restored architectural harmony. They were right to borrow these framing forms from the Greek style. For where else could they have found verticality and horizontality so beautifully represented or embodied as in Greek columns and cornices? Indeed, they contrived with great ingenuity to fit these parts as a whole into their arcuated system. Although they had no clear conception of the original source, they had a sense for what was attractive, sound, and truthful. (In the decoration of their temples they also retained Greek models—at least in their own estimation, although we see these only as faint shadows of the originals.)

From what has been said, it is evident that the vaulted covering is indeed an amplification of the preceding system but that aesthetically it does not represent a gain. It does not lead to the creation of new sculptural forms but only to a play of more vivid lines, which are similar to those surface decorations that tend toward the pictorial.* We shall see later that all succeeding arcuated styles were really only variations on the same theme: that is to say, they were attempts to free the arch—that segment of a circle—from its stern aspect and indeed from its dissonant appearance. This is what gives any arcuated style, in contrast to the classical repose of rectilinear structures, the character of restless immobility that I have already defined as Romantic.

With the decline of Roman power and greatness, a situation developed that was not favorable to architecture. The Romans with their comparatively sound artistic sense realized that the new element of the arch could not exist by itself but that to satisfy, it had to be wedded to something that was original, namely to *architectonic-sculptural* quality.† Yet the nations of the increasingly turbulent period that followed were unable to uphold this insight in its original vigor. It became more and more obscured, and the early stirrings of architectural creativity, stimulated by the first attempts to merge the new with the existing elements, were pushed into the

---

* *While the Greeks, with their system of straight lines, everywhere attained formal perfection, in the details as well as in the building as a whole, the Romans achieved it only in those rare cases where buildings could be covered with domes.*

† *It should perhaps be explained that I understand "the architectonic-sculptural"* [das Architektonisch-Plastische] *to be the result of arranging the forms in such a way that the functions of all structural parts, like the members of the human body, are clearly revealed, while at the same time the structural arrangement does justice to the particular nature of the material.*

background. Increasingly, people were content to borrow from existing works only the barest essentials. This, of course, meant that the arch form, a feature conspicuous even to the crudest sense, was given preference, especially because its construction required only small stones and consequently no great technical skill—a quality that was in short supply because of political upheavals, fragmentation of forces, and scarcity of means. Since traditional forms were apprehended with little mental effort and even less material expense, the sense of rightness became increasingly dulled.

As a result, the limitations that previous generations had wisely accepted (in the belief that the *architectonic-pictorial* form of the arch was scarcely akin to true architectural principles) were abandoned; instead, builders tried through chamfering to give the arch form a more sculptural appearance and to give the arch more than a purely linear function in the process of formal creation by providing columns for its support in place of square piers. It was no longer clear to them why the Romans of the best period had given up using them for this purpose, even though trabeated architecture had shown that columns were functionally adequate as supports. Their artistic sense being dulled, they thought to gain by using columns as a support for the arches, not only because space was saved with round columns but also because, for instance, they became easier to walk around.* Yet this entailed a change in the shape of the column by which it was divested of its particular charm. Gradually, the taper was lost, so that the column in its cylindrical shape at least had a perpendicular contour and thus fitted the arch better; the capital also acquired a square and massive form, which provided a tolerable continuation of the spring of the arch—carved, as it were, out of the wall—but made a poor match for the round shaft of the column. Thus the head was, so to speak, severed from the trunk, and the integrated, organic form of the column was torn open in order to make shift to join it with the new element, the hemispherical covering. Despite the crude ideas that the practical builders (who, at that time, were hardly more than artisans) entertained on these matters, they did not fail to realize that something more had to be done to make the form of the arch more pleasing, an objective that the Romans had tried to achieve by framing it with straight lines.

The Romans, as we have seen, had adopted the Greek forms for this purpose, using them only as lines that were to frame the arches as closely as possible. But this arrangement was now considered a luxury; the builder thought he had done enough by showing the arcades in a far vaguer relationship with the principal [horizontal and vertical] lines. This was achieved either through simple projections

Recently, some younger architects who are under the same illusion have recommended the further development of this style.

(lesenes), usually placed at the corners of the major parts of the building only, or through relieflike wall panels that framed the round shape of the arch, though at a greater distance, with vertical and horizontal lines. Or a relation to horizontality was achieved by the regular recurrence of arches of equal height, while at the same time the symmetrical divergence of the rising archivolts suggested perpendicularity; so that it was only the ends of this type of arcade that failed to resolve the dissonance. Although this principle gave only partial satisfaction, it was applied in many variations, especially in the construction of gables, which, because of the poor quality of the material used for roofing, became increasingly steep. In order to mitigate the disturbing impression of these unpleasantly steep slopes, a row of arches with or without piers was added, running below the cornice. Its contours were intended to counterbalance the sloping outline of the roof to which it was attached. Another way to soften the unpleasant effect of a steep gable and to bring its slope into better harmony with the basic [horizontal and vertical] lines was to raise it in steps, a method that later became quite common, although it entailed other irregularities.

For all that, steep roofs, especially at the gable ends, remained a great defect and were therefore toned down or kept out of sight as much as possible until, with the invention of bells, the introduction of church towers led to the unrestricted use of these misshapen and intractable monsters with which architects fight a constant battle. It was now possible to make the gables, flanked by towers, as high as one desired, without having to fear the disrupting effect of the high roof, at least not at the facade. In this respect, the sides of the building were totally neglected.

Just as the steep gables were the result of the poor quality of the material used for covering, so the unnecessary great strength of the thick walls was the result of insufficient technical effort. When not using the spoils gathered from Roman monuments (as is well known, many columns as well as marble tiles, etc., found in ruined buildings were used again), builders resorted to the first materials that came to hand, however poor. On the one hand, the great thickness of the walls seemed to obviate the need for local reinforcement, as used by the Romans to great aesthetic advantage through engaged piers, columns, and other vertical projections; on the other hand, it became desirable to chamfer the corners and to splay the windows and doors, or rather to increase their outer width, mainly to improve lighting. Since this kind of refinement, through chamfering, lacked any structural motivation, it encouraged a tendency toward carved form in architecture, which, once introduced, quickly spread and opened the way to the Gothic style. The beginnings of this style can best be observed in the Byzantine style, where doorways, stepped back in plan, are decorated with colonnettes, whose roundness continues past the capitals and converges in the arched portion of the doorway. Here already we meet the plantlike growth of the column, which is the basic principle of the medieval style.

The need to establish a connection between the arched line and the vertical contour, for the sake of which the Romans had replaced columns with rectangular piers, had been largely lost on the Byzantines;* and the Moors in Spain—who had received their influences partly from a few Roman remains but largely secondhand, from the remains (in a Byzantine style) left by their predecessors, the Goths—showed an even stronger tendency to treat the arched superstructure separately from the vertical support. Endowed with vivid imagination and love of adornment—qualities that in general are typical of the character of the Oriental and southern peoples—the Arabs or Moors were not satisfied with the forms their predecessors had given to the architectural elements. They were evidently far advanced in technical skill, and the squat heaviness of existing arches and columns seemed to them as superfluous as it was incompatible with their predilection for opulence and daintiness. Even so, it took them some time to free themselves from these defects, so that only their later works have the slender proportions and boldly constructed vaults that typify their style.

The first change they undertook concerned the form of the arch: they elongated the semicircle (a change that conformed better to the relation of its height to the narrowed distance between their slender columns) and brought its shanks round toward each other, so that it formed a three-quarter circle. This is of great interest for our present study because here we meet in the way the ends of the arch are brought closer together—so typical of the Moorish style—another attempt to complete the form of the arch and to provide the semicircle, which by itself leaves much to be desired, with a complementary form and so connect it in a more satisfactory way with the rising tangential lines. With the changed contour of the arch, totally unrelated to the perpendicular line of the support, any attempts to connect these two parts came to an end. Indeed their separation became even more complete with the insertion of a stone console on top of the Corinthian capital (still in use at the beginning) to ensure that the arch was provided with a better and widened baseplate, a practice that later became general.† How this arrangement and its details, especially the capital with its intermediate piece, evolved into different forms and how the arch

*The term "Byzantine style" is usually taken to refer to the architecture of all those nations that succeeded the Romans, although not only the Byzantines but also the Ostrogoths and Visigoths, the Langobards, and indeed the Romance peoples, all drew from the same source and consequently all built in this style with minor variations; as is known, it was also applied to the German buildings of the time.
†This particular baseplate appears here and there in the Byzantine style, although at a very early date when builders still wished to use ancient columns and had not yet thought of meeting the need to provide the arch with a stronger, square, and widely projecting support by altering the form of the capital.

assumed various shapes (with pointed forms already among them), I shall pass over. The Moors were guided by responses similar to those of the Byzantines but were also stirred by their own highly charged imaginations. I will only add that while the Moors committed the same mistake as the Byzantines and Goths and—unlike the Romans—separated support and arch, they nevertheless showed a refined taste in following the Romans' example of framing almost every arch with horizontal and perpendicular tangential lines.

        I now pass straightaway to the medieval style. All intermediate attempts, including the Saracen style in Sicily with its generally pointed arches, will be sufficiently explained by a discussion of the medieval style in which the rising contour of the pier is completely merged with the curve of the arch. All of a sudden, a totally new idea—that of a plantlike ascent, the first sign of which we met in the outlining of the arches in Roman art—became the basis of architecture. At the same time, the true basis of the art, namely the nature of the material as the source of all forms, was completely overlooked. Handed down over many centuries, these once natural elements came to be used without aesthetic sensitivity, and their all-pervading spirit was completely lost. Eventually, a new artistic age, brought about by changed circumstances, freed itself of the slovenly habit of lifeless imitation, gave completely new forms to the elements generally used, and cast off all the fetters of the past. An art formerly based on simple, natural, and easily understood motifs—as Greek and even Roman art had been—was now replaced by an arbitrary system that conformed to the emergent demands of [national] character. The same devout and almost fanatical spirit that stirred people to exert such enormous efforts in the conduct of the Crusades and instilled unity of purpose into the usually divided nations of the West, the same enthusiasm also inspired the practical artistic brains among the architects and led them to try to unify the various styles that had arisen out of the degenerate architecture of the Romans.

        Clearheaded as they were, they selected from the monuments of other nations with whom they frequently came into contact in those turbulent times whatever they found consistent with their ideas. With exquisite artistic sense for picturesque form and for the beauty of linear perfection, they rearranged what they had appropriated and added something of their own. As a sign of how much they drew from what already existed, it is interesting to note that a trend toward slender and daring forms is already evident in the Byzantine and Arabic styles, not only in the naves of churches and mosques and in the towers with their pointed roofs flanking the facades but also in the proportion of the colonnettes, those decorative elements used inside and out, which had been considerably lengthened with the steadily growing height and now only needed a slight increase to bring about the ascending impression that is the hallmark of the Germanic style. The strengthening wall piers or pilasters of the Romans, not used in the intervening styles, were the source of the buttresses that now created an overall diminution of mass toward the top, an insetting, freeing, and pointing of the upper parts, and an increase in the number of ascending forms and lines. Furthermore, it was quite natural for the Gothic builders to adopt the elongated Arabic arch in the form of the pointed arch, which allowed them to place the piers closer together than was possible with a semicircular arch and also conformed better to the increased spaces between them. They also adopted the Roman groin vault, a form they considered highly appropriate to their whole architectural system.* They had the rich decoration that covers the walls of all Arabic buildings constantly before them; and for the plantlike forms, ascending from the columns, their models were the Byzantine doorways, before mentioned. In short, they brought all the efforts of their predecessors to fruition and readied themselves to surpass all that had been done before. We admire the energetic effort that led them to such artistic perfection and harmonic order, although the mineralogical and structural basis upon which architecture had originally arisen vanished altogether. Their only purpose was to set up a powerful symbol of their religious aspiration.

Although the Germanic style reproduced much that had existed before, it nevertheless is of great interest to us in our examination of the many attempts in different styles that were made to counterbalance the curved line of the arch. Through a completely new approach, the Germanic style succeeded in achieving this effect with a perfection that will never be surpassed. For whereas the need to relate the semicircular arch to horizontal and vertical lines was obvious and for that reason a strong need arose to frame it with such lines or to indicate a relation to them in another way—a need that, as we have seen, was satisfied in various ways—the high pointed arch could only be surrounded by slanting and ascending lines that, as tangents, came together in one point (the pointed gable). Since these, however, were not in harmony with the principal directions of the building, the dissonance had to be resolved in some other way, which in the main consisted of flanking it with perpendicular parts, an arrangement derived from the Byzantine church facades with their high towers and steeply gabled roofs and later to be found again in buildings of the Germanic style.

The same vivid artistic sense that gave rise to this new way of counter-balancing the arch led to the brilliant invention of helm or pointed roofs (further mediated by foliated ornament), with which the ascending lines were satisfactorily terminated. The steep slopes of the roofs blended with the now-dominant perpen-

---

Because this vault presented them with lines and edges, which they could strengthen and adorn by applying ribs in conformity with the rest, whereas all other types of vaulting were formed by surfaces.

dicular lines in the same way as the contour of the Greek roof deviated as little as possible from the horizontal forms and lines that were then the dominant feature. Unfortunately, as I have often said before,* it was in the nature of things that the former was not so easy to achieve as the latter, so that sculptural perfection in the Germanic style could apply only to the minor parts of a building. Yet in fact both inventions are what is essentially new in the Germanic style.

However, this style, like others, could not stay for long at the level of perfection that (in one respect alone) it had reached. Lacking natural and structural motifs, it opened the floodgates to arbitrariness. The impulse to outdo each new formation as it appeared soon led to decline. Developing the style further, architects adopted the intricate, intertwining arch form (the so-called *style flamboyant*), of which the Münster in Ulm is the most prominent example. The Venetians also took up this style, though as a rule they kept more to the Byzantine and Arabic style (the curvilinear forms being less confusing here, because the plain walls made it possible to frame them with straight lines). These attempts, though attractive, were bound to lead to decadence and need not be pursued any further.

When, in the fifteenth century the discovery and study of antique works belonging to the sister arts aroused painters and sculptors to renewed activity, architects too were stimulated to follow them in their quest for a reborn art after the profound decline and the aberrations of preceding periods. Whereas other artists found among the ancient remains models that were superb and in most cases genuinely Greek, architects had only a few Roman remains to turn to, which had received the Greek spirit secondhand and gave only a weak reflection of it. Nevertheless, the surge of energy that the arts in general experienced at the time also affected our fellow architects and led them to attempt a revival of ancient architecture; although it must be admitted that they did no more than touch the surface. They had only a vague sense of the inner truth of those monuments and of its intimate links with material and construction in particular, and they consequently often strayed into the pictorial. Only Bramante, Sangallo, and Peruzzi followed,[4] as far as it was possible under these circumstances, a sound course from which, however, their successors soon diverged. Lacking a true understanding, they added a profusion of parts of the most arbitrary kind that conflicted with the original meaning of the forms; this led in the sixteenth century to the so-called Renaissance style.

What can I say now about our latest period? We are the heirs to all the acquisitions and accomplishments, to all the attempts and efforts on which I have

* *On Schinkel's Friedrich Werdersche Kirche in Berlin, see* Allgemeine Bauzeitung (Literatur…Beilage), *no. 1 (1842): 507; and on Ohlmüller's church in Munich, ibid., no. 2, 213.*

cast a fleeting light. Yet instead of profiting from these experiences and adopting only what is true and everlasting, we take pleasure in admitting into our art all the mistakes committed by our predecessors; and, moreover, we still cling to the misguided idea that we can succeed in inventing a new style that has never existed before. It is just this confusion of ideas that has prompted me to make this historical review. I have sought to show that real benefit cannot be expected to accrue from further attempts to create new styles but rather from the recognition that the great periods of architecture, those that brought real advances and added new architectural elements, ended with the climax of Greek (Ionic and late Doric) architecture. Furthermore, I have sought to show that the addition of the arch by the Romans represented a significant gain, though more of a material nature: an element that in appropriate places and in an appropriate manner we may have to introduce into our architecture. Since we have become acquainted with the original buildings, a privilege not granted to our medieval predecessors, and can make use of the advances achieved in aesthetics and the history of art—and, indeed, of all the groundwork done by so many experts and scholars—we would be unworthy of so many treasures if we were not to return to what alone is true and what fulfills all our requirements.

After what has been said, Professor Stier's question "What kind of originality can we expect to find in present day architecture?" finds its own answer. We are called upon to be new only in the sense of modifying and rearranging the architectural elements that naturally evolved in antiquity. This leaves for invention an admittedly finite but still extremely wide field, a terrain whose fertility will never be exhausted. Invention is restricted to demonstrating that the eternal laws and forms discovered by the ancients can be applied in many new ways that conform to the idea of each particular building, to the material conditions, and therefore also to the particular requirements of our age and our nation. In this, our guide can again be the careful observation and contemplation of the ancient models with their fine sense of what is appropriate.* However, we lack the vocation and the ability to create new forms and therefore must forgo the fame of having a national and truly original style. The character and—I am convinced—the merit of our period resides in the fact that art has relinquished the claim to be particular and national in order to become uni-

---

*In my reviews, I have frequently declared this to be the aim of present-day architecture. Therefore, I will never acknowledge—as some architects do, who generally pursue a more correct course—that it is pleasant and interesting here and there to encounter a little building recently erected in the Byzantine or Moorish style. All these various manners of building should nowadays appear only in historical paintings, vignettes, stage sets, etc., where their presence is historically justified as a kind of costume that helps us to imagine ourselves transported to the times to which these buildings belong.

versally valid. Even on this higher level, those differences between nations and countries that are rooted in nature will assert themselves, albeit in a subordinate way and only if they are not consciously sought. If every artist strives after what is true and right, then his work will in itself carry the imprint of his mind.

I will conclude by expressing the hope that no preconceived opinion will stand in the way of a general acceptance and propagation of this basic truth, upon which alone, in my opinion, our art can thrive. Of course, I can foresee that many dissenting opinions will first be raised: one might quote in this connection what Goethe once remarked in a letter to Schiller, "Many who resist truth do so simply because they would perish if they were to acknowledge it."[5] All who share this belief (however few in number) must therefore close ranks and with unwavering courage wrest the ground from the adversary, inch by inch. Art is of a rank equal to religion and philosophy; joined to these, it must extend and establish the realm of the spirit, as far as it is humanly possible. Let us start to sow the seeds from which will rise mighty trees that will afford no room for rampant weeds and spread their magnificent branches wide to choke the thistles and thorns. Then we shall fulfill the vocation that the age has imposed upon us as recognized at first by a few but later unfailingly by all.

Source Note: Johann Heinrich Wolff, "Einige Worte über die von Herrn Professor Stier bei der Architektenversammlung zu Bamberg zur Sprache gebrachten (und im Jahrgange 1843 dieser Zeitschrift S. 301 mitgetheilten) architektonischen Fragen," *Allgemeine Bauzeitung* 10 (1845) (*Literatur...Beilage*) 2, no. 17: 255–70.

Translator's Notes

1. Friedrich Wilhelm Ludwig Stier's paper, published in the *Allgemeine Bauzeitung* 8 (1843): 296–302, was entitled "Übersicht bemerkenswerther Bestrebungen und Fragen für die Auffassung der Baukunst in der Gegenwart und jüngsten Vergangenheit." Stier set out three questions on page 301 of his paper; Wolff quotes them verbatim in the body of his text.

2. Karl Theodor Ottmer (1800–1843). The building that Wolff had in mind when criticizing picturesque castles was Ottmer's Schloss Neu-Richmond near Braunschweig (1833–1838).

3. To understand the meaning of *"die Eintheilung des Quadrats in drei Intervalle,"* one has indeed to turn to Wolff's brochure, where he develops his aesthetic theory in greater detail. Equality, he explains, is the only proportion that satisfies absolutely. The "law of equality" is therefore best expressed in the square (p. 16). The square (i.e., the ratio 1:1) underlies the composition of any work of art, not by an accumulation of square parts but by arranging forms in such a way that their correlation is per-

ceived as a square. Thus, "the proportion of the single column does not contain (a square)...but must, in order to achieve the satisfying impression of equality, be brought into relation with other commensurate parts" (p. 41). In a colonnade of Doric columns, "the first three columns with two intervening distances [*Zwischenweiten*]...form a kind of square" (p. 81). This is different "with the arrangement of the slimmer Ionic column where—because the distance from the first to the third column could not equal the height—the fourth column was added to in order to form this kind of square where four columns with three intervening distances equal the height" (p. 82). In the article of 1844, possibly with the musical analogy in mind, he changed the term *Zwischenweiten* into *Intervalle*.

4. Donato Bramante (1444–1514), Antonio da Sangallo the Younger (1483–1546), and Baldassare Peruzzi (1481–1536), Renaissance architects.

5. Johann Wolfgang von Goethe (1749–1832), German poet and dramatist. Johann Christoph Friedrich von Schiller (1759–1805), German poet, critic, and dramatist and a close friend of Goethe.

THE PRINCIPLES OF THE

HELLENIC AND GERMANIC

WAYS OF BUILDING

WITH REGARD TO THEIR APPLICATION TO OUR

PRESENT WAY OF BUILDING

CARL GOTTLIEB WILHELM BÖTTICHER

IT WILL BE APPROPRIATE TO THE FESTIVE CELEBRATION OF THIS DAY, DIGNIFIED BY THE PRESENCE OF SO MANY HIGHLY GIFTED AND ENLIGHTENED MEN OF ART AND SCIENCE, IF WE DIRECT OUR ATTENTION TO ONE OF THE IMMEDIATE EFFECTS OF THE WORK OF THE MAN IN WHOSE MEMORY WE ARE GATHERED HERE. When we consider the relation of our time to the tradition of Hellenic architecture, we find that Schinkel alone revealed Hellenic forms to us through practical work and that his influence in turn stimulated architectural scholarship and established as its first priority a thorough examination of the essence of the Hellenic style. As the fruits of earlier artistic research testify, it was only after Schinkel's creations became known that it became possible to penetrate the essence of this art and turn its study into a science. An architect of genius today thus fulfills his appointed mission in two ways. On the one hand, by satisfying present needs through his work, he spurs others to emulate him. On the other hand, by clothing this work in a historical style and thus by seeking to elevate it to an object of history, he forces the science of art to investigate the style that, by adopting, he has clearly designated as fit for its purpose. There is no need here to preface these remarks by noting that by the science of ancient architecture we do not mean the mere knowledge of the works and art-forms that have come down to us—this we take for granted—but the knowledge of the essence and the original conception that is artistically embodied in those forms.

Yet, as we survey the benefits bestowed upon us by Schinkel's creative activity, it goes without saying that every time we remember his works we must also recollect in praise those noble individuals whose spirits nurtured his own, shaped it, and brought it to maturity. Among them we may recall with particular gratitude the name of the noble statesman and scholar who, in a time of dire need, became Schinkel's patron,[1] who saved him for us and for his destiny, freed him from material worries, and with great kindness eased the path he was to pursue, thus enabling his genius to unfold in undisturbed purity and freedom. To such men, since departed, Wilhelm von Humboldt, Hirt, Niebuhr, and others,[2] we still owe a debt of gratitude today.

Considering these circumstances and the standing of a man who personifies a moment in the history of art, we must deny ourselves too exclusive a predilection for this great artist, lest we later appear to have been partisan or shortsighted, lest it be said that because the judgment of his contemporaries was biased, the generation that followed was forced to restore the integrity of a corrupted history of art in order to form an unbiased and fair appreciation of the man. Therefore, in justice to historical truth we must first of all allude to a name whose bearer still today distributes the blessings of art among the people for the good of the fatherland, as he once, through Schinkel's hand, bestowed it on those works in which a princely mind impressed the seal of beauty on a rude and barren nature and transformed a desert into a Hesperidean garden. Schinkel himself spoke of the originator of these works in memorable words, declaring that he "would have to acknowledge Him as the foremost living architect, if such a thing could have been imagined." We too would be obliged to name Him, did not a profound respect impose a discreet silence.[3] Yet these very works, through the thoughts that they inspired, induced the austere art of Schinkel to change its rhythm and descend, as it were, from the cothurnus and turn to the idyll, taking up the shepherd's crook and panpipes, where, close to the Hippodrome and Piscina, beneath a leafy, Dionysian shade and beside a rippling fountain, a tranquil resting place beckons the astonished wanderer, in whom it raises the desire that—like Homer's happy Lotus-Eaters—he may forget the longing to return to his dear homeland and pass the days in an eternal dolce far niente. Schinkel's works in the severe style gave us an idea of the hieratic manner of Hellenic architecture; by contrast, these works that breathe the spirit of Virgil's *Georgics* were the first to let us see in reality the wondrous world of Roman urban and rustic dwellings, which had hitherto lived, like myths, only in the writings of the past.

To what heights have these works raised our knowledge of ancient life and art in the short span of three decades! Indeed, what higher task has art than to touch the pulse of life and to arouse in a whole generation a longing for nobility and beauty! Only then does the artist's work become an ethical force. If the needs of a generation reveal its state of moral and cultural development, then the work itself that meets these needs will serve posterity as testimony to the culture of the architect and to the spirit of its founder. If a man deserves our praise because his work has satisfied the needs of the time, then we must above all praise one who rose higher, whose thoughts were ahead of his time, and who, by setting a nobler example, raised his generation to his own level. For this is the poet's and the artist's mission: not to serve a commonplace reality and remain within its confines but to follow a higher calling by which, heedless of the applause or censure of the undiscerning crowd, they must accomplish the task the Deity has inscribed in their hearts. As there is an occasion for every great work of art and as that occasion springs from the will of the person who determines it, works of art are truly monuments to the fame, and lasting testimonies to the spirit, of the patron, the great man, the prince, who in his wisdom has chosen these noble means to elevate the spirit of his people and to lead it away from the base necessities of life toward the great and the sublime.

Those who, in our day, turn their attention to former ages and profess the study of the life and work of past generations are often asked by those on the other side, that is, by men who live only for the present and for their own interests: What is the purpose of such activity? What, they say, can be the use of turning back to an art of the past, of adhering to its traditions, and projecting oneself into its spirit? Could the greatest discovery that might be made in this sphere or the most important artistic revelation outweigh the benefit that will result from the completion of the most insignificant present-day project? These objections are especially directed against scholarly research undertaken in connection with architecture, the mother of the fine arts, and in particular against the architectural style we call the Hellenic, which, however, was only the ripened fruit and refined result of all the styles that evolved in pre-Christian nations (if we exclude the Roman beginnings of the arcuated system). To return to origins is dismissed as a one-sided or antiquarian fancy; to steep oneself in ancient traditions is seen as a retrograde step, a sign of inability to create anything that is new, modern, and progressive in conception.

Since the time when opinions concerning the antique and medieval styles began to be so diametrically opposed, the question of whether any benefit will be gleaned from the study of these two styles has been answered in widely differing ways. Yet these views have never touched upon the basic causes from which any judgment or comparison should start. All opinions for or against a particular style have referred only to the outer shell, that is, to the scheme of the building's art-forms, which were considered to be identical with the principle of a style. The true essentials have never been seriously considered; the discussion has never actually turned to the source of the art-forms and of the diversity of styles, namely, the structural principle and material conditions on which each is based.[4] And yet these two factors are crucial for any criticism. It is well known how unproductive and how far removed from what is really essential, the views expressed have been. The view that the schema of the antique style is the ideal or acme of all tectonic activity, which no style could ever surpass, has deprived the medieval style, and especially the style characterized by the pointed arch, of its due. Those who dismiss it as Germanic and barbaric overlook the enormous step forward represented by the medieval system of widely spanned spaces, with its escape from the structural limitations of material, in comparison with the limitations of the Hellenic post-and-lintel system, which was tied to a certain massiveness, short spans, and restricted forms of plan. According to those who hold the opposite view, the Hellenic is an alien importation, does not conform to our architectural conditions, and has so little impact on our emotions that we cannot possibly comprehend its forms. They go even further, cross themselves, and ask: How can we who are no longer pagans commit the sacrilege of profaning our sanctuaries by using such forms? Only the Middle Ages have given us forms that represent the Christian mind; these have entered our minds, and they are the only ones we understand; besides, they are native to our soil and represent the custom of our forefathers. As if the art-forms that express a truth valid for all times and all generations could ever be solely pagan or Christian, Hellenic or Germanic!

By presenting one style as uniquely true and valid while negating the other, each side has abolished one-half of the history of art, thus clearly revealing a failure to understand either the style that was favored or the style that was dismissed. What was overlooked was that these two styles, even though we see them as opposites, are not opposites in the sense of being conceived or created in order to cancel or destroy each other, but opposites that are complementary and, within the vast framework of the history of art, are therefore always conceived together. They signify two stages of development that have had to run their prescribed course before a third style can see the light of day, one that will reject neither of the two preceding ones but will base itself on the achievements of both in order to occupy a third stage in the development, a higher stage than either: a third style that is destined to be produced as a matter of historical inevitability, by the age that will follow us, and for which we have already begun to prepare the ground.

Regarding the two views mentioned above, it is evident that neither can help us to decide which of the two is right and valid for the pursuit of our aim. Closer examination leads to the following conclusion. If one gives credence to the latter view, then the antique style ought to be totally removed from our artistic sphere as something extinct that does not need discussing. If—with as much right—one accepts the former view, then the Germanic style too ought to be excluded as completely invalid. As a result, nothing would be left to us; we would find ourselves alone in an immense void, having lost all the historical ground that the past has provided for us and for the future as the only basis on which further development is possible. This leads us to two conclusions. First, we must for the time being hold on to what has been directly handed down to us, lest we lose the positive assets that we now possess. Indeed, to reject or negate tradition is as impossible as to reject history itself; for even the ephemeral configurations (lately presented to us by a few so-called original artists as manifestations of their deliverance from all tradition) seem to us—in the few places where they still contain some traces of truth—to be nothing more than misunderstood and misapplied traditional forms. By contrast, we see before us grandly conceived monuments that will forever have a place in history because they uphold tradition and at the same time fulfill present needs. Second, it follows that we must not make use of tradition for its own sake; through scholarly research we must penetrate its spiritual and material qualities in order to arrive at an apprehension of the essential nature of tradition and an understanding of its forms. Only then will we be able to decide what part of tradition merely belongs to the past, was valid only then, and therefore must be rejected and what part contains eternal truth, is valid for all future generations, and therefore must be accepted and retained by us. This would be true eclecticism, the eclecticism of the spirit that reigns throughout history and through which, in a gradually accelerating development, nature conducts the essence of each thing toward its supreme and ultimate goal.

Apart from these two views, we encounter a third that counsels a reconciliation and unification of the two extremes. Those who have put forward this view would have been right had they not again merely touched the surface and based their view on a negation—namely, the negation of those things in both styles that are their inviolable qualities. Their intention was nothing less than this: to clothe the structural skeleton of the Germanic style with the forms of the Hellenic style and in this way to give the arcuated system a kind of aesthetic education. They really thought to take the perfect product of a time-honored art, which embodies and reveals the artistic awareness and practical ability of a great nation, and use it like a model to be dressed at will. This was a most wretched and foolhardy idea; it was eclecticism at its lowest, which every time it has appeared in history has signified the relapse of a generation from a higher plane of tradition into ignorance and license. While shamefully disfiguring one style by robbing it of the inborn essence of its character, they violated the opposite style by forcing it into monstrous dress and cruelly degrading it into a buffoon of modern art. One may ask how the retention of an old style in a new dress could ever turn it into a new one that would embody the essence of both? Might this bring to light an original innovation or a new structural system, or would it only produce a hybrid form that would shamefully belie its paternal and maternal origins? Of course, something new would be produced but also something monstrous: something possible as a form but lifeless and stillborn. If the forms of Hellenic art had been right for the Germanic style, how did it happen—we may ask—that the arcuated system, although starting with the forms of the Hellenic style and first appearing in its dress, nevertheless sought to free itself from these forms in the course of developing its essential character and in the end, apart from a few reminiscences, cast them completely aside at the very moment it reached the highest degree of independence and manifested itself as their perfect antithesis?

When two styles have reached a stage in their development where their essential characters are fully expressed and are shown to be diametrically opposed, as in the case of the Hellenic and Germanic styles, then any eclectic transference of forms from one style to the other, because it stems from a deficient sense of the essential character of both styles, will in turn produce only senseless forms that by their contradictions destroy each other. History itself has marked such an attempt as a destruction of everything that makes architecture into an art. Wherever it has made its appearance in architecture, it has signaled the death of the idea of form. A similar process has taken place three times, and three times it has had the same result. Each time a generation has chosen this expedient, it has been hurled from the height that it had attained with the help of tradition down to the lowest level of form making: to the stage where chance reigns instead of necessity, arbitrariness in place of law.

The first example of this process was the way in which caves were hollowed out in India, which started after Hellenic art had reached its culmination. This practice cannot be called architecture, because, notwithstanding the enormous expense of energy that was involved, so impoverished was the creative invention of its makers that they were incapable of producing a free-articulated structure; in their indolence, they blindly surrendered to the fortuitous shape of their raw material.

When we look at these vast and depressing caves, their monolithic surfaces covered with lifeless, bizarre, and distorted schemata of the structural components and art-forms of the Hellenic style, we realize that history has displayed these works to show how far a nation's artistic understanding can sink below the level of a consciousness that it has either never possessed or else corrupted and permanently lost. Yet some people have seen in this Indian manner the origin of all styles, from which the conscious art of the Hellenic style might also have arisen.

The second example of such a process of architectural transformation is the Arabic style. Being incapable of grasping the essence of the antique style, the Arabs incorporated into their phantasmagoric art only the spaciousness that gratified their pursuit of enjoyment. Yet they destroyed its art-forms by covering the structural skeleton, carpetlike, with the geometrical patterns of their own floral world, thus overlaying their buildings with an opulent but meaningless coating.

The third occasion was during the fading years of Germanic art, at the time of the so-called Renaissance, when misunderstood antique forms were adopted to clothe buildings in the Germanic style. No lengthy critique of such a meaningless welter of forms is called for: the senseless and bizarre formations that were produced are too well known and too displeasing. This purely luxurious art, which stood in the service of princely profligacy, and which therefore frequently disposed of abundant resources, regrettably expresses little but an enervated lust for shallow pleasure that has outlasted mental capacity.

Therefore, this third school of thought, which counseled compromise as the source of a new style, also remained tied to the surface of things. No one realized that the origin of all specific styles rests on the effect of a new structural principle derived from the material and that this alone makes the formation of a new system of covering space possible and thereby brings forth a new world of art-forms. This third view does, however, show rather clearly that architects at least still acknowledged the need for tradition, although only in the superficial arrangement of its schemata. The outcome of all this arbitrary selection and rejection was, in fact, to refer us back to tradition. We were forced to accept and to take cognizance of tradition. Obviously, one has first to comprehend the particular structural principle of an architectural system, as well as the significance of each of its individual forms, before one can use it as a means to express one's own ideas, let alone lay down an absolute law for the use of its art-forms.

The situation would be different if we were to accept the validity of the two aforementioned views while disallowing any mutual negation, so that both styles and their forms could exist with their well-deserved historical rights untouched. This would entail continuing with tradition and making use of it wherever it could be of help in resolving modern issues, until in the course of time a new and more satisfactory style would arise that could then take the place of the traditional one. This, as can be clearly demonstrated, would be the course that would promote the evolution of art.

How does a new style arise, and how does it define itself in terms of principle?

The essence of any particular style is indicated by the system according to which the covering of a space is articulated into parts or structural units. For the possible form of an enclosed space is contingent on the possible form of the covering, and both the overall plan and its particular layout depend on the organization of that covering. With all styles the covering is the factor that determines the placing and configuration of the structural supports, as well as the arrangement and articulation of the walls by which space is enclosed, and finally the art-forms of all these parts related to it. Therefore, the covering reveals the structural principle of every style and constitutes the criterion by which to judge it. What comes first with any style is the development of a structural force that emanates from the material and, as an active principle, permeates the system of the covering. Only three structural forces can be used architecturally: they are inherent in the material, and in technical parlance they are known as absolute, relative, and reactive strength, or as the forces resisting tension, fracture, and compression. The secret of the structural dynamics of a material lies in its texture, that is to say, in the law of atomic order. The degree of coherence that makes the material suitable for building purposes depends on this law. In the unformed state of the material, these forces are dead or latent. The material is aroused and compelled to demonstrate its structural strength once it has been given a form that is appropriate to it and at the same time fits it to perform a space-creating architectural function: in other words, once it has been formed into architectural members. These represent the forces on which the system of covering—that is, the architectural system as a whole—is based. Yet the three forces are not equally strong in every kind of material. Therefore, when using a material, the inherent force and its strength must be investigated. From this knowledge automatically follows the law that lays down how the material should be formed to fulfill its specified function. In this way the structural form of the architectural part is determined, and the nature of the material is mastered and made useful. It was through such a process that relative strength became the active principle of the Hellenic system of covering, and reactive strength that of the vaulting system.

This structural subjugation of the material is at the root of all architecture. That is why this art has an advantage over sculpture and painting and is invested with a higher degree of practical independence than the two other arts. While architecture must first be victorious in its struggle with the material and, without a model as a guide, must establish a spatial system before it can enlist sculpture and painting to embellish it with art-forms, these two arts proceed straightaway to the representation of ideas by using familiar analogies taken from the outside world. Winckelmann and Schelling have shown that it is quite possible to comprehend the law and innermost essence of sculpture and painting without being a practicing artist; but the author of *Die Baukunst nach den Grundsätzen der Alten* [*Architecture According to the Principles of the Ancients*] and, following him, many authors of similar books have shown that nobody is able to enter into the material principle of this art and clarify the cause and meaning of its forms without having passed through a practical training in architecture and having become fully conversant with the subject.[5]

Every creative generation that has given birth to a new style has had to start from the beginning with this process of mastering the material. Any generation that has failed to do so, resting content with a traditional, ready-made style, has had no chance of inventing a new style. The need to start the process of formal creation from the beginning is an eternal law imposed on any generation destined to create a new style, a law from which it cannot escape. Although this law is first felt only as an unconscious urge, it will be clearly comprehended once it becomes a fact: that is to say, once it has passed from a mere idea into reality. Every generation that has such a destiny must therefore return to the beginning and start anew the process of developing the structural properties of its chosen building. However, this does not mean developing the same force that has been previously developed but another that lies still undeveloped within the material. Otherwise, man would, like Sisyphus, be condemned to a life of endlessly and fruitlessly repeated labor without ever reaching his goal. This is why history and tradition have, for man's benefit, preserved monuments that enshrine the principle of each style—the result of the processes that have gone before—so that on careful examination we may know what has already been developed and garner what will be fruitful. This is also the reason why beneficent nature has destroyed whole styles, except for those things that contained the germ of something new and superior, covering with an almost impenetrable veil all else that was valid only for the past. In this way, nature has contrived to force the following generation to become more independent and to seek in the still visible traces of the past for its true essence, not by groping around blindly but by consciously identifying and subordinating to its own style all that remains hidden.

Such are the blessings of tradition. For if history had found fulfillment in Hellenism, the Middle Ages would not have come about; and had the latter terminated the evolution, mankind would have come to an end. Should we find ourselves suddenly deprived of all the creative energy so lavishly accorded to earlier generations, we would be overcome with melancholy, if history had not clearly shown that there is an inner force that constantly produces something new and that the process of development by which one aspect of architecture became prominent with the Greeks and the opposite aspect with the Middle Ages must be continued by a future generation in a synthesis of both. Yet the joy of victory and the bliss of creating something new can be experienced only by a generation that is strong enough to endure the toil of mastering the material and the effort of exploration. If, however, it indolently shuns such toil, indulges the senses, and lazily rests on the soft bed of tradition, then there remains for such a generation only the shadow of the creative bliss that the previous energetic generation enjoyed in full—only the dross, so to speak, from which the precious metal has long been smelted away. Can one call one's own what is only the theft, the indolent appropriation, of someone else's mental property? How can anyone who takes a thing that is finished and complete in itself and merely peels away the husk of form speak of creative inventiveness? It makes no difference whether one makes eclectic use of the schemata of the art-forms or of the structural systems and spatial forms: neither will serve to conceal a lack of ideas.

The opposite to these eclectic pseudostyles was the work done by the energetic generation that was destined to contrast the Hellenic with a new style and to wrest from the material a new structural principle with which to create a space-covering system far superior to that of the Greeks. This was the generation that introduced into Roman architecture the arch and the vault that later evolved into the Germanic style. This generation went back to the beginning and started the process of developing the material anew; it bore the toil of mastering the material and fought its way to victory. Unable to find an art-form compatible with the new structural principle that was then still in its budding stage, the Romans used the traditional Hellenic forms and maintained them within their arcuated system. Yet these forms could not fulfill their new function; with the exception of those forms unrelated to the spanning of spaces, they had become an anomaly. In a system of covering that uses monolithic beams, relative strength is the sole active force; and in the Hellenic style this was clearly symbolized by the art-forms that adorned the architrave and upper parts of the entablature. These forms, characterized by relative strength, were therefore in conflict with an arch composed of many blocks, because with the arch reactive strength is the force that alone conditions the forms through which it can be adequately symbolized. The Hellenic schema was thus continued in a traditional yet completely illogical way.

The Hellenic art-forms gradually disappeared; they were finally eliminated from the system when structural explicitness came to be the aim. Only faint traces of the Hellenic element remained in certain parts of the Germanic style. Yet whether this style with its emancipation from the material—leading to a withdrawal from nature and the sensory world—replaced the Hellenic art-forms with others of equal value is a question to which we can only respond with a definite "no." With regard to our perception of style, the Middle Ages differ from antiquity. The works of the Christian style are still before us; they still serve the same purpose as when they were built. Their ethical and functional significance hold no mystery for us, and the structural system in all its evolutionary stages is clearly displayed: all it needs for a full perception is our willingness to see. It is quite different with antiquity. Not only have very few of its buildings survived—and these only in scarcely recognizable remains—but the arrangement and particular function of the interior is still hidden from us behind an impenetrable veil. We have neither the ability nor the desire to return to Hellenic art, because this would mean regressing by more than two thousand years at least. But it would be equally impossible to breathe new life into Germanic art. To seek to continue with either style would mean trying to perfect perfection. Both styles have had their existence and will never exist again. And yet another art will emerge from the womb of time and will take on a life of its own: an art in which a different structural principle will sound a more ringing keynote than the other two. Another style will be born but only after the other two have made their contributions. Because this style will have its origin and its basis in the principles of the two other styles, it cannot exclude either of them; but it will embrace both and allow them to serve it jointly.

Is it possible for yet another new style to be developed in addition to these two traditional styles, one specific to our generation, in which a structural force different from that of the other two styles acts as the principle of its system of covering? And what force would be its active principle? In view of what has just been said, it is possible without needing the gift of clairvoyance to answer this question. As always with things that are still coming into existence, no more than hints can be given, although there are clear indications that the beginning has already become a reality.

Aside from the fact that a single person cannot promulgate a style and that only a whole nation can cause its inception and a whole epoch suffice for its development, the truth of the matter can only be as follows.

Our contention that the manner of covering determines every style and its ultimate development is confirmed by the monuments of all styles. Equally evident is the truth that from the earliest and roughest attempts to cover spaces by using stone, to the culmination represented by the *Spitzbogen* vault, and down to the present time, all the ways in which stone could possibly be used to span a space have been exploited, and they have completely exhausted the possible structural applications of this material. No longer can stone alone form a new structural system of a higher stage of development. The reactive, as well as relative, strength of stone has been completely exhausted. A new and so far unknown system of covering (which will of course bring in its train a new world of art-forms) can appear only with the adoption of an unknown material, or rather a material that so far has not been used as a guiding principle. It will have to be a material with physical properties that will permit wider spans, with less weight and greater reliability, than are possible when using stone alone. With regard to spatial design and construction, it must be such as will meet any conceivable spatial or planning need. A minimal quantity of material should be needed for the walls, thus rendering the bulky and ponderous buttresses of the *Spitzbogenstil* completely superfluous. The whole weight of the covering system would be confined to vertical pressure, that is, to the reactive strength of walls and supports. Of course, this does not mean that the indirect use of stone vaulting, especially the system of ribbed and stellar vaulting, will be excluded; on the contrary, the latter will be widely used. But it does mean that, for those parts on which the whole system rests, another material will be used, one that makes it possible to transfer their structural function to other parts in which a different principle operates. It makes no difference whether the members to be replaced are buttresses or members that support the ceiling, such as ribs, bands, etc.

Such a material is iron, which has already been used for this purpose in our century. Further testing and greater knowledge of its structural properties will ensure that iron will become the basis for the covering system of the future and that structurally it will in times to come be as superior to the Hellenic and medieval systems as the arcuated medieval system was to the monolithic trabeated system of antiquity. Disregarding the fragile wooden ceiling (which in any case cannot serve as a comparison) and using mathematical terms, one can say that iron is indeed the material whose principle, yet unutilized, will introduce into architecture the last of the three forces, namely, absolute strength. In particular it will be active in those anchor bands that will replace buttresses and flying buttresses. In this way, absolute force will be established as the guiding principle of the system of covering. Therefore, if relative strength is the principle of the classical trabeated system and reactive strength that of the arcuated system, then the system of a vaulted stone covering with iron ribs can adopt from the arcuated system only its relative strength, to which—as its defining feature—it must add the absolute strength of the anchor bands. The relative strength of iron beams, replacing those made of stone in the trabeated system, can play only an indirect and minor role; to replace the Hellenic trabeated stone system with a trabeated iron system would represent only a change of material, not a change of principle. It would lead to one-sided and very limited progress and would prove as inadequate as stone beams for spanning wide spaces.

The structural principle is thus to be adopted from the arcuated system and transformed into a new and hitherto unknown system; for the art-forms of the new system, on the other hand, the formative principle of the Hellenic style must be adopted in order to give artistic expression to the structural forces within the parts, their correlation, and the spatial concept. This alone will create the true mediation, the right synthesis of the two preceding styles. In what manner and by what art-forms the structural and spatial character might be expressed within this newly formed system is a question that the thoughtful person will not find too difficult to answer. Nor is it necessary to say that it is technically possible to protect the forms of the iron parts against rusting with a tin or copper-plating process or that this coating should be sufficiently thick to outline the forms clearly in a way appropriate to each part of the vault.

To return to our theme: we have said that the acceptance and continuance of tradition, not its negation, is historically the only correct course for art. There is indeed a spirit alive within our generation that urges it in this direction in spite of all subjective and speculative ideas and holds it to this traditional course, leading it toward the destined emergence from tradition to a newborn, original, and unique style. In answer to the objection raised earlier as to why we still cling to tradition instead of striving for an original and completely independent style, we need only refer to the present state of the arts to prove that those who have challenged such fidelity to tradition or who have done no more than counsel a superficial accommodation are the last persons who could ever invalidate tradition and become the pioneers of a new era. If we contemplate developments in art, we find tradition and nothing but tradition, be it the tradition of the ancient world or that of the so-called Christian world. Nowhere can we see anything that transcends tradition, neither with regard to the original art-forms nor to structural systems, unless the first beginnings of a covering system in iron are taken into consideration. All our art-forms and ideas are rooted in the tradition that we have accepted and in which we move, although often unaware of it. Well may those to whom the positive values of the past seem like shackles desire to shake them off and to destroy tradition; but it still has not been established what we can put in its place. On the contrary, despite recent attempts on the part of some people, ignorant of the essence of art, to repudiate tradition, it has emerged in all its grandeur and splendor.

Spiritual progress can come about only through a clear perception of what already exists. As each generation presses forward, it must look back to what has been already created in order to become aware of a new truth, to accept what exists, and to develop it further. For this reason, when Raphael Sanzio painted the

Christian Virtues, he depicted Truth with two faces—one in the full bloom of youth, seeking to recognize itself and the present world in the reflection of reality, and the other an aged face that looks back to its origins and to the past, the source of all that exists, and shows a foreboding of a future state.

Having accepted tradition in architecture and recognized it as an undeniable fact, we should not, of course, stop there and adopt only the schematic plan, since this would mean that we would maintain the outer shell and not pursue, as we ought to do, the living spirit and essence of tradition. To reach the essence of tradition, we should not stop even when we come to what seems to be the last element but must go back to the one that preceded it and gradually ascend to the very first element and so penetrate to the source from which traditional ideas have sprung. If it is true that the style of the Middle Ages and the arcuated system in general already constitute the second stage of all architectural evolution—one that could appear only after the styles of antiquity had gone before—and if the origin of the medieval structural system is to be found in the Roman world, while the Roman art-forms are rooted in the Hellenic style, then we cannot remain with the traditional forms of the Middle Ages but must turn first to the Roman style to look for the origin of the arcuated structural system and then go back to the Hellenic style. If it is impossible to understand the Roman style without understanding the Hellenic style, then one cannot apprehend the essence of the Middle Ages without first apprehending the essence of the Hellenic style. This alone will reveal to us wherein the Germanic style is superior or inferior to the Hellenic style.

We have reached a point in our deliberations where the man whose name marks today's celebration brings his great authority to bear on our main theme. Schinkel's creations were destined by providence to guide his generation toward the right path of artistic development. In fact, the most important part of his appointed mission was to carry us beyond the tradition of the Middle Ages and lead us to the original source. He alone was capable of guiding us toward knowledge, because he himself sought only knowledge and did not lose himself in mere sensuous impressions. Moved by the grand monuments of the Romantic period, he too built in the Romantic style. He relived the Middle Ages in the warmth of his imagination, but he also penetrated it with his intellect. His designs of that period demonstrate this. Yet he could not stop there; his intuitive spirit urged him to probe deeper toward the original source. In time, after he had passed through this phase, his sensibility led him to see that the consecration of all art can derive only from the source from which the Middle Ages too had sprung.

Although the accounts of writers such as Stuart, Mazois,[6] and others had contributed before Schinkel to the knowledge of Hellenic monuments, it was

Schinkel's work alone, as an instrument of history, that led to the true perception of the Hellenic style by revealing to us its spatial and structural qualities in those of his buildings that followed the Hellenic scheme. These are the two qualities by which architecture differs from the other two arts. Whereas the painter finds fulfillment in a graphic representation on a flat surface and the sculptor in a form that can be enjoyed from the outside only, architecture employs both of these means to create enclosed space. Since the essence of architecture resides in its unique capacity to present the idea and set forth its theme through this structural-spatial combination, it follows that a work of architecture can be fully comprehended only if looked at and enjoyed spatially. This impression, however, cannot be fully gained either in a graphic representation or in a model but only through the presentation of the work on its true scale.

It is therefore evident that it was through Schinkel's work that the Hellenic tradition found a new home in our country. While Schinkel reached the immediate aim that he had set for himself, at the same time both he and his buildings had an invigorating and instructive influence on the historical study of art. He impelled us to consider in detail the style that he presented and to subject its principles and its ultimate origin to critical examination. But in truth this reproductive presentation still left us dissatisfied, because neither the structural principle of the style nor the idea underlying its forms was thereby revealed. These matters remained as obscure as they had been before. The thoughtful architect could not rest content with the fact that an artist as great as Schinkel had recognized this style to be the right style; he had to look for the reasons that had induced Schinkel to present it to us as the correct and valid one. Schinkel's works do not help us here. We cannot even judge whether Schinkel, when he allowed himself to deviate from the antique system, did so in conformity with ancient laws or not. He never wrote or spoke about it but simply displayed the antique forms. All we have from him in the way of instruction are the *Vorbilder für Fabrikanten und Handwerker* [*Designs for Artisans*], which do not even touch on this important problem.[7] According to Schinkel himself, the aim of this publication was to illustrate for the building tradesman the various parts of the Hellenic architectural system; yet even here he did not offer the explanations that at that time were already to be found in archaeological books. Thus, we still lack an explanation. Yet we cannot and must not leave it at that but must turn from Schinkel to the original source from which he drew, so that we can arrive at a full understanding. This is an indisputable necessity. Although Schinkel's works have helped us to rise above the fraud of eclecticism in general, they still have not helped us to get past eclecticism in particular, as applied to Hellenic art itself. Recent buildings show that eclecticism has become markedly more prevalent and that the beautiful proportions and exquisite taste that are the characteristic features of all of Schinkel's works have already lost much of their influence. When, in addition, persons who profess to teach architecture invoke the principle that out of respect for antiquity we may freely use and imitate ancient forms even if we do not understand them, then the trend in recent art and art theory can clearly be seen.[8]

Yet where will this purely manual dexterity lead when nothing is left to "eclecticize," when the forms of Schinkel's works and those of ancient monuments have been used up like so many transfer pictures? Perhaps to a reiterated Renaissance! Let it not be said: "Why trouble with research? The elect will find the answer given to them in their sleep!" Certainly, but "to everyone that hath shall be given," and another saying is "Who does not prepare the lamp, will never see the bridegroom." Knowledge alone leads to conception; only imaginative inquiry inspires thought and invention.

A direct examination of tradition thus being necessary, we must make a critical analysis of the monuments with regard to tectonics, construction, and artistic appearance, and we must seek out and make use of the aid that ancient literature can provide. Since architecture in all its different manners and forms emanates from the artistic consciousness of the generation that created it and is like every fine art only a mute manifestation of that consciousness, the relevant facts of the literary record must confirm the results of our examination of the monuments. We need the testimony of the ancient authors that the significance we ascribe to these forms was really the one that the ancients themselves originally attached to them. In order to test our findings, we must bring together and compare what both sources—literature and monuments—have transmitted and make up from one what is missing in the other.

Apart from the manner of how to enclose space, the first matter that has to be dealt with in our examination is the concept that lies behind the spatial organization of the building. It is self-evident that only the history of the religious and moral life of the Hellenes can provide some information on this. The understanding of ancient monuments starts with historical sources. Indeed, how can we explain the spatial form and arrangement of the temple, if we do not know the ritual of the cult for whose performance it was intended or the sacred objects for whose safekeeping the room was designed? All explanations given so far are nothing but oft-repeated conjecture. The reason for the interior and exterior arrangement of the *hieron* has remained hidden behind a dense veil. Again, how can one possibly know the purpose of the living rooms of a house without first finding out about the domestic life and habits of its occupants? Our lack of progress in this matter is shown by the fact that we are not even sure of the relation of the *atrium* to the *cavaedium*,[9] which after all affects the main room of the house.

Here the experience of the practicing architect is useful in the elucidation of the technical factors. The aim is to grasp the principle of the statics and construction and the law and form of each part of the structural system that characterizes the style in question. Once this is understood, then the key is found to the riddle of the art-forms that have been applied to these parts as a kind of explanatory layer. Since these parts have been made for the sole purpose of creating a spatial structure, any forms applied to them that do not serve this material purpose can only have been intended to symbolize this function and to make visible the concept of structure and space that in its purely structural state cannot be perceived. Therefore, the structural member and its art-form are initially conceived as a single whole. The architectural system in its purely structural form is a technical product; these perfected forms give it the artistic stamp. The structure itself is an invented form without a model in the outside world; the art-forms, though they too are mental creations, are taken from what exists in the outside world.

In this respect (in the creation of art-forms), architecture has common roots with the two arts of sculpture and painting and follows the same principle, although it joins the rank of representational arts only after it has fulfilled the material nature of its task, related to structure, and has invented a system of enclosing space. The only way in which the two fine arts can express ideas is by applying the metaphorical method of pictorial language, in which pictorial signs or artistic symbols take the place of the idea. Pictorial art cannot represent an idea as such, but must represent it through a symbol and thus embody it. Architecture follows the same method. It takes its symbols and art-forms only from those natural objects that embody an idea analogous to the one inherent in the members of the architectural system. Therefore, an idea for which no analogue exists in the external world cannot be represented by pictorial art nor for that matter by architecture. The essence of pictorial art and its relation to nature rests in this interaction between concept and object, between invention and imitation.

With regard to art-forms in general, their meaning can be explained by the general law of formal creation, the law that governs the evolution of all natural forms and by analogy also the forms of buildings. Yet neither the former proof of their essential nature, by reference to nature herself, nor the latter, by reference to art, can be universally valid, because there can be ideas that in themselves are true but that nevertheless have no relevance to the particular matter to which they are applied. If, however, it emerges from the written record that both agree and that the significance of the forms as deduced from the monuments is confirmed by ancient literature, if all the evidence of the art-forms—including their latest, almost unthinking uses—points to this meaning, then the inference has been documented as historically correct and becomes an irrefutable truth. The searcher has the great satisfaction of knowing that he has made no incorrect inference. Even the greatest authority will be unable to dispute the result. Since the research has been freed of all subjectivity and firmly based on science, only science can either prove it to be invalid or, when corrected or rather corroborated, recognize it as the simple truth. A summary rejection is no longer possible.

It is true that there are people who are not fond of science. They are of the opinion that they can easily succeed without its help and suppose themselves to have conquered the domain of art theory merely through their technical knowledge or, at best, through the adoption of some schematic view. Not only do they seek to exclude science as much as possible as a means to knowledge: they wish to reject it outright. Science, the tutelary spirit that guards all things positive, is for them not only a great nuisance but also a dangerous enemy, because it constantly contradicts their assumptions (which, of course, never go beyond mere hypotheses) and always seeks to hold the fanciful flights of their artistic imagination down to the level of mere fact. The adherents of this movement, who see things only by halves, are like those one-eyed Arimaspians of the ancient myth,[10] who did constant battle with Apollo's griffins for the possession of the god's golden treasure but who never vanquished them or took possession of the hidden hoard.

That we shall reach our goal through research is supported by irrefutable evidence. Any doubts that might remain will vanish if we glance at the period prior to Schinkel's works, a period when the greatness of an architect was measured by his ability to achieve effects by putting together the superficially attractive motifs that were used ad nauseam by the Italian and French architects on their facades. It was a sign of Schinkel's upright character that he always despised such a practice as a means to win the sympathy of the crowd and never used what is called the picturesque element in architecture to embellish his buildings, although he well knew how to do so and made full use of it in his designs for architectural dioramas and theater decorations. Remembering the ethical demand to be sparing in means (what the Hellenes called *sophrosyne*), he felt that a work of art in which the pure idea had passed unblemished into form had already attained fulfillment and that any additional form would, like an empty phrase, only harm it. We reject the idea that Schinkel's genius would have received an equal stimulus without the scientific revelations that preceded it. Must we not admit that it was through the research of Winckelmann that we experienced ancient sculpture reborn? Schinkel himself often confessed how much he treasured the work of Hirt on the history of art.[11] Truth can only be attained when the full knowledge of the architect's practical work unites with that derived from methodical research. The goal cannot be reached through one of these activities alone. On the one hand, research is the only path to the understanding of the spirit that permeates the types of the extant works of antiquity; on the other hand, only full knowledge of practical work can provide the key to the causes that gave rise to the architectural system of the Hellenes.

While penetrating in this way the essence of tradition, we simultaneously recapture an awareness of the principle, the law, and the idea inherent in traditional forms; destroy lifeless eclecticism; and once again tap the source of artistic invention. Unthinking veneration of those ideal art-forms, veneration that rests solely on the sensuous conception of their beauty, will be replaced by the clear perception of the causes of that beauty. It may be that those afflicted with the superficial mentality of today will dissent; but the time is not far distant when they will have to concede and accept what is right. The literary work bequeathed to us by the ancients is the holy scripture of their art. That is why practical work must always go hand in hand with scholarship, so that the latter provides the practicing architect with information he cannot obtain otherwise. As a great philosopher has said: only when practice and learning are joined can a learned practice arise; and that alone is art. Schinkel's genius and work vouches for that. I can only repeat what I once said to my friends of the Architekten-Verein:

> Ancient art is like a beautiful musical instrument, created
> by a great nation of poets in order that its harmonious sounds
> might arouse the dormant forces of nature and join them in
> a new and higher order. It is an instrument by whose sounds,
> according to the legend, the temples and walls of Thebes of
> the Seven Gates formed themselves, stone by stone, in the
> right rhythm and right form. Yet it is an instrument that
> has been silent for hundreds of years; since the passing of
> that race, its touch has been forgotten. But if ages later, men
> of kindred mind discover the way in which the instrument
> was used and resolutely strike the chords, then once again
> the raw stones will form themselves into new and magnifi-
> cent creations never seen before. As Memnon's statue is said
> to have greeted the return of his mother Eos with clear
> sounds, so did Schinkel's hymn in the name of the German
> nation greet the returning dawn of that original art as it arose
> in a new manifestation.

We should therefore keep to Schinkel's intentions and firmly pursue the course that he was the first to take, especially those of us who by virtue of their great intellectual gifts and good fortune have attained the splendid, yet arduous position of leaders of our artistic activity. They will be a model worthy of emulation, as he was; and, by their example and works, they will enlighten a younger generation more than the most selfless devotion to art theory and art education could ever achieve. Then—just as the Hellenes said that the nightingales nowhere better loved to build their nests and nowhere sang more sweetly than at the spot where Hesiod's urn was placed—the Germans may one day say that nowhere in the world does one build with greater distinction and nobility than in the city that houses the honored tomb of Schinkel.

Source Note: Carl Gottlieb Wilhelm Bötticher, "Das Prinzip der hellenischen und germanischen Bauweise hinsichtlich der Übertragung in die Bauweise unserer Tage," *Allgemeine Bauzeitung* 11 (1846): 111–25. (This is the text of a commemorative address given on the occasion of the birthday of Karl Friedrich Schinkel [1781–1841].)

Translator's Notes

1. The "noble statesman and scholar" was probably Wilhelm von Humboldt (1767–1835), the Prussian envoy in Rome, Vienna, and London and an eminent philologist whose works were influential in developing comparative philology. Humboldt was Prussian resident minister at the time of Schinkel's first stay in Rome in 1803. When Schinkel returned penniless from an expensive tour of Sicily, Humboldt "saved" Schinkel by helping him obtain funds from Berlin. It was in fact the minister Graf von Haugwitz who responded to Schinkel's urgent entreaty by sending him money immediately. See Maria Zadow, *Karl Friedrich Schinkel* (Berlin: Rembrandt Verlag, 1980), 14.

2. Aloys Ludwig Hirt (1759–1837) was an archaeologist and from 1796 a teacher at the Bauakademie, where two years later Schinkel became his pupil. Hirt was an outstanding representative of dogmatic classicism. Berthold Georg Niebuhr (1776–1831) was a diplomat and historian. His main works deal with Roman law and history.

3. Bötticher was referring to the king of Prussia, Friedrich Wilhelm IV (1795–1861), whom he thought it not proper to mention by name. For that reason he capitalized the pronoun, a spelling that, unless it refers to the deity, is as unusual in German as it is in English. In the same way, the word *Gründer* (used by Bötticher a few lines further down) is in this connection a strange expression in German. Therefore it is translated literally by using the word *founder*, which is equally strange in this context.

Friedrich Wilhelm (who only succeeded to the throne in 1840) not only took great interest in architectural matters but had an almost professional understanding of the problems involved in the various building projects that he wished Schinkel to execute. Schinkel fully acknowledged how much he owed to the Crown Prince's stimulating suggestions (A. von Wolzogen, *Aus Schinkel's Nachlass* [1861], 3: 377–78). On Friedrich Wilhelm's work as architect, see Ludwig Dehio, *Friedrich Wilhelm* von Preussen: *Ein Baukünstler der Romantik* (Berlin: Deutscher Kunstverlag, 1961); and Eva Börsch-Supan, *Berliner Baukunst nach Schinkel: 1840–1870* (Munich: Prestel Verlag, 1977), 14, 89–90.

4. Considering the importance that Hübsch and other writers ascribed to structure and material as the determinants of style, Bötticher's remark was certainly unjustified. He, nonetheless, repeated it again, see p. 153.

5. Johann Joachim Winckelmann (1717–1768) was a German archaeologist and art critic. Friedrich Wilhelm Joseph von Schelling (1775–1854) was a prominent German philosopher. The author of *Die Baukunst nach den Grundsätzen der Alten* was Aloys Ludwig Hirt (see note 2). Although Bötticher maintained toward the end of his speech that Schinkel himself "treasured the work of Hirt on the history of art," this is not confirmed by the notes Schinkel made when reading Hirt's book. Schinkel opposed Hirt's basic attitude; he criticized his failure to understand the new principle governing medieval architecture, and he even denied that Hirt had a true perception of the Greek spirit, "since he demeans himself to vulgar imitation." Goerd Peschken, *Das Architektonische Lehrbuch* (Berlin: Deutscher Kunstverlag, 1979), 28–29.

6. James Stuart and N. Revett, *The Antiquities of Athens* (London: J. Haberkorn, 1762); a German translation appeared in 1829. François Mazois, *Le Palais de Scaurus, ou description d'une maison romaine* (Paris: F. Didot, 1819); German translation, *Der Palast des Scaurus* (1820). The book contains a description of a Roman house written by Merovic, the founder of the Merovingian dynasty, who visited it in the fifth century A.D.

7. The editor of this book was Christian Peter Wilhelm Beuth (1781–1853). He asked Schinkel to be in charge of the first two parts; the first complete edition appeared in 1830, the second in 1837. (See the comprehensive article by Barbara Mundt on the beneficial effect this publication had on the applied arts in: *Berlin und die Antike* [*Aufsätze*] [Berlin: Deutsches Archäologisches Institut, 1979], 455–72.)

8. This refers to Wilhelm Stier's paper "Architrav und Bogen" in *Allgemeine Bauzeitung* (1843) and his declaration "that we can imitate without hesitation ... even when we cannot instantly see the reason for it" (p. 329). Bötticher severely criticized Stier's article in the same journal two years later.

9. The atrium was the main room of the Roman villa around which the other rooms were arranged. From early on it became the custom to open the roof of the atrium; whence the name *cavaedium* (*cavis aedium* = hollow or vaulted room) as another name for atrium. See H. Blümer, *Die römischen Privataltertümer* (Munich: C. H. Beck'sche Verlagsbuchhandlung Oskar Beck, 1911), 30–31.

10. According to Herodotus, the Arimaspi were a race of one-eyed men who lived among the Scyths in the north of Europe where there was more gold than in any other region. They were constantly at war with the gold-guarding griffins.

11. See note 5.

THE DIFFERING VIEWS OF

ARCHITECTURAL STYLE

IN RELATION TO THE

PRESENT TIME

HEINRICH HÜBSCH

FINALLY, WE APPROACH OUR TRUE GOAL—THE LIVING ART FOR WHICH THE COMPARATIVE DESCRIPTION OF VARIOUS EARLIER WAYS OF BUILDING HAS PREPARED US. I trust that in the foregoing discourse I have not, with a novice's enthusiasm, overrated some aspects nor with a doctrinaire perfectionism disregarded the less perfect. My aim has been to appreciate in an unbiased and objective way all aspects of every manner of building and to distinguish their different qualities. From this it emerges that apart from those qualities that are exclusively its own, almost every form of architecture contains a number of other qualities taken over from earlier ones. Of course, this is not meant to imply that an organic architecture can be put together from any eclectic mixture but is addressed to those who measure the artistic efforts of the present time by a super-purist standard and are quick to accuse it of eclecticism. They must be made aware that by adopting this attitude—out of naïveté or for other reasons—they set an impossible task for modern art, one that has never before been accomplished. It is indeed strange that the art critic who produces no art himself, and who is perhaps too enthusiastic in praising the past, at times looks down upon the productive artist from an icy, negative sphere far above the realm of living warmth.

For modern architects the task has been made even more difficult by the many erroneous and contradictory demands to which architectural style has been exposed. These must be refuted in order to arrive at a sound basis. They can be reduced to the following.

First, it is denied—in line with a commonly held aesthetic cosmopolitanism—that architecture's connection with religion and morals is so close as to restrict the architect to only one style. The indispensable main forms of a building are taken simply as a mechanical framework over which architecture proper in its role as a fine art should spread its veil of exquisite form; and it is argued that in our equitable times, which freely accept the beauty of every age, the simultaneous use of every beautiful style is permitted. Yet such a motley fashion of building has never existed since the creation of the world. Of course, it is possible—*per fòrza*—to foist any style whatsoever onto any building but only by doing one of two things. Either the style is modified to fit the present, just as in the theater an antiquated dress is adjusted to fit the fashion of the day: this is called a free treatment of style. Or by here and there stretching and compressing the essential structural and spatial forms of the building on a Procrustean bed: this operation when carried out without too severely mutilating the functions in question is called architectural skill. Thus, with a lack of character that makes the age of periwigs—which at least kept to one style—look like an epoch of high achievement, the Gothic style is chosen today for a church, the Greek style tomorrow for a theater, the Byzantine style for a palace, or possibly the other way around, so that we might just as well have drawn lots.

It may well be possible to use many different styles on those temporary sham buildings that are knocked together with boards for a festive occasion, but real—that is, monumental—buildings last far too long for any such playful improvisation. However opulent and ornate they may be and however hard the architect may have tried to play his part consistently, they tend to reveal much that is rough and contradictory to the discerning eye.[1] Of necessity, such an architectural carnival can produce only buildings that are not thoroughly thought out, are false in conception, or are carelessly planned. For, just as a man can converse in several languages but can think and feel in only one, so the imaginative artist has only one language, only one style in which he really believes. Anyone who claims that he can feel in several styles has no genuine feeling in any of them: his feeling is at best purely archaeological and conventional. His sense of beauty is as far beneath the true sense of beauty as the polygamous love of the Turk is beneath the love of the Christian. How numbed and confused must the visual sense become when the formal extremes of two thousand years—the Gothic and Greek styles—are presented in close proximity! With artistic sensibility already weakened by our hurried and fragmented times, can the observer by some sleight of hand derive equal pleasure from the thin, spiky, and restless forms he sees on his right and from the solid, horizontal, and tranquil forms he sees on his left? Can his structural sense respond to lightness and slender proportions today and to heaviness and massive proportions tomorrow—that is to say, to proportions as different as those of Gothic and Greek architecture? It is of course understood that this criticism refers only to new buildings, not to restorations of older monuments. The splendid project for the completion of the Cologne cathedral is certainly praiseworthy: first as a protest against modern materialism and second as a patriotic enterprise.[2] Let us hope that it will endure; and where mistakes are made, may they be corrected!

Second, in contrast to the first-mentioned, characterless point of view, many Germanomaniacs demand an exclusively German style.[3] This demand stems from a failure to distinguish the style from the actual building. It is true that buildings in Germany, designed according to specific or local circumstances, differ from those in England, France, and Italy just as customs and climate do. Customs and climate in these countries are not, however, so different as to alter significantly the structural forms of monumental stone buildings. Nor for that reason can they bring about a significant variation in style, which, as is known, embraces only the structural forms related to the general spatial character and those formal articulations and architectural ornaments that do not express any function. Therefore, since the time of Charlemagne, only one style has prevailed in all these countries at any one time, and its decorative variations have usually been caused by factors other than climate and national character. The characterization of Gothic architecture as a national German style—often lightly made—can at best be substantiated only by the fact that in its leafwork (which compared to its many geometrical patterns was not very conspicuous) the southern acanthus leaf, so much favored in earlier times, was replaced by other leaves indigenous to the north, such as oak, clover, etc. The difference between the German and Italian styles being so small, a slight touch of the German can be given with little effort to any architectural style whatsoever.

There might in fact be better reasons to draw a distinction between a north German and a south German style, because the latter uses more ashlar as a building material, the former more brick. Furthermore, Protestant north Germany agrees in religion and customs almost more with Scandinavia than with the Catholic south.

Third, the recognition of a characteristic trend in architecture encounters a great deal of emotional arrogance and indolence. In our time of glorified subjectivism and widespread sentimental impertinence, a good many insignificant persons parade as aesthetic authorities, flaunting their recently acquired—or even their anticipated—sense of beauty. With great self-assurance (being sure that they cannot be caught lying), they present these feelings as supreme inspirations to which the new style will have to conform. It is indeed difficult to say anything to these aesthetic Tartuffes except that they should keep quiet until their feelings have undergone at least some training. Other persons, being indolent, expect that they will respond at once to the new style and will love it as if it had always existed. They would like to be transported in cozy comfort to a new sense of beauty without having to judge or to think: two activities that people are often inclined to take as antagonistic to true feeling. They forget that today we no longer enjoy the youthful prerogative that belonged to those past ages when feeling came before thought. Unfortunately, an instinctive feeling for beauty has become as rare with us as instinctive innocence, and our supposed inspirations are often sick and fickle. Those who possess some capacity for self-criticism and who know their own minds and hearts will admit that their feelings for beauty in early life were a chaotic mixture of conventional and novel ideas that shifted, chameleonlike, often but imperceptibly; that sober reflection, when it proved right, turned gradually (though not overnight) into warm feelings; and that it was those feelings that remained closest to their hearts.

Fourth, many imagine the hoped-for new style as something like a happily chosen catchword that must immediately bring about an irresistible passion for art even among the most prosaic persons. They confuse style with the production of a work of art. Yet, as we have seen before, it is the poetic conception and organic presentation of the actual object and its artistic decoration that causes enthusiasm and delight, rather than the style, which concerns only the more general qualities of the work of art and in fact has to do with cold logic.

Fifth, and finally, many people understand the maxim (in itself certainly true) that "modern art must be a clear expression of the present" to mean that a contemporary architectural style, and indeed any contemporary art, must reflect the present as it is today with all of its whimsical qualities and must for that reason be completely new. Above all, they want our time to be seen as an absolutely new and extraordinary birth, radically different from all previous times. True, the present (and I do not want to underestimate its good qualities) is indeed new and unique in one respect: it has an unprecedented illness—that is to say, the speed with which the so-called modern part of mankind again and again changes its appearance, so that in this respect it no longer has a "being" (however brief) but—in Hegelian terms—only a "becoming." Even in the age of periwigs (although restless fashion was already then very active), the Baroque taste in dress and posture lasted for at least a whole generation, long enough for people to get somewhat accustomed to it and—according to the proverb *consuetudo est altera natura* [custom is a second nature]—for human appearance to retain some kind of naturalness. Today, however, fashion—and with it the form, posture, and immediate environs of the person—changes every ten or fifteen years; in which time one can master only its rudiments, even with relentless drilling. Hardly has the eye become half-used to the new fashions when they give way yet again to the latest cut, the latest gait, the latest coy glance, and people at once discard as outmoded their youthful airs and graces imposed by custom and by training in order to run with apish nimbleness for the latest fashionable ideals. Such headlong rapidity of change has produced on the one hand an excessive vanity that has distorted natural beauty and, on the other hand, a rather coarse and superficial visual sense. For there is never sufficient time to accustom the eye to the subtle detail of a form but only to notice and to appreciate crudely exaggerated forms that might just as well be sensed by touch.

This frenetic pace of change in our dress and our surroundings is not the result of the speed of intellectual development, which was equally swift in some earlier periods. The cause, rather, is the massive and autocratic power of industry. Encouraged, unfortunately, by the customers' vain aspirations, industry has become rich by filling our rooms with a host of luxuries. By promoting rapid changes of fashion, it gives our whole appearance an unnatural look and barbarizes our visual sense. This picture of our society will not be thought at all exaggerated by those who have had the opportunity to compare us with the nations of the south, who are less affected by modern luxury and who, moreover, belong to more beautiful races.

With regard to naturalness we are thus divided, as never before, into two factions representative of essentially different points of view. With the modern faction, a description of which has just been given, outer appearance and custom change faster than inner life; and since the outer person is no longer shaped by his inner self, all expression is affected and only half-true. Yet there is, thank goodness, a second, old-fashioned faction, whose outer appearance and custom have not markedly changed over many generations and whose expression is still true and natural. Unfortunately, this second faction is actively represented only by the rural population, although it also has some passive members in the more idealistically orientated, educated class of society. Although in appearance these educated people do not completely dissociate themselves from modern influences—partly out of indolence and partly in deference to the prevailing climate of modernism—they nevertheless recognize the damaging effect of the modern faction and deplore it as an aesthetic and even a moral calamity.

Must, or can, art depict the physiognomy of the modern faction of mankind—that is to say, the fast-moving foam carried along by the river of time—as recommended in the many daily papers that propagate the spirit of the age? Obviously, this blurred and fast-changing face of the present cannot be the subject for monumental art. These forms of today and yesterday, these latest affected airs and gestures of the beau monde, hardly maintain themselves as signs of youthful grace long enough for a great painting or statue to be finished. Even less can the most monumental art of all, that of architecture, pander to the fashions in forms and colors found on mirror frames and wallpapers that are introduced by industry and are, unfortunately, as widely accepted as they are quickly abandoned. Before a great building can possibly be completed, the vulgar taste rushes toward another fancy. This would require every decade to have a new style of architecture, at least with regard to form. Today's commercial culture, whose gift to art and science is flexibility, seeks to make its poetic effects by coming out with foreign fashions and customs—Arabic and Chinese, for the present. This new routine often colors architecture on every level, from interior decoration to the dwelling and from there to every public building.

Considering the pedantic and irresolute attitude of the middle classes, true art exists only for the better-educated elite and, as far as religious content is concerned, for those who form the healthy core of the population and still have natural feelings. Art would be destroyed if artists were to embrace the prosaic spirit and the coarse vision of the fickle and childishly vain world of modern materialism, which staggers from one extreme of bad taste to the other.

Therefore, high art can and must represent only the more constant and the more noble face—that is, the better aspect—of the present. But what is today's better aspect? Is it completely new and different from every earlier period? To answer this question, we shall relate and compare our own time with the main periods of the past, which can be characterized in the following way.

Since Christianity gave mankind a new meaning, there have been, apart from the distant Oriental nations, only three main, distinctively different trends in moral development and aesthetic production. The first was the classical early Christian period. Its spiritual religion and morality led people to despise the pagan religion as inadequate, although they did not reject the classical intellect and formal education but rather assimilated these into the higher ideal. The result was the substantial literature of the early Fathers, the august music of the early Church, and the early Christian art that lasted for almost five hundred years. Without prejudice to its magnificent ethical character, this art, as shown earlier, adopted with the same consistency the formal aspect of classical art (because otherwise one suddenly would have had to procure quite different eyes). It retained the clarity of classical art but unfortunately lost much of its refinement.

This period was followed by the second, the Romanesque Christian period, which, beginning and ending with the Middle Ages, was characterized almost exclusively by religious spirit, sincere piety, and self-denying asceticism. Yet with regard to the forms of daily life, these times, especially among the Germanic nations, lacked formal refinement even more than the first period. Classical details were retained in art but only as a second or thirdhand tradition. More and more, the orderly classical clarity of presentation was lost, and during the second half of the Middle Ages artists indulged in boundless exuberance. Yet the characteristic aspect of this art revealed a world of deep emotion and great monumental dignity.

Whereas this trend was centered in northwest Europe, the third period developed in Italy. It should be called the classical neo-Christian because there, at the end of the fourteenth century, the classical culture (never entirely extinguished in Italy) was strongly revived and formed a new bond with Christianity. The spirit of the times changed from a visionary and pious view of life and religion to a more reflective and contemplative attitude, and intellectual concerns now included secular as well as religious ones.

It is obvious that the better aspect of the present still belongs within this third period. Christianity is still its faith, and even for the convinced atheist, it is Christian morality that is the measure by which character and all profane matters are judged. In the same way, our intellect and formal education are still mainly classical, and this finds an echo to some extent even among the people. Admittedly, there are symptoms—namely a brand-new religion and morality, tolerant in matters of faith and conscience, under the patronage of a rough-and-ready culture—that threaten the advent of a new and totally different period, the fourth. Should half-educated and wholly arrogant persons really take control over spiritual and aesthetic matters, then indeed there can no longer be any talk of true poetry and art. Instead of the monumental church, the sleek industrial hall built of cast iron will become the architectural prototype—painted in shiny, fashionable colors and appointed with the pseudomonumental, dazzling shine of mirrors and gold-fringed velvet curtains to attract the *haute volée*.

However, the core of the population is not yet infected; there still exists, though small in numbers, an intellectual aristocracy that withstands the anti-idealistic onslaught of shallow, rational utilitarianism and materialistic Epicureanism. Educated people are now devoting themselves—far more than in the last, freethinking century—to a contemplative Christian way of life. It is to be hoped that they will abandon not only the modern mania for change but in time also the vanity and affectation that distorts outer appearance. With this hope we continue to pursue our aim in art and emphasize again that the rapidly changing appearance of modern man has become an affectation and a half-truth; it has become a mask that does not conform to his inner self, and taste staggers from one extreme to the other. Yet alongside this scarcely natural world of fashion, this craving for change and constant flux, there still exists another, more natural world of being that embraces the better spiritual qualities of the present and does not differ in essence from the third period, which we called the classical neo-Christian period. Today's fine art can and must envisage and represent this true face alone (although it should also take into account certain valuable recent nuances). That other, ephemeral, ever-changing face is best left to the lower art of genre painting, which characteristically diverges today more than ever from truly poetic art. Whenever the latter seriously tries to perpetuate the latest modern face, those who have good taste and fine vision are horrified by the affected physiognomy that grimaces out at them. This does not seem to disturb those who preach with specious logic that living art must above all represent life in its latest form, meaning modern man. Unmodern man they consider to be already antiquated.[4]

Source Note: Heinrich Hübsch, "Die verschiedenen Ansichten über Baustil gegenüber der heutigen Zeit," *Die Architektur und ihr Verhältniß zur heutigen Malerei und Skulptur* (Stuttgart and Tübingen: J. G. Cotta, 1847), chap. 14, 184–97.

Translator's Notes

1. A few years later in *Der Stil* (Frankfurt-am-Main: Bruckmann, 1860–1863), 1: 229–30, Semper also referred to these "improvised structures," which at festive occasions were covered with carpets and decorated with garlands, festoons, and bands. In contrast to Hübsch, yet in line with his theory of dressing, Semper perceived them as the roots from which monumental architecture had evolved.

2. The decision to complete the cathedral was made in 1842 and was enthusiastically received throughout Germany as a great patriotic act and symbol of German unity. Rebuilding progressed slowly, so that by 1847 the church was still in the same unfinished state as it had been since work on it had stopped in the sixteenth century. See W. D. Robson-Scott, *The Literary Background of the Gothic Revival in Germany* (Oxford: Clarendon, 1965), 292ff.

3. Hübsch might have been thinking of the following publications: Rudolf Wiegmann, "Gedanken über die Entwickelung eines zeitgemäßen nazionalen Baustyls," *Allgemeine Bauzeitung* 6 (1841):

207ff; Friedrich Wilhelm Ludwig Stier, Das Centralmoment bei der historischen Entwicklung des germanischen Baustiles," *Allgemeine Bauzeitung* (1844): 301ff; August Reichensperger, *Die Christlich-germanische Baukunst und ihr Verhältniß zur Gegenwart: Nebst einem Berichte Schinkel's aus dem Jahre 1816, den Cölner Dombau betreffend* (Trier: F. Lintz, 1845); Ferdinand Wilhelm Horn, *System eines neugermanischen Baustyls* (Potsdam, 1845), and also an article in the *Zeitschrift für praktische Baukunst* (1845), 243ff.

4. The last six lines of the chapter refer to rhetoric and music; they have been omitted from the translation.

BOOKS

1821   *Vorbilder für Fabrikanten und Handwerker: Auf Befehl des Ministers für Handel Gewerbe und Bauwesen herausgegeben von der Technischen Deputation für Gewerbe.* Pls. 2-25. Berlin: Schellenberg, 1821.

1830   *Lexicon Taciteum; sive, De stilo C. Cornelii Taciti, praemissis de Taciti vita, scriptis ac scribendi genere prolegomenis, scripsit Guil. Bötticher.* Berolini: Sumptibus C. G. Nauckii, 1830.

1834   *Zeichnungen nach Darstellungen auf Kirchenteppichen des Mittelalters.* Berlin: n.p., 1834.
        Ornamenten-Buch: Zum practischen Gebrauche für Architecten, Decorations- und Stubenmaler, Tapeten-Fabrikanten, Seiden-, Woll- und Damastweber u.s.w. 5 vols. Berlin: Ernst & Korn, 1834-1844. Reprint. 1 vol. 1834-1856.

1836   *Die Holzarchitectur des Mittelalters: Mit Anschluß der schönsten in dieser Epoche entwickelten Produkte der gewerblichen Industrie: In Reisestudien gesammelt und auf Stein gezeichnet.* Berlin: Privately published, commissioned by Schenk & Gerstäcker, 1836 (vols. 1 & 2); Berlin: Schenk & Gerstäcker, 1836-1842 (vols. 3 & 4).

1838   *Ornamenten-Schule: Ein Studien-Cursus für die Zeichnung und Erfindung des Ornamentes, nach dem von der antiken Kunst gegeben Karakterisirungsprinzipe architectonischer Formen: Als Lehrbuch für Kunst- und Gewerbe-Schulen wie auch für das Selbststudium bearbeitet und dem Herrn Königl. Ober-Bau-Director Herrn Schinkel zugeeignet.* Vol. 1. Berlin: n.p., 1838.

1839   *Dessinateur-Schule: Ein Lehrkursus der Dessination der gewebten Stoffe; als Handbuch für den Lehrer, so wie als Leitfaden für den Selbstunterricht.* Berlin: Eigentum des Verfassers, 1839.

1844   *Die Tektonik der Hellenen.* 2 vols. Potsdam: Ferdinand Riegel, 1844-1852 (atlas published in 1862). 2nd ed. 2 vols. and atlas. Berlin: Ernst & Korn, 1869-1881.

1846   *Andeutungen über das Heilige und Profane in der Baukunst der Hellenen: Eine Gedächtnißchrift zur Geburtstagsfeier Schinkels.* Berlin: J. Petsch, 1846.

1847   *Der Hypäthraltempel, auf Grund des Vitruvischen Zeugnisses gegen Prof. Dr. L. Ross erwiesen.* Potsdam: Ferdinand Riegel, 1847; Berlin: Ernst & Korn, 1847.
        Architektonische Formenschule in Ornament-Erfindungen, als Vorbilder zum Unterrichte für technische Institute, Kunst- und Bauschulen, Architecten, Bauhandwerker. Potsdam: n.p., 1847.

1850   *Ornament-Zeichnen: Cursus für künftige Bauführer 1849/50.* Berlin: Bauakademie, 1850.

        Ornamenten-Werk, als Vorbilder zum Unterrichte. Potsdam: n.p., 1850.

1851   *Der Poliastempel als Wohnhaus des Königs Erechtheus nach der Annahme von Fr. Thiersch. Beleuchtet und seinen Freunden in der archäologischen Gesellschaft, zugeeignet.* Berlin: J. Petsch, 1851. Reprint. Berlin: Gebauer, 1854.

1854   Kopisch, August. *Die königlichen Schlösser und Gärten zu Potsdam: Von der Zeit ihrer Gründung bis zum Jahre MDCCLII: Auf Allerhöchsten Befehl Sr. Majestät des Königs.* Edited and with a preface by Carl Bötticher. Berlin: Ernst & Korn, 1854.

1856   *Der Baumkultus der Hellenen nach den gottesdienstlichen Gebräuchen und den überlieferten Bildwerken dargestellet.* Berlin: Weidmann, 1856.

        Gesammelte Werke von August Kopisch. Edited by Carl Bötticher. 5 vols. Berlin: Weidmannsche Buchhandlung, 1856.

1857   *Karl Friedrich Schinkel und sein baukünstlerisches Vermächtnis: Eine Mahnung an seine Nachfolge in der Zeit in drei Reden und drei Toasten an den Tagen der Geburtstagsfeier des Verewigten gesprochen.* Berlin: Ernst & Korn, 1857. 2nd ed. Edited by Clarissa Bötticher, introduction by W. P. Tuckermann, with an addendum, "Aesthetische Sentenzen und kleinere Gedichte." Deutsche Bucherei 61. Berlin: Neelmeyer, 1906.

1858   *Das Grab des Dionysus: An der Marmorbasis zu Dresden: Nebst Nachschrift des Herausgebers und einer Abbildung.* Berlin: W. Hertz, 1858.

        Ornament-Vorbilder. Berlin: n.p., 1858–1860.

1859   *Der Omphalos des Zeus zu Delphi: Nebst Nachschrift des Herausgebers und einer Steintafel.* Berlin: W. Hertz, 1859.

1862   *Nachtrag zu dem Friedrich'schen Kataloge.* N.p., 1862.

1863   *Bericht über die Untersuchungen auf der Akropolis von Athen im Frühjahre 1862.* Berlin: Ernst & Korn, 1863.

1864   *Dirke als Quelle und Heroine: Nebst einer Bildtafel.* Berlin: Besser, 1864.

1865   *Athenischer Festkalender in Bildern: Bildtafel aus Philologus Bd. XXII, nebst Übersicht des daselbst erklärten Inhaltes der Darstellungen.* Göttingen: Dieterich, 1865.

1870   *Mittheilungen aus der Sammlung der Sculpturen und Gypsabgüße des königlichen Museums.* Berlin: G. Reimer, 1870.

1871   *Königliche Museen: Erklärendes Verzeichniß der Abgüße antiker Werke.* Berlin: Ernst Kühn, 1871.

        Zwei Hermenbildniße der Sappho. Berlin: G. Reimer, 1871.

1872   *Von dem Berliner Museum: Eine Berichtigung an A. Conze in Wien.* Berlin: Ernst & Korn, 1872.

1875   *Der Zophorus am Parthenon hinsichtlich der Streitfrage über seinen Inhalt und dessen Beziehung auf dieses Gebäude.* Berlin: Ernst & Korn, 1875.

1880   *Die Thymele der Athena-Nike auf der Akropolis von Athen, in ihrem heutigen Zustande: Nach der tektonischen Untersuchung im Frühlinge 1878.* Berlin: Ernst & Korn, 1880.

1883   *Evangelisch! Zum vierhundertsten Geburtstage Luthers.* Berlin: n.p., 1883.

1888   *Zur Thronbesteigung Kaiser Wilhelms II.* Berlin: n.p., 1888.

1894   *Eros und Erkenntnis bei Plato in ihrer gegenseitigen Förderung und Ergänzung.* Wissenschaftliche Beilage zum Jahresbericht des Luisenstädtischen Gymnasiums zu Berlin 64. Berlin: R. Gaertners Verlagsbuchhandlung Hermann Heyfelder, 1894.

1895   *Das Wesen des religiösen Glaubens im Neuen Testament.* Wissenschaftliche Beilage zum Programm des Luisenstädtischen Gymnasiums zu Berlin 64. Berlin: R. Gaertners Verlagsbuchhandlung Hermann Heyfelder, 1895.

ARTICLES, ADDRESSES, AND PAMPHLETS

1833   "Allegorien in altchristlichen Ornamenten." December 1833 [address delivered at the Architekten-Verein].

1834   "Erklärung der interessantesten Allegorien der christlichen Kunst des Mittelalters, die sich in Kunstprodukten bis auf unsere Zeiten erhalten haben." *Museum* 2 (1834): 57-61.

1835   "Ausbildung der Details beim Ausbau altdeutscher Gebäude." July 1835 [address delivered at the Architekten-Verein].

1836   "Technisches der Webkunst." May 1836 [address delivered at the Architekten-Verein].

1840   "Entwickelung der Formen der hellenischen Tektonik." *Allgemeine Bauzeitung* 5 (1840): 316-40.

1844   "Tektonik der Hellenen." Winter 1844-1845 [lectures delivered at the Architekten-Verein].

1845   "Polemisch-Kritisches." *Allgemeine Bauzeitung* 10 (1845) (*Literatur... Beilage*) 2, no. 18: 281-320.
        "Neugriechische Kostüme nach Stackelberg." April 1845 [address delivered at the Architekten-Verein].

1846   "Das Prinzip der hellenischen und germanischen Bauweise hinsichtlich der Übertragung in die Bauweise unserer Tage." *Allgemeine Bauzeitung* 11 (1846): 111-25 [address delivered at the Schinkelfest].
        "Hypaethraltempel." June 1846 [address delivered at the Architekten-Verein].

1848   "Rede am Schinkelfest zu Berlin am 13. März 1848 vor einer Versammlung von Architekten und anderen Künstlern und Verehrern des Gefeierten." *Allgemeine Bauzeitung*

13 (1848): 143-48 [address delivered at the Schinkelfest].

1852   "Über den Parthenon zu Athen und den Zeus-Tempel zu Olympia, je nach Zweck und Benutzung." *Zeitschrift für Bauwesen* 2, no. 6-7 (1 June 1852): 194-210; no. 11-12 (1 December 1852): 498-520; 3, no. 1-2 (1 January 1853): 35-44; no. 3-4 (1 March 1853): 127-42; no. 5-6 (1 May 1853): 269-92.

1855   "Schwatlo über die Auffassung der dorischen und ionischen Architektur nach Bötticher." April 1855 [address delivered at the Architekten-Verein].

1859   "Über die letzte bauliche Untersuchung des Erechtheion auf der Akropolis von Athen." *Zeitschrift für Bauwesen* 9 (1859): 203-16, 317-36.

1861   "Über agonale Festtempel und Thesauren, deren Bilder und Ausstattung." *Philologus* 17 (1861): 385-408, 577-605; 18 (1862): 1-54, 385-417, 577-603; 19 (1863): 1-74.

1863   "Meine Untersuchungen auf der Akropolis von Athen im Frühjahre 1862." *Zeitschrift für Bauwesen* 13 (1863), no. 4-6: 195-224; no. 7-10: 405-70; no. 11-12: 557-608.

1864   "Ergänzungen zu den letzten Untersuchungen auf der Akropolis in Athen." *Philologus* 21 (1864): 41-72; 22 (1865): 69-98, 221-84, 385-436, 576-77, 755-57; 24 (1867): 227-42; 25 (1868): 13-42, 193-211; 3rd supplement, no. 3 (1878): 285-448.

1871   "Mittheilungen aus der Sammlung der Sculpturen und Gypsabgüsse des königlichen Museums." *Archäologische Zeitung*, n.s. 3 (1871): 59-64.

1872   "Zwei Hermenbildnisse der Sappho." *Archäologische Zeitung*, n.s. 4 (1872): 83-86.

1880   "Tektonische Untersuchungen auf der Akropolis von Athen im Frühjahre 1878, betreffend die Thymele des Niketempels und die Südhalle der Propyläen." *Zeitschrift für Bauwesen* 30 (1880): 71-88, 209-28.

SELECTED SECONDARY SOURCES

Blankenstein, Hermann. "Karl Bötticher, sein Leben und Wirken." *Centralblatt der Bauverwaltung* 9 (1889): 315-17, 326-29.

Börsch-Supan, Eva. *Berliner Baukunst nach Schinkel: 1840-1870*, pp. 71-72, 556-58. Munich: Prestel Verlag, 1977.

Curtius, Ernst. *Der Tektonik der Hellenen* by Karl Bötticher. *Kunst-Blatt*, no. 11 (6 February 1845): 41-43; no. 12 (11 February 1845): 45-46; no. 13 (13 February 1845): 49-51; no. 14 (18 February 1845); 56-57.

Goethert, Friedrich. "Bötticher." In *Neue Deutsche Biographie*, compiled by Historische Kommission bei der bayerischen Akademie der Wissenschaften, vol. 2, 412-13. Berlin: Duncker & Humblot, 1971.

Gurlitt, Cornelius. "Karl Bötticher." *Deutsche Bauzeitung* 24, no. 64 (9 August 1890): 384-87; no. 66 (16 August 1890): 393-95.

Lohde, Ludwig. *Die Architektonik der Hellenen nach C. Bötticher's Tektonik der Hellenen. Nachträge zur fünften Auflage von Mauch's architektonischen Ordnungen der Griechen und Römer und der neueren Meister*.... Berlin: n.p., 1862.

Lohde-Bötticher, Clarissa. *Aus dem Leben Karl Böttichers*. Gotha: n.p., 1890.

Michaelis, A. "Karl Bötticher." In *Allgemeine Deutsche Biographie*, compiled by Die historische Commission bei der königlichen Akademie der Wissenschaften, vol. 47, 144–53. Leipzig: Duncker & Humblot, 1903.

Nagler, G. K. "Karl Bötticher." In *Neues Allgemeines Künstler-Lexicon*, vol. 2, 2. Munich: E. A. Fleischmann, 1835.

Streiter, Richard. *Karl Böttichers Tektonik der Hellenen als ästhetische und kunstgeschichtliche Theorie. Eine Kritik*. Beiträge zur Aesthetik 3. Hamburg and Leipzig: Leopold Voss, 1896.

BOOKS

1822   *Über griechische Architectur.* Heidelberg: J. C. B. Mohr, 1822.

1823   Heger, Franz, and Heinrich Hübsch. *Malerische Ansichten von Athen.* Darmstadt: n.p., 1823.
       Architektonische Verzierungen für Künstler und Handwerker. Vol. 1. Frankfurt am Main: n.p., 1823.

1824   *Über griechische Architectur: Mit einer Vertheidigung gegen Herrn A. Hirt.* 2nd ed. Heidelberg: J. C. B. Mohr, 1824.

1825   *Entwurf zu einem Theater mit eiserner Dachrüstung.* Frankfurt am Main: W. L. Wesché, 1825.

1828   *In welchem Style sollen wir bauen?* Karlsruhe: Chr. Fr. Müller Hofbuchhandlung und Hofbuchdruckeren, 1828. Reprint. Afterword by Wulf Schirmer. Karlsruhe: C. F. Müller, 1984.

1838   *Bau-Werke.* 1st series. Vols. 1 and 2. Karlsruhe and Baden: Marx, 1838.

1847   *Die Architektur und ihr Verhältniß zur heutigen Malerei und Skulptur.* Stuttgart and Tübingen: J. G. Cotta, 1847. Reprint. Berlin: Beeken, 1985.

1852   *Bau-Werke.* 2nd series. Vols. 1 and 2. Karlsruhe: J. Veith, 1852.

1859   *Bau-Werke.* 2nd series. Vol. 3. Karlsruhe: J. Veith, 1859.

1862   *Die altchristlichen Kirchen nach den Baudenkmalen und älteren Beschreibungen und der Einfluß des altchristlichen Baustyles auf den Kirchenbau aller späteren Perioden.* 2 vols. Karlsruhe: W. Hasper, 1862-1863.

TRANSLATIONS

1866   *Monuments de l'architecture chrétienne depuis Constantin jusqu'à Charlemagne et de leur influence sur le style des constructions religieuses aux époques postérieures.* Translated by M. l'abbé V. Guerber. Paris: A. Morel, 1866.

ARTICLES, ADDRESSES, AND PAMPHLETS

1836   [Heinrich Hübsch?]. "Bemerkungen über die verschiedenen Baukonstrukzionen der neueren Griechen." *Allgemeine Bauzeitung* 1, no. 21 (1836): 163-66.

1837   "Die ideelle Formenbildung in der Architektur." *Allgemeine Bauzeitung* 2, no. 29 (1837): 239-41.

1853   *Über christliche Baukunst.* Karlsruhe: 12 September 1853 [pamphlet].

1854   "Das bedeutendste Denkmal altchristlicher Kunst zu Mailand." *Deutsches Kunstblatt* 5, no. 47 (23 November 1854): 415-19.

1855   "Das bedeutendste Denkmal altchristlicher Kunst zu Mailand." *Deutsches Kunstblatt* 6, no. 20 (17 May 1855): 177-79; no. 21 (24 May 1855): 184-86.

        "Sollen wir heute unsere Kirchen im gothischen oder im altchristlichen Style bauen?" *Beilage der Augsburger Postzeitung*, no. 26 (6 February 1855).

        "Rezension von Salzenbergs *Altchristlichen Baudenkmalen in Constantinopel.*" *Wiener Kathol. Lit. Zeitung*, no. 13 (1855).

1857   "Über die aesthetischen Principien der monumentalen Architektur." *Deutsches Kunstblatt* 8, no. 26 (25 June 1857): 221-24; no. 27 (2 July 1857): 229-31; no. 28 (9 July 1857): 239-43.

1860   "Einige Bemerkungen zur Recension der 'altchristlichen Kirchen von Hübsch,' welche im X Jahrgang, Heft I u. ff. der *Zeitschrift für Bauwesen* enthalten ist." *Zeitschrift für Bauwesen* 10 (1860): 625-28.

SELECTED SECONDARY SOURCES

Bergdoll, Barry. "Archaeology vs. History: Heinrich Hübsch's Critique of Neoclassicism and the Beginnings of Historicism in German Architectural Theory." *The Oxford Art Journal* 5, no. 2 (1982): 3-12.

Drücke, Eberhard. "Heinrich Hübsch." In *The Macmillan Encyclopedia of Architects*, edited by Adolf Placzek, vol. 2, 435. New York: The Free Press, 1982.

Göricke, Joachim. *Die Kirchenbauten des Architekten Heinrich Hübsch.* Studien zur Bauforschung 8. Stuttgart: Der Koldewey-Gesellschaft, 1974.

Hirsch, Fritz. "Heinrich Hübsch." In *Allgemeines Lexicon der bildenden Künstler von der Antike bis zur Gegenwart*, edited by Hans Vollmer, vol. 18, 50-52. Leipzig: E. A. Seemann, 1925.

Klein, Bernhard. "Heinrich Hübsch und die evangelische Ludwigskirche, Anmerkungen zur Rekonstruktion der Zisterzienser-Klosterkirche Tennenbach in Freiburg im Breisgau." *Zeitschrift des Breisgau-Geschichtsvereins* 101 (1982): 275-98.

Merz, Fr. H. Review of *"Die Architektur und ihr Verhältniß zur heutigen Malerei und Skulptur* by Heinrich Hübsch." *Kunst-Blatt*, no. 50 (12 October 1848): 197-200; no. 52 (24 October 1848): 205-8.

Schirmer, Wulf. *Heinrich Hübsch 1795-1863: Der Große Badische Baumeister der Romantik.* Exh. cat. Karlsruhe: C. F. Müller, 1983.

Valdenaire, Arthur. "Heinrich Hübsch: Eine Studie zur Baukunst der Romantik." *Zeitschrift für die Geschichte des Oberrheins* 39 (1926): 421-44, 527-56; 40 (1927): 181-206.

Vilmar, Gernot. "Heinrich Hübsch." In *Neue Deutsche Biographie*, compiled by Historische Kommission bei der bayerischen Akademie der Wissenschaften, vol. 9, 723-24. Berlin: Duncker & Humblot, 1972.

Waskönig, Dagmar. "Konstruktionen eines zeitgemäßen Stils zu Beginn der Industrialisierung in Deutschland: Historisches Denken in Heinrich Hübschs Theorie des Rundbogenstils." In *"Geschichte allein ist zeitgemäß": Historismus in Deutschland*, edited by Michael Brix and Monika Steinhauser, 93-105. Lahn-Gießen: Anabas, 1978.

BOOKS

1830 *Über die Entstehung und Bedeutung der architektonischen Formen der Griechen.* Berlin: n.p., 1830.

1837 Clemens, J. F., Mellin, Friedrich Albert Immanuel, and Rosenthal, Carl Albert, eds. *Der Dom zu Magdeburg.* Magdeburg: Creutz, 1837-1852.

1841 *Vollständige Übersicht der Geschichte der Baukunst von ihrem Ursprunge an bis auf die neueste Zeit im organischen Zusammenhange in sich und mit der allgemeinen Culturgeschichte für Geschichtsforscher, Baumeister und überhaupt für denkende und gebildete Leser.* 2 vols. Berlin: G. Reimer, 1841-1842.

ARTICLES, ADDRESSES, AND PAMPHLETS

1830 "Über die Entstehung und Bedeutung der architectonischen Formen der Griechen." *Journal für die Baukunst* 3 (1830), no. 2: 232-42; no. 3: 276-326.

1839 Übersicht der Geschichte der Baukunst, mit Rücksicht auf die allgemeine Culturgeschichte." *Journal für die Baukunst* 13 (1839), no. 1: 52-81; no. 2: 188-206; no. 3: 255-81; 14 (1840), no. 1: 1-39; no. 2: 183-98; no. 3: 199-255; 15 (1841), no. 1: 1-49; no. 2: 160-79; no. 3: 231-69; no. 4: 310-57; 16 (1842), no. 3: 197-246; 17 (1842), no. 1: 46-84; no. 2: 97-123; no. 3: 236-59; 18 (1843), no. 2: 129-72; 20 (1844), no. 1: 32-68; 22 (1845), no. 2: 97-132; 25 (1847), no. 1: 1-32; no. 3: 216-51; no. 4: 323-68; 26 (1848), no. 1: 48-96; no. 4: 351-78; 27 (1849), no. 1: 62-92; no. 4: 244-74; 28 (1850), no. 1: 57-90; no. 2: 126-46; no. 3: 177-98, 345-62.

1842 "Kurzer Überblick des Entwickelungsganges der Baukunst." *Zeitschrift für praktische Baukunst* 2 (1842): 282-90.

1844 "In welchem Style sollen wir bauen? (Eine Frage für die Mitglieder des deutschen Architektenvereins)." *Zeitschrift für praktische Baukunst* 4 (1844): 23-27.
"Was will die Baukunst eigentlich?" *Allgemeine Bauzeitung* 9 (1844): 268-74.
"Gefängnisgebäude." *Zeitschrift für praktische Baukunst* 4 (1844): 275.

1845 "Das neue Rathhaus zu Neustadt bei Magdeburg." *Zeitschrift für praktische Baukunst* 5 (1845): 286-87.

1856 "Der Dom zu Magdeburg." *Allgemeine Bauzeitung* 21 (1856): 281-93.

SELECTED SECONDARY SOURCES

Börsch-Supan, Eva. *Berliner Baukunst nach Schinkel: 1840-1870,* p. 27, no. 109. Munich: Prestel Verlag, 1977.

BOOKS

1836   *Die Malerei der Alten in ihrer Anwendung und Technik insbesondere als Dekorations-malerei.* Foreword by Hofrathe K. O. Müller. Hannover: Hahn, 1836.

1839   *Der Ritter Leo von Klenze und unsere Kunst.* Düsseldorf: J. H. C. Schreiner, 1839.
Über die Konstruction von Kettenbrücken nach dem Dreiecksystem. Düsseldorf: n.p., 1839.

1842   *Über den Ursprung des Spitzbogenstils: Mit einem Anhange betreffend die Bildung eines Vereins für die Geschichte der mittelalterlichen Baukunst.* Düsseldorf: J. Buddeus, 1842.

1846   *Grundzüge der Lehre von der Perspektive für Maler und Zeichenlehrer.* Düsseldorf: J. Buddeus, 1846. 2nd ed. 1876.

1847   *Die Malweise des Tizian: Nach Ergebnissen der von dem Maler J. Dräger angestellten Untersuchungen und Versuche mitgetheilt.* Düsseldorf: J. Buddeus, 1847.

1856   *Die königliche Kunst-Akademie zu Düsseldorf: Ihre Geschichte, Einrichtung und Wirksamkeit und die Düsseldorfer Künstler.* Düsseldorf: J. Buddeus, 1856.

ARTICLES, ADDRESSES, AND PAMPHLETS

1829   "Bemerkungen über die Schrift: *In welchem Styl sollen wir bauen?* von H. Hübsch." *Kunst-Blatt* 10 (1829), no. 44: 173-74; no. 45: 177-79; no. 46: 181-83.

1841   "Gedanken über die Entwickelung eines zeitgemäßen nazionalen Baustyls." *Allgemeine Bauzeitung* 6 (1841): 207-14.
"Werke der höheren Baukunst: Für die Ausführung erfunden und dargestellt von Dr. J. F. Schinkel." *Allgemeine Bauzeitung* 6, no. 43 (August 1841) (*Literatur... Beilage*): 403-10.

1842   "Über den Ursprung des Spitzbogenstils." *Allgemeine Bauzeitung* 7 (1842): 37-61.
Über eine Konstrukzion sich freitragender Brücken aus Holz und Eisen ohne Wider-lager." *Allgemeine Bauzeitung* 7 (1842): 267-69.
"Polemisches." *Allgemeine Bauzeitung* 7 (1842) (*Literatur...Beilage*): 498-500.

1846   "Gegensätze: Die Tendenz des Hrn. Prof. J. H. Wolff und 'Die Christlich-germanische Baukunst und ihr Verhältniß zur Gegenwart von A. Reichensperger, Trier 1845,' nebst einer Schlußbetrachtung." *Allgemeine Bauzeitung* 11 (1846) (*Literatur...Beilage*) 3, no. 1: 1-19.

1855 "Die Wiederherstellung des Domes zu Speyer nach dem Plane des Großh. Badischen Baudirektors H. Hübsch." *Deutsches Kunstblatt* 6, no. 37 (13 September 1855): 324–26.

SELECTED SECONDARY SOURCES

Daelen, Eduard. "Rudolf Wiegmann." In *Allgemeine Deutsche Biographie*, compiled by Die historische Commission bei der königlichen Akademie der Wissenschaften, vol. 42, 390–91. Leipzig: Duncker & Humblot, 1897.

Nagler, G. K. "Rudolf Wiegmann." In *Neues allgemeines Künstler-Lexicon*, vol. 21, 391–92. Munich: E. A. Fleischmann, 1851.

Pfeffer, Klaus, "Spätklassizismus in Düsseldorf." *Düsseldorfer Jahrbuch* 51 (1963): 133–43.

Trier, Eduard, and Willy Weyres, eds. *Kunst des 19. Jahrhunderts im Rheinland*. Düsseldorf: Schwann, 1980.

Johann Heinrich Wolff Bibliography

Books

1831 *Über Plan und Methode bei dem Studium der Architectur.* Leipzig and Darmstadt: Carl Wilhelm Leske, 1831.

1834 *Beiträge zur Aesthetik der Baukunst oder die Grundgesetze der plastischen Form, nachgewiesen an den Haupttheilen der griechischen Architektur.* Leipzig and Darmstadt: Carl Wilhelm Leske, 1834.

1854 *Die wesentlichste Grundlage der monumentalen Baukunst: Historisch dargelegt an den Meisterwerken der alten Architectur. Eine Abtheilung geschichtlicher Vorträge.* Göttingen: George H. Wigand, 1854. 2nd ed. 1857.
Lutherische Antwort auf die Denkschrift der theologischen Facultät zu Göttingen. Stade: n.p., 1854.

1856 *Handbuch der höheren Kunst-Industrie für Gewerbetreibende und Künstler, sowie für Lehranstalten....* Kassel: n.p., 1856?

1862 *Zum Kirchenfrieden.* Stade: n.p., 1862.

Articles, Addresses, and Pamphlets

1827 Review of "Georg Moller, *Entwürfe ausgeführter und zur Ausführung bestimmter Gebäude. Heft 1. Das großherzogliche Hoftheater zu Darmstadt.*" *Kunst-Blatt* 8, no. 83 (15 October 1827): 331-32; no. 84 (18 October 1827): 334-36; no. 85 (22 October 1827): 337-38.
Review of "Heinrich Hübsch, *Entwurf zu einem Theater mit eiserner Dachrüstung.*" *Göttingische gelehrte Anzeigen* 3 (1827), no. 199: 1977-84; no. 200: 1985-99.
"*Sammlung architektonischer Entwürfe* von Schinkel, enthaltend theils Werke welche ausgeführt sind, theils Gegenstände deren Ausführung beabsichtigt wurde: Erstes Heft." *Göttingische gelehrte Anzeigen*, no. 6-7 (11 January 1827): 49-64; no. 8 (13 January 1827): 65-79.
"*Sammlung architektonischer Entwürfe* von Schinkel, enthaltend theils Werke welche ausgeführt sind, theils Gegenstände deren Ausführung beabsichtigt wurde: II Heft." *Göttingische gelehrte Anzeigen*, no. 45 (19 March 1827): 441-48; no. 46-47 (22 March 1827): 449-62.

1828 "*Sammlung architektonischer Entwürfe* von Schinkel, enthaltend theils Werke welche ausgeführt sind, theils Gegenstände deren Ausführung beabsichtigt wurde: Drittes Heft." *Göttingische gelehrte Anzeigen* (14 June 1828), no. 95: 937-44; no. 96: 945-56.

1842   "Einige Bemerkungen über das von Schinkel erbaute neue Wachthaus zu Dresden." *Zeitschrift für praktische Baukunst* 2 (1842): 241-45.

"*Sammlung architektonischer Entwürfe, welche ausgeführt oder für die Ausführung entworfen wurden von L. v. Klenze.*" *Allgemeine Bauzeitung* 7 (1842) (*Literatur... Beilage*), no. 47 (January): 451-58.

"*Sammlung architektonischer Entwürfe*, enthaltend theils Werke, welche ausgeführt sind, theils Gegenstände, deren Ausführung beabsichtigt wurde; bearbeitet und herausgegeben von Schinkel: Sechstes Heft." *Allgemeine Bauzeitung* 7 (1842) (*Literatur... Beilage*), no. 49 (March-April): 469-75.

"*Sammlung architektonischer Entwürfe* von Schinkel enthaltend, theils Werke, welche ausgeführt sind, theils Gegenstände, deren Ausführung beabsichtigte wurde, u.s.w. Dreizehntes Heft." *Allgemeine Bauzeitung* 7 (1842) (*Literatur... Beilage*), no. 52 (September): 507-17.

1843   "Polemisches." *Allgemeine Bauzeitung* 8 (1843) (*Literatur... Beilage*) 2, no. 1: 1-5.

"Entwürfe ausgeführter und zur Ausführung bestimmter Gebäude: Herausgegeben von Dr. Georg Moller." *Allgemeine Bauzeitung* 8 (1843) (*Literatur... Beilage*) 2, no. 1: 5-11.

"*Sammlung architektonischer Entwürfe* von Schinkel, enthaltend theils Werke, welche ausgeführt sind, theils Gegenstände, deren Ausführung beabsichtigt wurde u." *Allgemeine Bauzeitung* 8 (1843) (*Literatur... Beilage*) 2, no. 7: 103-10.

1845   "Einige Worte über die von Herrn Professor Stier bei der Architektenversammlung zu Bamberg zur Sprache gebrachten (und im Jahrgange 1843 dieser Zeitschrift S. 301 mitgetheilten) architektonischen Fragen." *Allgemeine Bauzeitung* 10 (1845) (*Literatur... Beilage*) 2, no. 17: 255-70.

"Die Mariahilfkirche in der Vorstadt Au zu München: Von Ohlmüller." *Allgemeine Bauzeitung* 10 (1845) (*Literatur... Beilage*) 2, no. 16: 243-50.

1846   "Ein Prinzip und keine Parteien!" *Allgemeine Bauzeitung* 11 (1846): 358-67.

1847   "Polemisches." *Allgemeine Bauzeitung* 12 (1847) (*Literatur... Beilage*) 3, no. 9: 178-87.

1852   "Einige Worte über die Nothwendigkeit naturgemäßer Motive in allen Gestaltungen der Architektur wie der Technik," *Allgemeine Bauzeitung* 17 (1852): 237-40.

1858   "Noch ein Wort über die Grundfragen der Baukunst." *Allgemeine Bauzeitung* 23 (1858) (*Notizblatt*) 4, no. 16 (December): 235-39.

1863   "Welches ist die zweckmäßigste innere Anordnung der protestantischen Kirchen?" *Allgemeine Bauzeitung* 28 (1863) (*Notizblatt*) 5, no. 15: 261-64.

Dehio, Georg. *Handbuch der deutschen Kunstdenkmäler*, vol. 3, pt. 1, 9. Berlin: Deutscher Kunstverlag, 1935.

Vollmer, Hans, ed. *Allgemeines Lexicon der bildenden Künstler von der Antike bis zur Gegenwart*, vol. 36, 209-10. Leipzig: E. A. Seeman, 1925.

Carl Gottlieb Wilhelm Bötticher

Bötticher was born at Nordhausen, near Erfurt, in 1806. In 1827 he entered the Bauakademie in Berlin. Influenced by Christian Peter Wilhelm Beuth's radical reorganization of teaching methods in the industrial arts, Bötticher concentrated his studies on ornamentation and particularly on textiles. During the next fifteen years he was engaged in teaching these subjects at several of Beuth's new technical schools, and from 1839 he taught at the Bauakademie where, having passed his final architect's examination in 1844, he was appointed professor of architecture.

On Karl Friedrich Schinkel's advice, Bötticher turned to the study of the ornamental and structural forms of the Greek temple. These studies resulted in the conception of the "core-form" and the "art-form," two different but interrelated forms that he felt to be the basic elements of any architectural work. This concept formed the main thesis of Bötticher's *Die Tektonik der Hellenen* (*The Tectonics of the Hellenes*), a book that influenced the architectural thought of many succeeding generations.

After the complete *Tektonik* had appeared in 1852, the author's outstanding contribution to scholarship was recognized by two academic distinctions: an honorary doctorate from the Universität Greifswald and an exceptional appointment as a lecturer (*Privatdozent*) in archaeology at the Königliche Friedrich-Wilhelms-Universität Berlin. In 1868 he was appointed director of the department of sculpture at the Neue Museum at Berlin. Eight years later, following criticism of the principles that he had established concerning the display of the museum's large collection of casts molded from antique sculptures, he resigned from this post and from all of his teaching positions. He died in 1899.

Heinrich Hübsch

Hübsch was born in 1795 in Weinheim, near Mannheim. In 1813 he entered the Ruprecht-Karls-Universität Heidelberg as a student of philosophy and mathematics but moved to Karlsruhe two years later to study architecture at Friedrich Weinbrenner's private school. Weinbrenner was a leading architect of the Neoclassical movement, and undoubtedly, Hübsch owed his thorough architectural training to the outstanding experience of this teacher. Yet even as a student, Hübsch's predilection for medieval architecture made him doubt that the classical style could be of benefit to the development of contemporary architecture.

In 1817, as a continuation of his training, Hübsch traveled to Rome where he stayed for the next four years. From Rome he visited Greece and Constantinople. In 1821 he returned to Germany to take his final examination, and he soon after finished his first book *Über griechische Architektur* (*On Greek Architecture*), which contained a critique of a major tenet of the classical doctrine: imitation. His arguments were angrily rebutted by the renowned archaeologist Aloys Ludwig Hirt.

In 1824 Hübsch was appointed teacher at the Städelsches Kunstinstitut at Frankfurt. His first major building, a church in Wuppertal-Barmen, was designed and subsequently executed during the three years he worked at the Kunstinstitut. Following Weinbrenner's death in 1826, he was called to Karlsruhe to assume the post of principal government architect. In 1832 he was appointed director of the architectural department of the newly formed Polytechnische Hochschule. His architectural practice was extensive. His most important buildings in Karlsruhe were the Finanzministerium (1829-1833), the Polytechnische Hochschule (1833-1835), the Kunsthalle (1836-1845), and the Hoftheater (1851-1853); and in Baden-Baden, the Trinkhalle (1837-1840). He was commissioned to design many churches of which St. Cyriacus in Bulach (1834-1837) and the Ludwigskirche in Ludwigshafen (1858-1862) are the most well known. Through these buildings, as well as through his writings, Hübsch became the foremost exponent of the *Rundbogenstil*. Despite his extensive professional work, he traveled widely, mainly to Italy, but also to Paris, Berlin, and Munich. In 1850 he converted to the Catholic faith, and he died in Karlsruhe in 1863.

CARL ALBERT ROSENTHAL

Rosenthal was born in 1801 in Sudenburg, near Magdeburg. In 1819 he enrolled as a student at the Bauakademie in Berlin. Having passed the final examination in 1823, he entered government service where he remained until his retirement fifty years later; by that time he had reached the rank of privy government councillor. Nothing is known about Rosenthal's architectural career except that from 1824 on he worked with other architects on the restoration of the Magdeburg cathedral (completed in 1852). His contributions to the discussion on style extend from 1830 to the middle of the century. They reflect a development in his architectural thought away from the classical canon, which was instilled in him during his years of study at the Bauakademie, toward the recognition of the supreme spiritual—and artistic—superiority of Gothic architecture.

RUDOLF WIEGMANN

Wiegmann was born in 1804 at Anderson, near Hannover. After completing his education at a gymnasium in the latter city, he moved to Darmstadt to study architecture under Georg Moller. He completed his studies in Italy, where he lived from 1828 to 1832. On his return, he settled in Düsseldorf and began to work as an architect. He received commissions to build several private houses, among them one completed in 1838 for Wilhelm von Schadow, the director of the Königliche Kunstakademie. It was probably on Schadow's recommendation that Wiegmann was asked to submit plans for the rebuilding of the Apollinariskirche at Remagen. Although he was not successful (the church was built according to the design of his competitor Ernst Friedrich Zerner), Wiegmann was appointed professor at the Kunstakademie in 1838 and given responsibility for teaching architecture and perspective.

Wiegmann became known mainly through his literary work. His articles on theoretical matters concerning contemporary architecture formed an important part of the discussion on style. Although he had been highly critical of Hübsch's *In welchem Style sollen wir bauen?* (*In What Style Should We Build?*) when he reviewed it in 1829, he later came to favor adoption of the *Rundbogenstil*, recognizing its latent possibilities.

A gifted painter himself, he was also interested in the painting techniques of both modern and ancient times, a subject on which he wrote several books. The conclusion he drew in *Die Malerei der Alten* (*The Paintings of the Ancients*) was criticized by Leo von Klenze. In response Wiegmann wrote a book in which he not only rebutted Klenze's arguments concerning this particular matter but attacked Klenze's general attitude toward art and architecture. Wiegmann taught at the Kunstakademie for almost thirty years. He died in 1865.

JOHANN HEINRICH WOLFF

Wolff was born in 1792, probably in Kassel. At an early age he was given some architectural instruction when he assisted Leo von Klenze, who from 1808 to 1810 executed Grandjean de Montigny's design for changing the main staircase of the Museum Fridericianum in Kassel into a parliament or *Ständehaus*. In 1814 Wolff went to Paris to study architecture under Charles Percier at the Ecole des Beaux-Arts. He lived in Rome from 1816 through 1818.

After his return to Kassel, Wolff worked as an assistant to the court architect, Johann Konrad Bromeis. He began teaching at the Akademie der Künste in 1821 and was appointed professor of architecture in 1832. As a teacher, art critic, and theoretician, his influence on contemporary architectural thought was considerable. With great consistency he stressed the importance of upholding classical tradition. Wolff died in 1869.

INDEX

Akademie der bildenden Künste. *See* Munich: Akademie der bildenden Künste

Alberti, Leon Battista, 48

Alexander the Great, 78

Altes Museum. *See* Berlin: Altes Museum

Athens: Parthenon, 77, 106, 110; Propylaea, 75, 77; Temple of Theseus, 72

Baden-Baden: Kurhaus, 21; Trinkhalle, 16, 21-22

Bad Kissingen: Trinkhalle, 43

Bauakademie. *See* Berlin: Bauakademie

Befreiungshalle. *See* Kelheim: Befreiungshalle

Benedictine abbey of Maria Laach. *See* Koblenz: Benedictine abbey of Maria Laach

Berlin: Altes Museum, 31; Bauakademie, 33, 35-38, 40, 56 n. 141; cathedral, 46; Friedrich
    Werdersche Kirche, 31; Petrikirche, 35; Schauspielhaus, 100 n. 2

Boisserée, Sulpiz, 2, 51 n. 1, 101 n. 10

Bötticher, Carl Gottlieb Wilhelm, 10, 33-35, 40-41, 44-45, 46

Bramante, Donato, 48

Brunelleschi, Filippo, 48, 81-82

Bulach: St. Cyriacus, 16-17, 20

Cimabue, 109

Cistern of the Thousand Columns. *See* Constantinople: Cistern of the Thousand Columns

Cologne: Cathedral, 2, 93

Colosseum. *See* Rome: Colosseum

Constantinople: Cistern of the Thousand Columns, 88; Hagia Sophia, 87

Curtius, Ernst, 33

Dresden: Dresden Opera House, 48

Engelhardt, J. D. W. E., 48

Fiesole, Fra Angelico da, 109

Friedrich Werdersche Kirche. *See* Berlin: Friedrich Werdersche Kirche

Gärtner, Friedrich von, 7, 16, 22-29, 31-33

Goethe, Johann Wolfgang von, 2, 51 n. 1

Gruppe, Otto Friedrich, 46, 50

Hagia Sophia. *See* Constantinople: Hagia Sophia

Hallmann, Anton, 8, 45

Hamburg: Nikolaikirche, 11

Hannover: Royal Opera House, 31

Hirt, Aloys Ludwig, 3, 100 n. 1

Hogarth, William, 100 n. 5

Horn, Ferdinand Wilhelm, 47

Irene, Empress, 112 n. 3

Jatho, L., 50

Karlsruhe: Polytechnische Hochschule, 16, 20

Kelheim: Befreiungshalle, 31

Klenze, Leo von, 6, 7, 9, 12, 29, 46, 54 n. 83

Koblenz: Benedictine abbey of Maria Laach, 91

Konrad III, Emperor, 112 n. 3

Kopp, Ernst, 37

Kugler, Franz, 6, 22, 37, 47-48

Kurhaus. *See* Baden-Baden: Kurhaus

Laugier, Marc-Antoine, 100 n. 1

Laves, Georg Ludwig Friedrich, 31

Ludwig-Maximilians-Universität. *See* Munich: Ludwig-Maximilians-Universität

Ludwigskirche. *See* Munich: Ludwigskirche

Manuel I, Emperor, 112 n. 3

Maria-Hilfskirche. *See* Munich: Maria-Hilfskirche

Maximilian of Bavaria, King, 9, 35

Metzger, Eduard, 6-8, 9, 42-44, 45, 46, 50

Michelangelo, 48, 109

Munich: Akademie der bildenden Künste, 9; Ludwig-Maximilians-Universität, 16; Ludwigs-kirche, 22-25; Maria-Hilfskirche, 31; Polytechnikum, 7; Staatsbibliothek, 16, 22, 25-29

Neumann, Balthasar, 112 n. 2

Neumann, Franz Ignaz Michael, 112 n. 2

Nikolaikirche. *See* Hamburg: Nikolaikirche and Potsdam: Nikolaikirche

Ohlmüller, Daniel Joseph, 31

Palace of Diocletian. *See* Spalato: Palace of Diocletian

Palladio, Andrea, 48

Parthenon. *See* Athens: Parthenon

Pausanias, 75

Pericles, 69, 76, 77, 78, 105

Peruzzi, Baldassare, 48

Petrikirche. *See* Berlin: Petrikirche

Plutarch, 77

Polytechnikum. *See* Munich: Polytechnikum

Polytechnische Hochschule. *See* Karlsruhe: Polytechnische Hochschule

Potsdam: Nikolaikirche, 31; Schloß Charlottenhof, 31

Propylaea. *See* Athens: Propylaea

Quast, Ferdinand von, 48-49

Raphael, 109

Regensburg: Walhalla, 29, 46

Reichensperger, August, 14, 15, 37, 47

Romberg, Johann Andreas, 8, 47, 48

Rome: Church of Santa Balbina, 86; Colosseum, 79; Temple of Peace, 85; Theater of Marcellus, 79

Rosenthal, Carl Albert, 6, 10

Royal Opera House. *See* Hannover: Royal Opera House

Rumohr, Carl Friedrich von, 4, 6

St. Cyriacus. *See* Bulach: St. Cyriacus

San Marco, Church of. *See* Venice: Church of San Marco

Santa Balbina, Church of. *See* Rome: Church of Santa Balbina

Scamozzi, Vincenzo, 48

Schauspielhaus. *See* Berlin: Schauspielhaus

Schinkel, Karl Friedrich, 31, 33, 35-38, 48, 54 n. 78, 100 n. 2

Schlegel, Friedrich von, 2, 9

Schloß Charlottenhof. *See* Potsdam: Schloß Charlottenhof

Schorn, Johann Karl, 4

Semper, Gottfried, 7, 11, 48

Spalato: Palace of Diocletian, 85

Speyer: Cathedral, 108

Staatsbibliothek. *See* Munich: Staatsbibliothek

Stieglitz, Christian Ludwig, 3-4

Stier, Friedrich Wilhelm Ludwig, 10, 38-41, 45

Strasbourg: Cathedral, 2

Sulzbach, Berta von, 112 n. 3

Temple of Peace. *See* Rome: Temple of Peace

Temple of Theseus. *See* Athens: Temple of Theseus

Theater of Marcellus. *See* Rome: Theater of Marcellus

Trinkhalle. *See* Baden-Baden: Trinkhalle and Bad Kissengen: Trinkhalle

Venice: Church of San Marco, 87

Vitruvius, 100 n. 1

Wagner, Martin von, 33

Walhalla. *See* Regensburg: Walhalla

Weinbrenner, Friedrich, 2, 21-22

Wiegmann, Rudolf, 5, 10-16, 33, 46, 54 n. 83

Winckelmann, Johann, 3
Wolff, Johann Heinrich, 10, 11-16, 41-43, 46, 47, 50, 100 n. 2

IN WHAT STYLE SHOULD WE BUILD?
THE GERMAN DEBATE ON ARCHITECTURAL STYLE

Introduction and Translation
by Wolfgang Herrmann

Wolfgang Herrmann has lived an extraordinary life. Born in Berlin on 17 August 1899, he studied philosophy at the Albert-Ludwigs-Universität Freiburg and art history at the Königliche Friedrich-Wilhelms-Universität Berlin (Adolf Goldschmidt), Ludwig-Maximilians-Universität Munich (Heinrich Wölfflin), and the Universität Leipzig (Wilhelm Pindar) where he received his Ph.D. in 1924. Soon after, he became active in the contemporary architectural scene, working in both the Berlin Kunstgewerbemuseum and Staatliche Kunstbibliothek. In 1933, however, he was dismissed for being politically "unreliable," that is, for being of Jewish descent. After emigrating to England, Herrmann entered into private business for nearly thirty years before "retiring" and again devoting himself to the history of architecture. His books on Marc-Antoine Laugier (*Laugier and Eighteenth Century French Theory*, 1962) and Claude Perrault (*The Theory of Claude Perrault*, 1973) established new standards for historical studies; his more recent works devoted to Gottfried Semper (*Gottfried Semper im Exil*, 1978; *Gottfried Semper theoretischer Nachlass*, 1980; *Gottfried Semper in Search of Architecture*, 1984) have virtually single-handedly resurrected the most important German theorist of the nineteenth century. Herrmann's very first book, *Deutsche Baukunst des XIX und XX Jahrhunderts*, written in 1932-1933, was published for the first time in its entirety in 1977. Wolfgang Herrmann and his lovely wife, Anni, live in Hampstead, London.   —Harry F. Mallgrave

Designed by Laurie Haycock Makela
Composed by Archetype, Toronto,
in Bodoni type (introduction), Caslon 74 type (translation),
Caslon 540 type (essay titles), and Stymie type (heads and running heads).
Printed by The Castle Press, Pasadena,
on Mohawk Superfine 80lb, white and off-white.
Bound by Roswell Book Bindery, Phoenix.

TEXTS & DOCUMENTS
Series designed by Laurie Haycock Makela and Lorraine Wild

LIBRARY OF CONGRESS CATALOGING-IN-PUBLICATION DATA

In what style should we build? : the German debate on architectural
style / Heinrich Hübsch...[et al.] : introduction and translation
by Wolfgang Herrmann.

    p.   cm.–(Texts & documents)
Includes bibliographical references (p. 178) and index.
ISBN 0-89236-199-9: $29.95.–ISBN 0-89236-198-0 (pbk.): $19.95.
    1. Architecture. 2. Architecture–Composition, proportion, etc.
3. Architectural design. I. Hübsch, Heinrich, 1795–1863.
II. Herrmann, Wolfgang, 1899-   . III. Series.
NA2500.I5 1992
720'.1–dc20   91-22702
                                                        CIP

END//:44